CLIMBING:
Expedition Planning

MOUNTAINEERS
OUTDOOR EXPERT
series

CLIMBING:
Expedition Planning

Clyde Soles and Phil Powers

THE MOUNTAINEERS BOOKS

Published by
The Mountaineers Books
1001 SW Klickitat Way, Suite 201
Seattle, WA 98134

First edition, 2003

Published simultaneously in Great Britain by Cordee, 3a DeMontfort Street, Leicester, England, LE1 7HD

Manufactured in the United States of America

Project Editor: Laura Slavik
Editor: Don Graydon
Cover and Book Design: The Mountaineers Books
Layout Artist: Peggy Egerdahl
Photographer: All photographs by Clyde Soles unless otherwise noted

Cover photograph: *Loading the bus* © Phil Powers
Frontispiece: *Two years in planning, two months to get here, and still over two thousand meters to go on Gasherbrum II (8,035m)* © Clyde Soles

Library of Congress Cataloging-in-Publication Data

Soles, Clyde, 1959-
  Climbing : expedition planning / Clyde Soles and Phil Powers.— 1st ed.
      p. cm. — (Mountaineers outdoor expert series)
Includes bibliographical references and index.
  ISBN 0-89886-770-3
  1. Mountaineering. 2. Mountaineering—Equipment and supplies. I. Title. II. Series.
  GV200.S615 2003
  796.52'2—dc21
                                 2003009366

Contents

Dedication

You cannot stay on the summit forever; you have to come down again. . . . So why bother in the first place? Just this: What is above knows what is below, but what is below does not know what is above.

One climbs, one sees, one descends, one sees no longer, but one has seen. There is an art of conducting oneself in the lower regions by the memory of what one saw higher up. When one can no longer see, one can at least still know.

—Rene Daumal, *Mount Analogue*

Preface

This book is for dreamers who want to become doers. Many climbers have a vague notion that they'd like to go on an expedition. But the logistics appear overwhelming and the idea never comes to fruition. The purpose of *Climbing: Expedition Planning* is to provide information and encouragement for safely breaking the barriers to your dreams.

The book is written primarily for intermediate and advanced climbers who seek to broaden their experience in other parts of the globe. While you may have technical expertise on rock and ice, that is but a fraction of the knowledge and skills required for success in a remote wilderness. This book will help with researching the goal, assembling the team, and selecting the gear and food—familiar issues that take on new meaning when talking about an expedition to the opposite side of the planet.

This is also for beginners who think big: Denali, Aconcagua, Everest. These are all achievable for most people with sufficient desire and willpower. And it is for those who would like to break out from guided climbing to venture on their own. Although this is not an instructional manual on climbing techniques (see the other titles in the Mountaineers Outdoor Expert Series), it does provide important information for planning your expedition apprenticeship.

Even those with no desire to climb on high or distant peaks may gain insight. A great many books relate tales of expedition daring or disaster. Here you will discover what it takes to organize an expedition—and hints on why many failed.

If you venture forth, this book will enhance your enjoyment and help prevent disappointment. Rather than learning solely in the school of hard knocks, you can use the collective wisdom within these pages to ensure a great adventure and a lifetime of vivid memories.

Although *Climbing: Expedition Planning* is centered upon mountaineering in the great ranges, the most complex of expeditions, it fully applies to backcountry climbs of any duration—it's just a matter of scale. The concepts of planning a climbing expedition cross over to adventures of all sorts: rafting, caving, diving, exploration, scientific research, deep-water sailing.

Whatever your dream, it is almost certainly achievable if you think it through.

A NOTE ABOUT SAFETY

Safety is an important concern in all outdoor activities. No book can alert you to every hazard or anticipate the limitations of every reader. The descriptions of techniques and procedures in this book are intended to provide general information. This is not a complete text on climbing or training technique. Nothing substitutes for formal instruction, routine practice, and plenty of experience. When you follow any of the procedures described here, you assume responsibility for your own safety. Use this book as a general guide to further information. Under normal conditions, excursions into the backcountry require attention to traffic, road and trail conditions, weather, terrain, the capabilities of your party, and other factors. Keeping informed on current conditions and exercising common sense are the keys to a safe, enjoyable outing.

The Mountaineers Books

Acknowledgments

Many thanks to all my teammates from all my adventures! There are too many to list, but without your friendship, experience, and support, I wouldn't have been able to write this book—or have such great trips. Special thanks to Fred Barth, who contributed much to this project and has been a great partner.

Since I haven't been everywhere (yet), I've consulted many experienced climbers, including Conrad Anker, John Catto, Eric Coomer, Gary Neptune, Jake Norton, Paula Quenemoen, Jack Roberts, Eric Simonson, and Rich Wachtel. Sadly, two of the climbers who appear in my photos—Anatoli Boukreev and Freddie Snalam—are no longer with us; they were inspirations and friends who are missed but not forgotten.

—*Clyde Soles*

CHAPTER 1

Moose's Tooth (10,355 feet, 3,156 meters), Alaska

Expedition Dreaming

It's a loaded word, *expedition*. Immediately it conjures up images of exotic destinations, of epic struggles and heroic triumphs, and of gripping disasters. But implicit in that picture are months of preparation, heaps of equipment, potential personality conflicts, and weeks without a shower.

Mention to someone that you're going on an expedition, even without stating the goal, and their eyes reveal a range of emotions. Some will look at you with curiosity while they silently question your sanity. Others can barely contain their envy as they contemplate their normal, dull existence. A few exhibit a knowing twinkle and a wistful reflection upon their own adventures.

An expedition is a call to action. There is a contagious energy that builds within the group: it empowers everyone to push their own physical, mental, and emotional limits. When people return from an expedition, they are often changed at heart—and many pounds lighter.

WHAT IS AN EXPEDITION?

People sometimes think of a climbing expedition as a large, military-style undertaking with hundreds of porters and horrendous logistics. But this approach is now the exception rather than the norm. These days, a more typical expedition consists of four to six climbers heading into a spectacular mountain range for a few weeks of hard effort and fun. It may take a week or so, using all manner of transport, just to get to the destination. But once there, the expedition members do all the work on the mountain by themselves.

An expedition can even be as simple as two friends teaming up for an extended climb in a remote corner of the Rocky Mountains. While this may not appear to be an expedition, it shares many of the characteristics and complexities of larger, more elaborate excursions.

Mountaineering expeditions have a

number of traits in common:

A precise objective. An expedition has a definite goal, big or small, that bonds the team together. The objective could be to climb a specific route or peak, traverse a range, circumnavigate a mountain, descend a river, explore an unknown region, even conduct medical research in the field. On an expedition, you seldom hear this conversation: "What do you want to do today?" "I dunno, what do you want to do?" When you travel with an objective, much of the agenda is preordained.

Responsibility to others. Members of an expedition take on responsibilities that begin with their obligations to each other: commitment to the goal, assisting with tasks, providing moral and physical support when the chips are down. An expedition also entails contracts, real or implied, with many other people. If your country's alpine club helps you obtain permits or gather information, a report on your activities is often expected. Sponsors want media coverage and feedback on equipment. An expedition also carries a responsibility to the groups that follow in its footsteps. As strangers in a foreign land that perhaps sees few Westerners, you may be viewed—like it or not—as representing your entire country. The people in the region you are visiting will look on you as simply an American, Canadian, Brit, or whatever the case may be. Through your deeds, you can prop the door open for others to follow, or slam it shut.

Extended duration. An expedition requires a significant time commitment, typically four to six weeks. Many ventures last only two to three weeks, however—still plenty of time to get into amazing places. Nowadays it's rare for a trip to last more than three months. Even though modern expeditions demand a good bit of time, the commitment pales in comparison with adventures of the past. During the golden age of Himalayan mountaineering

An expedition often travels great distances to exotic lands for spectacular goals.

in the mid-twentieth century, expeditions could last four to six months. Explorations of the polar regions and the interiors of Africa and Australia a century ago often took two years.

Remote location. The usual venue for an expedition's efforts is a place far off the beaten path. If a day's walk from the mountain will bring you to a paved road, flush toilets, and a cold beer, you're probably not on an expedition.

THE OBJECTIVE

Selecting an appropriate goal for your expedition isn't easy. This step requires significant introspection to honestly evaluate your own abilities and those of the people on your team. Dream big, but temper the dream with reality.

For first expeditions, most climbers choose popular peaks and trade routes, such as the West Buttress on Denali (Mount McKinley) or the Via Normal on Aconcagua. They may not be bold or glamorous ventures for veteran climbers, and you certainly won't have an uncrowded wilderness experience. But these climbs provide learning opportunities that no book or weekend trip can replicate. Such excursions give you a chance to find out if you can handle high altitude and the pressures of climbing big mountains, while you're still relatively close to civilization and on a modest-budget expedition.

Once you've served an apprenticeship, working your way up a progression of adventures, it may be time to start thinking about more challenging goals. It's possible to move up faster if you're fortunate enough to have a mentor take you under-wing, or if you hire a guide. But skipping

Photo by Fred Barth

Denali's West Buttress is a worthy objective even for Himalayan veterans.

ahead too fast without guidance invites disaster; blind ambition can count on only so much luck.

IN SEARCH OF A DREAM

So you're ready for an adventure. How do you choose a goal? Guidebooks for major climbing destinations are good starting points. You might peruse books like *Himalaya Alpine-Style* (The Mountaineers Books, 1995), *Climbing the World's 14 Highest Mountains* (The Mountaineers Books, 2000), and *World Mountaineering* (Bulfinch Press, 1998).

Climbing magazines can expose you to new areas. They carry news about recent expeditions and often have articles on classic climbs with up-to-date information. For detailed expedition accounts, read the annual journals published by alpine clubs and exploration societies. Once you've narrowed your area of interest, guidebooks may be able to fill in many of the specifics.

Other climbers and adventurers can get you headed in the right direction. Attend slide shows at every opportunity, both for motivation and for networking. Network by joining your local climbing club, grotto (caving group), or mountain rescue team. Contact members of previous expeditions to the area you're interested in.

Inspiration can come from unlikely places, so keep your eyes and mind open. After observing a distant mountain range out of a plane window, Chris Bonington made three expeditions to the area and nearly achieved the first ascent of a striking Tibetan peak (Sepu Kangri, 22,800 feet)

Classics attract mountaineers from around the world. Basque climbers high on Gasherbrum II.

that was virtually unknown to Westerners. A look at a postcard picture of a spectacular peak was all that it took for four friends to mount an expedition to make the first ascent of the 3,000-foot east face of Cerro Cathedral in Torres del Paine, Chile. The discovery of a mislabeled mountain on a map was the impetus for Clyde and three others to attempt the first ascent of a 21,800-foot peak in Nepal.

Your expedition doesn't have to be about a first ascent, however. The mountaineering classics can provide a great cultural experience because you'll meet climbers from around the world. These aren't the climbs to choose if you're looking for solitude, but they can be fun and instructive.

WORTHY GOALS

When considering options, think about the merit of your adventure. If you are climbing purely for yourself, this is simply a matter of taste, and others' opinions don't matter as long as you act ethically. But when the climb concerns people other than just you and your teammates, greater obligations are involved. For example, exploration in all of its forms—first ascents of peaks or routes, first descents of rivers, traverses of uncharted terrain, scientific research—is usually worthwhile, but you owe it to your predecessors and peers to publish the information.

A goal that is primarily chosen to raise money for your own pleasure invites indignation. The so-called environmental cleanup expeditions are sometimes just scams for cheap trips; their real benefit may be minimal. Likewise, charity climbs on occasion contribute little to the coffers of their supposed beneficiary, hampering the effectiveness of efforts that are sincere. An "all-women expedition" that employs male guides can be yet another hypocrisy for exploiting sponsors. Contrived media events—such as "solo" ascents on crowded routes or "fastest" ascents using helicopters—are soon forgotten by historians. Attempts to become the youngest or oldest person to scale a peak are foolhardy at best; these meaningless records inevitably lead to injury or death.

Although the world is full of new and worthy mountaineering challenges, many climbers are still drawn to the biggest and most obvious objectives—often ones that are done again and again. By the year 2000, almost 2,800 people had stood atop an 8,000-meter peak (a summit higher than 26,250 feet). Cho Oyu, with easy access and relatively low difficulty, had the highest number, almost 1,000. Everest was second with 874, followed by Gasherbrum II with 456.

As of this writing, ten climbers have reached the summit of all fourteen of the world's 8,000-meter peaks, so the only real competition for this distinction is to see who will be the first woman to make it. More than a hundred people have climbed the highest peak on each continent, the so-called Seven Summits. And eleven adventurers have reached the Three Poles (North Pole, South Pole, Mount Everest).

This doesn't mean these feats are no longer worthy goals, just that it's time for fresh ideas. Most of the major peaks have been climbed by fewer than a dozen routes (and only a few of those have had repeat ascents), with plenty of room for more. Some of the Big 14 have yet to receive alpine-style or winter ascents. There are endless opportunities for traverses of mountains, linkups of peaks, and circumnavigations, in the Himalaya and elsewhere.

Do you sometimes feel like everything has already been climbed? From the summit of one of the giant peaks on a clear day, the view is of a sea of mountains—unnamed, unclimbed, and striking in grandeur and challenge. Reinhold Messner was right: "Nothing is done."

Looking down the Baltoro Glacier. So much to do, so little time.

MOUNTAIN ETHICS

We hold this truth to be self-evident: that the mountains, and the people who live among them, must be respected. While this is common sense for most of us, it evidently is not a universal sentiment. All too often, expeditions have acted with disregard for the environment, culture, and people of the countries they visit.

Practices that may have been accepted when expeditions were few and far between are no longer tolerated. The UIAA (*Union Internationale des Associations d'Alpinisme*), to which all national mountaineering clubs belong, has established principles that are a consensus on ethical behavior in the mountains.

- Ensure that all members of the team are aware of the regulations set by the host country.
- Adopt a sporting approach to the expedition's objectives and do not use equipment or other resources out of proportion to these objectives.
- Conduct the expedition in a way that maintains the safety of its members and especially those it employs.
- Whenever possible, provide technical advice and training to members of the expedition from the host country.
- Give an accurate report about the expedition to the appropriate bodies.
- Do not use equipment and materials owned by other expeditions without permission, and be prepared to help local people or other expeditions if the need arises.
- Leave the mountain environment as clean as possible at the end of the expedition.

A MATTER OF TIMING

Given enough determination and patience, it's possible to climb almost any peak at any time of the year. Considering the cost of mounting an expedition, however, most people will want to maximize their odds of success by picking the most favorable season.

You don't need to select the exact dates right away, because further research will help narrow the travel window. But it would suck to make plans for a trip, only to discover too late that it's monsoon season when the annual monthlong windstorm blows.

The duration of your expedition is another critical decision. The leading cause of expedition failure, after personality conflicts, is insufficient time to accomplish the goal.

Sometimes you get lucky. Two friends went to climb the Super Couloir on Fitzroy in Patagonia, where people often sit for weeks waiting out storms. They arrived in a spell of perfect weather, climbed the route, and were headed home in a few days. Another friend and his team climbed Denali in a week, plane to plane, while most people need three to four weeks.

More often, climbers underestimate the time needed, and people quit the expedition because they have to get back to work. You *must* expect delays, and budget time for them. Delays can be caused by any number of misfortunes: bad weather, illness, bureaucracy—you name it. But count on it.

Don't be fooled by some of the fast times on 8,000-meter peaks; these claims can be misleading. The actual expedition was probably two to three months long, just as with most standard ascents. The acclimatization was simply done on nearby peaks, or the climbers came from another expedition and were already acclimatized. Either way, nobody goes from sea level to a high summit in a few days since your body must adapt to thin air.

If you're lucky and there's time left over at the end, great! Go sightseeing, or stop off at a warm sport-climbing area on the way back home. After a long expedition, it's nice to have a few days to mentally reacclimatize instead of jumping right back in to your hectic life.

PRIME CLIMBING SEASONS: Give or take a month

■ Best time
☐ Not recommended or known

	JANUARY	FEBRUARY	MARCH	APRIL	MAY	JUNE	JULY	AUGUST	SEPTEMBER	OCTOBER	NOVEMBER	DECEMBER
Alaska					■		■					
Antarctica: Vinson Massif	■										■	■
Argentina/Chile: Aconcagua	■	■										■
Argentina/Chile: Patagonia	■	■										■
Argentina: Lake District	■	■	■									
Bhutan			■		■				■	■		
Bolivia					■	■	■	■	■			
Canada: Baffin Island						■	■	■				
Canada: Coast Range					■	■	■	■	■			
Canada: Rockies						■	■	■	■			
Canada: St. Elias Range						■	■					
Chile: Tierra del Fuego	■	■										
China: Tibet				■					■	■		
Colombia/Venezuela	■											■
Ecuador	■	■						■				■
Greenland						■	■	■				
India			■						■	■		
Indonesia: Carstensz Pyramid				■				■				
Kazakhstan: Tien Shan							■	■				
Kenya	■											■
Mali	■											
Mexico	■											■
Mongolia: Altai Mountains							■	■				
Morocco: High Atlas Mountains				■	■							
Nepal			■	■	■					■	■	
New Zealand	■											
Norway						■	■	■				
Pakistan						■	■	■				
Peru						■	■	■				
Russia: Caucasus Mountains							■	■				
Tajikistan: Pamirs								■				
Tanzania: Kilimanjaro	■	■							■	■		
Turkey/Iran							■	■				
Uganda/Zaire: Ruwenzori Mountains	■					■	■					■

Photo by Jack Roberts

Every climber has their own level of acceptable risk.

A MATTER OF RISK

Though most climbers aren't the adrenaline junkies that the general public believes, we do thrive on uncertainty. If there was no risk and the outcome was assured, most climbers would take up some other pursuit. In choosing a goal, your expedition will decide what constitutes an acceptable level of risk and then try to pick an appropriate climb.

Given that there is always an element of danger, no matter how "easy" the climb, the trick lies in matching the route's difficulty to the climbers' comfort zone. There's a world of difference between the standard West Buttress route on Denali, which is appropriate for the competent mountaineer, and that peak's far more demanding Cassin Ridge, better suited to the strong, experienced alpinist. Of course, it isn't always desirable to stay within your comfort zone—pushing the envelope is how we improve—but it's best to do this incrementally instead of in one huge leap.

The risk can be reduced by selecting a style of ascent that offers greater safety, although this may involve actions that some climbers don't consider "fair means." Installing fixed ropes allows retreat in severe weather. Employing high-altitude porters saves climbers' energies. And using supplementary oxygen essentially lowers the altitude. All of these possibilities need to be discussed and weighed to see if any of them are right for your particular venture.

No simple answer applies to all climbers or all expeditions. Those who are new to this game should start from the viewpoint of which hedges can reasonably be eliminated; veteran climbers, on the other hand, often begin from a bare minimum and add only what is necessary.

There is a strong correlation between increasing altitude and a higher death rate. This doesn't prove causation, since many other factors are involved, but basically, higher peaks are more dangerous. Although only 2,674 feet (815 meters) separate the height of the lowest and highest 8,000-meter peaks (Gasherbrum II and Everest), the death rate of summiters during the descent from Gasherbrum II was 0.6 percent, while that on Everest was 8.3 percent. (These statistics are for climbers without supplemental oxygen; with oxygen, the descent death rate on Everest dropped to 3 percent.)

At elevations much above 20,000 feet (6,000 meters), progress over fifth-class rock and ice is drastically slowed. Teams must be efficient climbers long before they arrive. Less-technical terrain allows much faster progress, a crucial factor at high altitudes. Simulclimbing is a fast technique where both partners move simultaneously over moderately technical terrain while roped and the leader places protection. Although more dangerous than belaying one at a time, the increased speed can offset the risk (if both climbers are competent). When climbing between storms—the case on almost any expedition—it's often a race against time.

Consideration must also be given to a route's objective hazards. Even when the climbing is not technically difficult, it may be extremely dangerous due to moderate-angle snow slopes that are prone to avalanche. Some icefalls are relatively stable, allowing safe passage, while others are shifting death traps. Ridges don't usually suffer the rockfall common on big faces and in couloirs, but instead may be heavily corniced. Routes on the side of a mountain opposite from the prevailing winds provide little to no warning of impending storms. And don't overlook options for descent and escape; you only succeed when you make it home.

Another hazard is even less predictable: the other climbers on the mountain who aren't part of your team. Relatively easy routes on big peaks are popular and often attract a percentage of gumbies and poseurs who knock rocks down, trigger avalanches, and can't take care of themselves in an emergency. Be realistic about your own abilities when you choose a climb, and don't become a member of this dangerous crowd.

Also keep alert to reports of political turmoil in a region. Guerrilla warfare and insurrections are probably more adventure than most climbers care to experience. Ignoring warnings from the U.S. State Department is what got four young American climbers into trouble in Kyrgyzstan; they were taken hostage and just barely managed to escape with their lives.

A FEAR OF OTHERS

It's inexcusable for any climber to act as if he or she is independent on a crowded climb; irresponsible behavior places other people in danger. Even more reprehensible is to pretend that you have no obligation to others on the mountain.

Our team was the first to arrive at Gasherbrum Base Camp in 1997 and we had the mountain to ourselves, aside from the nearby Pakistan Army base. This was a mixed blessing. The trade-off for the relative solitude was the several weeks it took to establish a trail through the icefall. We felt like rats in a maze but it helped us acclimatize.

By the time we had finished packing a trail to advanced base camp, the other seven expeditions on our route up Gasherbrum II had arrived; an additional seven expeditions shared most of the same trail to a fork leading to Gasherbrum I (Hidden Peak). With the benefit of our trail to ABC, it was easy to move up to an elevation of 20,000 feet in a day. The Japanese brought Sherpas who promptly fixed lines damn near to the summit.

With a virtual handrail to the top, any moron could move up as fast as lungs would allow. Evidence of stupidity was aplenty: people walked around on the glacier unroped. We knew the anchors for the fixed lines in the icefall were unreliable after they had melted out by the sun, and snow bridges were disappearing fast, yet people acted as if the ropes were bombproof.

Prior to our summit bids, we were all concerned that another team would screw up our climb. Earlier in the trip, we found a dead climber in the glacier, and we also loaned our Gamow Bag air-pressure chamber and emergency oxygen to save the life of a Pakistani soldier; death wasn't an idle possibility.

Unlike the Indians and Dutch on Everest in 1992, it was certain that we would try to help another team if someone was sick or injured. There are times when nothing can be done—the first rule of rescue is look out for number one—but there is never a time when an attempt should not be made, merely because it ruins your plans.

Whether you like it or not, there is a bond between climbers in remote locations. If you act irresponsibly, you are in fact endangering people you may have never met. Should you ever be placed in the situation of having to decide whether to go for the summit or help someone, you will find the latter immensely more rewarding in the long run.

Thankfully, nothing serious went wrong during our climb, and nine out of the original eleven on our team made it to the summit. During the trek out, our expedition used the Gamow Bag again to save a porter from pulmonary edema. For a final bit of excitement, several of our team members saved the life of a pregnant woman by carrying her in a porter's basket for many miles over rugged terrain. It was a good expedition.

— *Clyde Soles*

A MATTER OF STYLE

A big step in preparation is deciding upon the style of your expedition. There is no right or wrong answer here; it's primarily a matter of preference, and each style has its pros and cons. But this choice will directly impact every other aspect of your climb.

EXPEDITION STYLE

Once the most common type of expedition, the traditional massive assault with dozens of climbers and Sherpas is now viewed by many climbers as about as outdated as wood-shafted ice axes and wool knickers. Yet there are still advantages to a large group (typically eight to twelve people) for sharing expenses and labor, particularly on big mountains.

There can be a lot of variation in the use of high-altitude porters above base camp in this style of operation. The expedition may hire porters to move gear to the base of the route, to ferry loads up the mountain, or even to support the effort right to the summit. Or expedition members can decide to do all of the work themselves.

In expedition style, after the route to the first camp is established, team members or porters carry gear up to stock that camp. Ropes are often fixed over climbing difficulties so that individuals can make their way back and forth between camps without the need of a belay from another person. In some cases, thousands of meters of rope are fixed for this purpose.

Once the first camp is stocked sufficiently to sustain a climbing team, climbers inhabit Camp 1 and begin the process of pioneering the route to Camp 2 and stocking it. This process continues until your planned series of camps is complete. If the climb demands a lot of fixed rope and you are using supplemental oxygen, the process of preparing the mountain for the summit bid can take a great deal of time. Even on trips that use little fixed line and no oxygen bottles, plan on many forays up the mountain before the camps are prepared.

Assuming a route has three camps above base camp, you might make six or more round trips to Camp 1, four to Camp 2, and two to place tents and food at Camp 3 to prepare the mountain for one attempt by a team of two. A lot of work, yes, but it also helps your body acclimatize; those who don't ferry loads run a greater risk of altitude illness.

Traditional expedition style offers a good chance at success and a relatively high degree of safety. The climber, in his or her final summit bid, has access to more resources than with other styles of ascent. The summit climber may be better acclimatized due to earlier work on the mountain and has the benefit of pre-placed camps for the entire descent. If you are traveling far from home and investing a lot of time and money, the appropriate use of expedition style can help you return with a summit.

Many teams overestimate the amount of food they need high on a mountain. To take full advantage of the expedition style, eat well and rest thoroughly at base camp, then make quick attempts on the summit. Excessive stays at camps above 20,000 feet use precious resources and do not help with acclimatization.

When weather or other conditions deteriorate, smart climbers descend to base camp and then go back up again, rested and strong, when things improve. While you might be tempted to stay above base camp for a head start when the weather improves, it's unlikely that the mountain will be in safe climbing condition immediately after a storm.

The major drawback to this traditional style of expedition is the vastly increased complexity from having so many people involved; good communication is vital. There is also a greater risk of personality clashes, even the formation of warring cliques.

If an expedition of this sort does not use high-altitude porters, it's possible for the team to spend too much energy in preparing the fixed routes and camps for the summit bid. In the struggle to move resources up the mountain, teams sometimes fail to rest adequately. Guard against exhausting yourselves to the point where you are unable to complete the climb.

CAPSULE STYLE

As an alternative to a traditional expedition, the capsule style works well with smaller groups (two to eight people) of experienced climbers. Instead of establishing a series of fixed camps and moving a pyramid of supplies upward, a capsule expedition has either one or two camps that move up and down the mountain with the team. Climbers establish the route and ferry loads to the upper campsite. Once it is stocked, they remove the previous camp and carry their sleeping bags and tents to the upper camp to start the process again for the next camp. On the first forays to the camp above, the lower camp remains in place so climbers have a sanctuary at the end of the day.

Like traditional expedition style, capsule style facilitates climbing high and sleeping low. Climbing higher prompts one's body to acclimatize to the altitude. Sleeping back at a lower elevation staves off altitude illness and allows for the quality sleep necessary for peak performance.

Keep in mind that our bodies are asked to acclimatize to many things on a big climb. Capsule style and expedition style both allow us to get used to the altitude, the cold, and the intricacies of the route itself. In most cases, you will arrive at a higher camp with more energy if you have made the trek once or twice before.

A more elaborate use of capsule style employs two complete sets of camping gear. Instead of just pioneering the route and placing a small amount of food and gear at the higher camp, the team completely establishes the higher camp. Then the lower camp can be transported into position as the next camp above that. This method of leapfrogging camps involves more equipment, but it offers the advantage of a second full camp on the mountain, which can become important for safety as the team moves higher. Altitude sickness can usually be diminished by retreating a few thousand feet in elevation to a lower camp.

An early example of capsule style was the 1962 Sayre expedition to Mount Everest that hoped to pull off a great coup, the first American ascent. Woodrow Wilson Sayre developed the technique on Denali in 1954, and he and his team then used it on Everest for their daring (and illegal) foray into Tibet from a base camp more than 25 miles away. They reached only 25,500 feet (7,772 meters), but clearly demonstrated that a climbing team can operate away from base camp for over a month by employing the capsule style of camps.

Teams that venture far afield but operate on relatively small budgets often adopt capsule style. It offers many of the advantages of expedition style, but with a smaller investment in equipment and less time preparing the mountain. There is one significant difference: every time you move the camp up in capsule style, you cut the umbilical cord to retreat. In the event of a storm, the team must sit tight instead of recuperating comfortably in base camp.

Capsule style has become popular on major big-wall climbs, where progress can be slow. Climbers might spend days pioneering the route up a significant distance. For harder routes, the distance between camps may be governed by the amount of rope the team carries. At the end of each climbing day, the team rappels back to the camp. Once the route is established to the limit of available rope, the climbers move the camp up to repeat the process.

ALPINE STYLE

For many climbers, the purest form of ascent is putting on a pack and climbing until the top is reached. This simplicity, combined with a small group (usually just two to four climbers), makes planning easier but greatly increases the challenge. A direct consequence of adopting an alpine style is a finite limit on the amount of gear that can be carried. Furthermore, you must be able to climb with a load on your back or have a system for hauling it up sections that are too difficult to lead with a pack.

Using expedition or capsule style, a team can place a large amount of food and equipment on the mountain. Alpine-style climbing typically limits teams to minimal camping and climbing gear and only a supply of food.

For a climb that is mostly on snow, and with the gear divided between two team members, the most that is practical to carry is nine or ten days of slim rations. On a difficult rock route, the weight of the hardware will reduce the amount of food that can be carried. If winter conditions prevail, the portion of the load reserved for food is diminished even further. Alpine style reduces the margin of safety because it restricts you to carrying only a minimum of food and equipment. Your ability to weather storms and wait for good conditions is virtually eliminated.

Alpine-style ascents can be perfect for objectives that do not demand a lot of travel or complex planning. For climbers who live in the Rocky Mountains, it's easy to pack up and head off for a three- or four-day alpine attempt on a mountain or big wall. The ability of ski planes to land near the base of climbs in Alaska, plus the long days, makes this region conducive to alpine ascents.

If you travel farther afield, perhaps to Asia or South America, the planning is more involved. It would not make sense to travel so far for just a single alpine attempt. Though your goal is an alpine ascent, you would take enough food and gear for an acclimatization climb in the area before trying your alpine route. If you failed on your alpine attempt because of weather or other reasons, you would want to try again. So plan your trip with a number of attempts in mind.

Of course this creates a dilemma: if you have to retreat from some point partway up your alpine route, what will you do with any food, fuel, or climbing gear that you don't need for the descent? It's likely that you will leave it at your high point so it can be used on the next attempt. If you believe you can get back to your high point in a one-day push, perhaps you will leave your bivouac gear as well.

Yet leaving anything changes your next attempt into something other than a pure alpine ascent. Your first try becomes an effort in which you pioneered some of the route and ferried a load to your high point. Your second try makes use of the cached food and gear. There is nothing wrong with

Photo by Jack Roberts

Ski planes allow short approaches; one reason Alaska is popular with alpinists.

this, assuming the climb is reported accurately. Indeed, it can be an excellent strategy. But it does change the nature of the climb you had envisioned.

An alpine ascent is certainly worthy of praise for its apparent simplicity and purity. It means no porters to help you get gear up the mountain, no camps below to which you might retreat, with every ounce of climbing and sleeping gear, food, fuel, and cooking equipment on your back.

This bold style demands contingency planning and escape options. Make plans for turning around if you fail to keep a pace that will put you over the top and en route back down before you run out of fuel (to melt snow for water) or food. Anticipate how you might retreat from various points on the route.

In general, adopting an alpine style limits the duration of a climb and the size of the mountain on which it can be used. Unless you are superhuman, 45-pound (20-kg) packs are about the maximum for alpine climbing. For most of us, this limits technical, alpine-style attempts to four or five days in winter conditions and about a week in the summer. This is definitely a case where less is more. Every pound of hardware and foul-weather gear you add to your load reduces climbing speed.

EXTREME ALPINE STYLE

Applying alpine techniques to routes that most would agree are too big and demanding to ascend in one push and without support is called extreme alpinism, or super-alpinism. The key to success is traveling exceptionally fast and light, usually without a tent, to get up and down before weather or altitude sickness can wreak havoc. Only a handful of people are capable of even attempting such climbs, and all of the planets must align for them to be successful.

Extreme alpinism arguably began with Hermann Buhl's 1953 ascent of Nanga Parbat (8,125 meters). What started out as a traditional expedition turned into a stunning solo alpine climb in which Buhl, by himself, became the first person to set foot on the summit of this Himalayan giant. Four years later, Buhl, Kurt Diemberger, Markus Schmuck, and Fritz Wintersteller proved that a small, fast team can accomplish wonders as they made the first ascent of Broad Peak (8,047 meters).

The next major leap in super-alpine style came with a three-day ascent in 1975 of a new route on Gasherbrum I, also known as Hidden Peak (8,068 meters), by Reinhold Messner and Peter Habeler. This breakthrough event opened the floodgates to new possibilities, including the solo ascent of Everest by Messner in 1980, and the first traverse of two 8,000-meter peaks, in which Messner and Hans Kammerlander in 1984 climbed Gasherbrum II and continued from there to the summit of Gasherbrum I. In the mid-1980s, a method described as "rush tactics," in which nearly all equipment is left behind, was employed on a series of remarkable Himalayan speed ascents by Erhard Loretan and partners.

With few exceptions, even the most amazing feats of skill and endurance are not truly super-alpine efforts. Instead, there is often a fair amount of expedition-style preparation, or at least some support from others. One-day round-trips on Everest and K2 have, to date, been supported by the fixed lines, established trail, or even food and shelter of others.

COMBINED STYLE

Clearly there are many gradations within a style. A traditional expedition-style ascent could mean full Sherpa support with bottled oxygen and fixed lines, but nowadays it could also be the climbers themselves who are setting up the series of camps, without the aid of others or mountains of equipment. Another possibility is a combination of styles within an expedition.

Expedition style is often used to stock lower camps, while the upper portions of the route employ a more portable style, closer to the capsule or alpine approaches. This program may be planned from the beginning or, as with Buhl on Nanga Parbat, it may turn out that way due to circumstances. Style decisions are part of planning, but changing or modifying styles must be considered throughout the expedition to help ensure safety and success.

On the Abruzzi Ridge of K2, Phil's team used a combination of expedition and alpine style. They established and stocked Camps 1 and 2 and then visited the location of Camp 3. This process helped them become comfortable with the routefinding and set the team up for a fast summit push. After they were acclimatized and rested, they set off for the summit from base camp at 16,500 feet (5,029 meters). Carrying the gear and food needed for the upper mountain, they

left base camp and climbed straight to Camp 2 at 22,500 feet (6,858 meters); from there they climbed to Camp 3 at 24,500 feet (7,468 meters) and slept. The next morning they climbed on to just above 26,000 feet (7,925 meters) and slept (barely) before leaving on the successful summit bid.

This combination of expedition and alpine styles works well if you do not need an excessive amount of equipment high on the mountain. Difficult rock climbing, and the heavy hardware it demands, or use of oxygen bottles might require that you employ expedition style right up to the highest camps.

There's no need to place values or judgments on the relative quality of these various climbing styles. Almost every mountaineering endeavor employs some version of expedition style at some point. For example, ferrying a load or two of supplies and equipment to the base of a big-wall route, in order to get a head start on an alpine-style attempt, is truthfully combination style.

COMMERCIAL EXPEDITIONS

A commercial expedition is quite different from a mountain adventure planned by a group of individuals. When you pay someone to do the organization and planning, there's likely to be less emotional involvement with the team and the goal. On the other hand, going commercial can save you huge amounts of time and energy and, in theory, ensure competent partners. For some people, going with a guide service can mean the difference between realizing a dream and never even making an attempt. Others may wish to gain experience on a guided climb before organizing their own expeditions.

After the 1996 disaster on Everest in which three guides and two clients died, the industry took a hard look at itself and tightened standards and procedures. Yet there remains a wide range in services and prices. Some low-budget commercial expeditions are borderline planned disasters, with inadequate provisions and surly or inexperienced guides. As with many things, you usually get what you pay for. It's smart to check with a guide's previous clients before laying down the dinero.

Although many think of a commercial expedition as a guided climb, this is not necessarily the case. Some outfitters do all the organization and provide support on the mountain, including a personal Sherpa if you wish, while allowing you to essentially climb on your own. Others will practically baby-sit you the entire way, for a heftier price.

Try to keep tabs on what's going on so you can feel sure that critical items (such as food, fuel, sleeping bags, tents, oxygen) are in the right place at the right time. It's not uncommon for clients to go hungry, for fixed ropes to not be ready when needed, or for Sherpas to not be provided. Be sure the guide service's obligations are spelled out in writing, and speak to the expedition leader if the company doesn't deliver.

Under no circumstances are you, as a guided client, allowed to disconnect your brain, especially when it comes to personal safety. You may have paid the guide service a small fortune, but it doesn't mean the company can foresee every possible contingency—or that it has its act together.

It's likely that in a life-threatening situation high on a mountain, you'll have to save yourself. In truth, there is only so much that even superheroes can do for someone else above 8,000 meters. Although it's important to trust your guide, avoid placing yourself in a position that you can't get out of on your own.

MILESTONE EXPEDITIONS

All climbers and armchair mountaineers should put modern achievements in context. This list identifies groundbreaking high-altitude expeditions that served as signposts for the future due to the introduction of new technology, new techniques, or sheer boldness. Many similar events have occurred in the rich history of climbing, but this roster focuses on the higher mountain ranges, where the distances are far and the air is thin.

1883

William W. Graham of the United Kingdom brings a small party, including a professional guide, for the single purpose of mountaineering in the Himalaya. His claims to have summited Kabru (24,080 feet; 7,341 meters) and other high peaks in the Garhwal of India are disputed. Of more importance, this was the first expedition devoted solely to climbing in the Himalaya, and it introduced the concept of a small team moving in alpine style.

continued on page 32

continued from page 31

1892

Martin Conway (United Kingdom) leads a large expedition to explore the Karakoram, and it becomes a model for traditional expeditions to follow (such as the Duke of the Abruzzi's K2 expedition of 1909 and the British Everest expeditions). The goal was to explore, map, and climb peaks of the Baltoro region. Conway introduced the concept of "large" to exploratory mountaineering; his team included scientists, surveyors, guides, and artists. It was one of the first expeditions to employ Sherpas and Gurkhas.

1895

Albert F. Mummery (United Kingdom) leads a small group of climbers, without guides, to climb Nanga Parbat (26,660 feet; 8,125 meters) in the Karakoram. This is the first serious attempt to climb an 8,000-meter peak. Mummery, along with two Gurkhas, disappeared on the climb. He underestimated the huge scale and difficulty of the mountain, but reinforced the idea of a small, mobile expedition.

1902

Oscar Eckenstein, an Englishman who was with Conway in 1892, leads a small expedition to K2 (28,250 feet; 8,611 meters). Attempting the Northeast Ridge, they encountered many problems, not the least of which was the party's realization that 8,000-meter mountains were much more than a larger version of the Alps. The Swiss doctor Jacot-Guillarmod recognized symptoms of high-altitude pulmonary edema in one of the members and saved his life by evacuating him to lower altitude.

1906

American Fanny Bullock-Workman reaches the top of Pinnacle Peak in the Nun Kun mountains of India, setting an altitude record of 22,810 feet (6,957 meters) for women climbers.

1907

Tom Longstaff (United Kingdom) and party make the first ascent of a 7,000-meter peak, Trisul (23,360 feet; 7,120 meters) in the Garhwal of India. The summit party included Alexis and Henri Brocherel, professional guides from Courmayeur, Italy, and the Gurkha Karbir. Bottled oxygen was brought to aid in climbing, but the system was so impractical it was not used.

1922

Charles G. Bruce (United Kingdom) leads the first serious attempt to climb Everest. George I. Finch and Geoffrey Bruce established a height record of 27,500 feet (8,380 meters) and introduced the use of supplemental oxygen and down clothing (Finch's down jacket).

1934

British mountaineers Eric Shipton and Bill Tilman, along with three Sherpas, use lightweight alpine-style tactics to discover the route to Nanda Devi (25,645 feet; 7,816 meters) in India (after

1980

Reinhold Messner climbs Everest solo, without oxygen or any other support. His climb is done during August, the monsoon period, when there are no other climbers anywhere on the mountain.

1984

Messner and Italian Hans Kammerlander make the first traverse of two 8,000-meter peaks, climbing Gasherbrum II (26,360 feet; 8,035 meters) and then Hidden Peak (26,470 feet; 8,068 meters) in one continuous push.

1985

David Breashears assists Dick Bass of the United States to the summit of Mount Everest in the first guided ascent of an 8,000-meter peak. Commercial expeditions to Everest and other Himalayan peaks soon follow.

1985

Polish climber Vojtek Kurtyka and Austrian Robert Schauer climb the steep and difficult 2,500-meter (8,200-foot) West Face of Gasherbrum IV (26,000 feet; 7,925 meters) in eleven days. The ascent of such a technical and committing route by so small a team in alpine style is a first.

1989

Tomo Cesen of Slovenia solos the 2,800-meter (9,200-foot) north face of Jannu (25,288 feet; 7,710 meters) in 23 hours. This is the first time such a difficult technical route is accomplished by a solo climber.

1990

In April, Tomo Cesen climbs the 10,000-foot (3,300-meter) South Face of Lhotse, solo. This difficult face has both steep rock, vertical to overhanging, and ice. The ascent has been controversial and is generally not believed to have been to the true summit of the peak.

1990

Sergei Bershov and Vladimir Karatayev, part of a Russian expedition, make the first ascent of the Lhotse South Face to the summit (27,940 feet; 8,516 meters) in the post-monsoon season. This highly technical route is widely considered one of the most difficult climbs in the world.

1999

Tomaz Humar of Slovenia does an incredible solo ascent of the 4,000-meter (more than 13,000-foot) South Face of Dhaulagiri (26,795 feet; 8,167 meters), although not to the summit. The nine-day climb is considered an outstanding achievement because of its sustained technical difficulty (M7+), serving as a signpost to the future.

— *Fred Barth*

DEFINING THE MISSION

The power of a few carefully chosen words is great. That's why it can be helpful to draft a brief mission statement for your expedition. This clearly focuses everyone on just what the expedition plans to do.

A mission statement is a simple sentence or two that defines the expedition's goals and methods. It distills this consensus into a guiding principle that you can keep in your head. The statement reinforces areas of agreement, and its creation helps clarify areas of disagreement. Later, individual decisions can be made and justified by referring to the statement.

This device can help keep motivation up within the team as everyone unites around a common goal. Equally important, a mission statement agreed upon in advance can prevent arguments at base camp and on the route. If you intend to seek sponsorship, it's essential to sum up your expedition in a few sentences that can be used for marketing.

The process of creating a mission statement forces discussion that helps everybody understand common goals. Overly simple statements do not fully engage teams in this sort of discussion. "To climb to the summit of Cho Oyu" is easily agreed upon, but is inadequate. "To climb to the summit of Cho Oyu at any cost," though it's a statement that few climbers would agree with, certainly does get to the heart of several key issues. Participants in constructing such an unlikely statement would all be aware that they are members of a group willing to sacrifice life itself to reach the summit.

A more realistic mission statement would include your main objective, the style of your anticipated climb, and any important goals that your team agrees upon. Here's one that does a thorough job of defining a team's direction: "To climb to the summit of Cho Oyu in alpine style, keeping safety a priority and without the use of supplemental oxygen."

An expedition may also have secondary objectives, but be aware that they can sometimes be at odds with the primary goal. For example, the secondary goal of filming the Cho Oyu climb might hinder the climb itself. The secondary goal of making a film or climbing additional peaks in the region could sap energy or result in an injury that jeopardizes the main objective. Team discussions leading to a mission statement should help define conflicts like this and point to solutions.

WIND STORY

As we cleared the dinner dishes, a rogue gust of wind threatened to rip the mess tent from its grommets. The six of us and our cook, hustled to tighten the guylines. Once the group tents were secure, we each scurried to our own sites to put them in shape. There were high, jet-stream clouds to the north over China, no precipitation, and clear skies above.

No other gusts brought the force of that initial one, but it remained blustery through the evening and night. Slowly we reconvened at the mess tent to consider the repercussions this storm might have on our plans. Those of us who had spent time in the Karakoram sent curious glances at one another: down on the glaciers, in the base camps, we had never seen a wind that fierce.

Our expedition had come to climb Hidden Peak. We hoped to start with an ascent of the Italian route—a route that was well within our ability and could serve to help us acclimatize and prepare for something harder. We had already established a camp in the upper portion of the Gasherbrum Glacier and another at 22,000 feet at the base of the Japanese Couloir on Hidden Peak, from which we hoped to make an alpine-style push to the summit. Once familiar with the descent and well-acclimatized, we had the dream of completing a direct line on the South Face. The bottom two-thirds of the route had been climbed by Vojtek Kurtyka and Jerzy Kukuczka but they had traversed off to easier ground, avoiding a difficult finish. We planned to leave our highest camp on the Italian route in place. Climbers who completed the new route would use that camp for shelter and a margin of safety on their descent.

We had been high on the mountain several times but had not yet launched a real summit attempt. The weather had been changeable with only brief periods of clear weather. The route from base camp to our first camp was threatened by avalanche and we usually had to wait after each storm to start climbing; this fact had hurt our ability to take full advantage of the shorter periods of good weather. That day, we descended again. From Camp 2, an odd-looking cloud on the distant northern horizon concerned me and we retreated. It was not a simple decision and some in the group thought it unnecessary.

Unbeknownst to us, Scott Fischer and Rob Hess—friends of ours guiding a team up Broad Peak only a few miles away—left their high camp for the summit a few hours before we began our descent. They reached the summit that morning and were well down the mountain before the winds rose. From their base camp, they witnessed (through spotting scopes and by listening to radio conversations) one of the great tragedies in the history of the Karakoram.

Individuals from several teams continued their struggle toward the summit of K2 at the time the gust of wind hit our base camp. It was 6 P.M., dusk, terribly late to be high on any 8,000-meter peak, much less K2 in a windstorm. It's difficult to imagine the terror of that wind high on a mountain that rises almost 2,000 feet higher than any other in the region. By the time it was all over, eight people were dead.

continued on page 38

continued from page 37

The storm was fierce but ended quickly. In the few pleasant days that followed, our team continued to work toward summit. The weather was never again as threatening as it was on that tragic day. Eventually, the low-pressure systems pumped at us by the coming monsoon to the south began to hamper our efforts again.

We stayed until mid-September, when the snows began to stick in base camp rather than melt in the afternoon. We stayed until we were not sure we could get porters in to carry our camp out of the mountains. We stayed in hopes of one last period of good weather, one last shot at the summit, and because to leave would admit defeat too easily.

As I look back on the trip, I wonder how much of a chance we ever really had at climbing Hidden Peak. More specifically, I wonder whether my conservative approach to the mountain kept our expedition from taking advantage of the few opportunities that did exist.

It was 1995 and I had been coming to the Karakoram with some regularity since 1987. With each trip my climbing objectives became a bit more challenging. And with each trip—and added year in my life—my tolerance for risk diminished. This is not a clear-cut picture. Every climber becomes more adept at managing taller risks as his or her skill increases. Even as caution rises, the skill to manage risk might outpace it.

The reward could be another 8,000-meter summit, maybe via a new route. The risk was a fate like that of those fragile people high on K2. My goals for personal and group safety and my desire to climb a route that was technically challenging at high altitude governed every decision. I'm proud of keeping our group safe. Unfortunately, the strength of safety goals meant that, in the fickle-weathered Karakoram, we were unlikely to succeed on our basic climbing objective, much less our ambitious desire to complete a new, direct line on an 8,000-meter peak.

In retrospect, I consider our Hidden Peak adventure only a mild success. More thorough conversations and greater introspection about our main goals and climbing objectives could have changed the attitudes with which we approached the mountain. Safety goals are not something you can really modify; they are part of your personality. Once you know your attitude toward risk and create a like-minded team, climbing objectives can be chosen to match.

Given the attitudes toward risk that I had and that the team shared for the most part, I wonder what the slightest modification of our climbing objective might have meant for us that summer. Instead of simply climbing the Italian route, the hope for a new route loomed in the back of our minds. What impact did this have? Did it reduce our fervor for the Italian route? Did it cause us to save our energy in any way for something else? Did it change the character of our initial attempts from true attempts into exercises in acclimatization?

Here in the comfort of a sunny room it is easy to look back and speculate. I believe that if our expedition had chosen a single climbing objective that truly matched our ideals for health and safety—and written that into a mission statement—we would have had a much greater chance at reaching the top.

—Phil Powers

CHAPTER 2

Orizaba (18,410 feet, 5,611 meters), Mexico

Teamwork Is Everything

The true mark of a successful expedition is not whether you make the summit, but that everyone returns, and returns as friends. Read a few expedition accounts and you'll soon realize the absolute importance of a compatible team. Failure to make high-quality choices in people not only can cause your team to lose the summit, but may also turn the entire trip into a thoroughly miserable—even deadly—experience.

The rich history of K2 expeditions is replete with discord. Paul Petzoldt and his teammates never mended the rifts that grew out of their reconnaissance in 1938. The following year, Fritz Wiessner accused Jack Durrance of removing all the support camps and abandoning their K2 climb while he, Wiessner, was still up at 25,000 feet. Nearly fifty years after the first ascent of K2, Walter Bonatti still contends that his teammates tried to kill him during their summit bid.

Perhaps the clearest example of assembling a strong team that couldn't possibly work together was the unsuccessful 1971 International Everest Expedition attempt on the unclimbed Southwest Face. With twenty-two prima donnas from nine different countries and no common language, the effort was doomed from the start and cost one climber his life. Yet only a year later, another international expedition repeated the same mistake—with the same unfortunate outcome.

When you join a climbing team, you certainly don't expect it to be dysfunctional, but it happens frequently. Many considerations go into choosing the people with whom you will spend weeks in a difficult, often dangerous environment. Expedition planners have a lot of tough decisions to make as they consider how many people should be on the team, and exactly who they should be.

SIZE MATTERS

The goal often dictates the size of the team, at least until you enter the ranks of the elite. The decision on size is also affected by the planned style of ascent.

The bigger the peak and the farther you have to travel, the more climbers you will probably want on your team. A major peak, far from your home country, suggests at least six team members and possibly up to a dozen. The extra manpower is needed because attrition from illness, injury, or flagging desire is common. Large teams have significant drawbacks, however, including greater potential for personality conflicts, communication problems, and organizational hassles.

In general, the more technical routes are best climbed by smaller parties of no more than four people. These teams usually are more efficient, so they can move faster and take advantage of windows of good weather.

If the terrain on the approach is not heavily glaciated, or you're climbing late in the season when crevasses are no longer hidden, a team of two experienced climbers may be the fastest option. Rather than swinging leads (alternating pitches) on the climb itself, it can be more effective to lead in "blocks"; one climber leads several pitches in a row while the second has a better opportunity to recuperate.

Of course, there can be considerable risk when it's just you and a friend in a remote mountain setting. A classic example is the epic of Joe Simpson and Simon Yates on Siula Grande in Peru. During a harrowing descent, Yates was forced by circumstances to cut the rope as Simpson, already with a broken leg, dangled over a cliff above a crevassed glacier. Simpson's book *Touching the Void* (Johnson Cape Ltd., 1988) is mandatory reading for all alpinists. Few climbers fully appreciate the consequences if one member of a roped pair falls deep into a crevasse; even without injury, getting the fallen climber out requires a major effort.

In many cases, a team of three rather than two makes the most sense on long, technical climbs. Other than a slightly larger tent, if one is carried, very little additional gear is needed for a third person. Three climbers are scarcely slower than two, since the leader can climb with a lighter pack and then belay both followers at the same time by using an appropriate belay device. The extra person greatly increases safety on glaciers, on corniced ridges, and in the event of emergency. On a big wall, the second can quickly jug up to the leader so they can start the next pitch while the third person ascends the rope using mechanical ascenders and cleans the pitch.

A team of four offers even more safety and is well-suited to long, moderate routes. This size provides for two, independent rope teams that can still work together and share a climbing rack and ropes. If somebody gets hurt, one person can remain with the victim while the others seek help or

Small expeditions require less of everything, which is part of the attraction.

additional resources. With a foursome, a group attitude is important, since there is a risk of the two pairs becoming fractious.

Finally, there is the solo option. A true solo effort is the undertaking of a single person, without a support team and without taking advantage of other people's work (like packed trails, fixed ropes, and camps). If you're ready for that step, you probably don't need to read this book, since you are either an expert or a fool—it's a fine line.

CREATING THE TEAM

An expedition is just an idea until you find yourself sitting down with possible team-mates, sharing thoughts and committing to the first steps toward the dream. As you assemble your team, consider such key factors as personalities, skills, risk toler-ance, and commitment.

Finding team members that meet your criteria isn't always easy, particularly if you don't live in a climbing center; sometimes you have to cast a wide net. In addition to looking for the right people, you'll need to determine who has the time and resources to join the expedition. All too often, the perfect partner must bow out due to an inescapable commitment or a lack of funds.

Your first choice in expedition mates will probably be longtime climbing partners who live nearby. A typical scenario has you inviting a couple of climbing friends to join the expedition, only to discover that one is planning to get married, while the other

Large expeditions bring together a broad range of experience and talents.

recently lost his job and now has the time, but no money. Then, feeling guilty for not staying in touch, you start ringing up old climbing partners who now live a thousand miles away. Even though the distance makes organization more of a hassle, it's preferable to go on an adventure with people you know.

Only after that well has run dry do you start considering the local climbers you don't really know, but who are perhaps friends of your climbing partners who can't make the trip. This adds a huge variable to your expedition, but at least these people are local. You'll be able to go on shakedown climbs together, and there will be helping hands nearby as departure time approaches.

If your roster still comes up short, you may have to try distant climbers whom you haven't met. While less than ideal, this can work if everyone involved keeps an open line of communication and works extra hard to get along.

Finally, you may need to consider inviting nonclimbers if they offer a particular skill or are otherwise uniquely qualified. This might be a doctor, a videographer, even a world-class chef. Naturally, this can present problems and you'll need to keep a watchful eye over them, and perhaps give some on-the-climb training. If you choose wisely, they might surprise everyone and turn in a stellar performance.

When your team is spread out across the country, or around the globe, the Internet becomes an invaluable resource, and all members should be encouraged to check their email at least once a day. By copying messages to everyone, each person is kept in the loop, fostering teamwork and motivation. Using email also minimizes the hassles of different time zones and playing phone tag.

PERSONALITIES

Personality conflicts have probably ruined more expeditions than either bad weather or accidents. The issue of compatibility is so vital to success that it bears more careful consideration than climbing talent or other skills. When selecting team members, or considering joining a team, the "job interview" needs to be far-ranging and revealing.

If you don't already know the potential candidates well, the Expedition Application form in Appendix A is a good starting point for learning about them. In addition to requesting basic information that will be needed if they join the team, the form includes questions that are often overlooked in a casual conversation. These are intended to stimulate discussion and head off trouble.

With completed applications in hand, or at least a blank form as a reminder of questions to ask, everyone can begin the process of sharing information about themselves and understanding their new friends. If you've never been on a long expedition, this process of discovery might seem too probing and intimate. After you've spent a month in cramped confines together, you may wish you had asked even more private questions ahead of time!

This is the best time to find out if they can laugh when the food sucks, the weather's crappy, and they have diarrhea—not when it actually happens. Discovering that two climbers are sports fanatics who are rabid fans of opposing teams might cause a rethinking of rope teams.

Still, even the most thorough investigation of teammates will be only a best guess. The intangible factors that determine harmony under normal circumstances can evaporate when people are stuck in a storm for days on end. Expeditions can create levels of stress far greater than what most people encounter in normal life. You may discover a new side to someone, a side that has never come to light even if you've known the person for years.

If an expedition's team members don't know each other well, pre-trip excursions to test equipment and temperament are

When stormbound for days, great personalities make the situation tolerable.

vital. These shakedown trips won't reveal all, but they can provide clues to whether everyone will get along, and to each person's strengths and weaknesses. Try to organize these trips early in the planning process so there is time to make adjustments to the team if necessary.

In an ideal team, about half the members will have a gung-ho attitude toward climbing while the other half will tend to the side of caution. The resulting yin-yang balance charges up the team for greatness, yet keeps everyone safe.

SKILLS

In any group of climbers, there is usually a wide range of skills. Even among elite partnerships, someone is bound to be a bit stronger on rock while another person is faster on sketchy ice. Determining these strengths and weaknesses in advance, and then exploiting them, creates a synergy within an expedition. Ignoring these differences and treating everyone as "equals" is the path to mediocrity.

While it may seem desirable that all climbers on a team be equally competent, that isn't necessarily the case. Assuming they are reasonably fit and possess common sense, it's probably better to invite an unskilled person with a great attitude than a phenomenal climber who is a jerk. Skills can be acquired, but no amount of talent can justify the misery inflicted by people who are grumpy and argumentative or who act as if they are God's gift to the climbing world (even if they are). Domineering climbers on ego trips are no fun to be around, and they could endanger others.

If personality is not a problem, then it may be wise to bring a "rope gun"—a strong climber who can be counted on to lead a section, no matter the difficulties. If your route involves mostly moderate snow climbing but has a few technical sections, having one rock expert along, even if that person hasn't done much on snow, can get a team with less-experienced rock climbers to their goal.

During the shopping-for-partners phase of your expedition, decide on a minimum set of skills that are required for the climb, and either eliminate candidates who don't measure up or allow time for learning. Plan a training schedule that gets everyone up to speed on the critical skills.

You might be an Emergency Medical Technician, but that is of little benefit if you're the unconscious victim. If you insist that everyone take a Wilderness First Responder course or equivalent first-aid training, they will likely need six months to find and complete a course. Similarly, there's really no such thing as being too

Acquire crevasse rescue skills before entering an icefall.

experienced in the use of avalanche beacons in searching for victims. Encourage everyone to take an avalanche avoidance course, and schedule beacon practice sessions.

When your goal entails glacier travel, everyone should be proficient at crevasse rescue techniques. It's common for climbers to be technically proficient at alpine climbing yet have minimal experience with crevasse rescue, simply because there aren't any glaciers nearby. They tend to underestimate the difficulties until it's too late. While a relatively easy skill to acquire, crevasse rescue does require practice.

It may be necessary to enlist a specialist for certain aspects of your expedition. If the approach trek requires numerous river crossings, someone trained in swift-water rescue could be a lifesaver. For travel in some parts of the world, it's helpful to include a person with knowledge of the region and the language. And you may want a professional photographer along to appease sponsors. You may believe that you or one of your companions can deliver high-quality photos or video, but a true profes-sional will capture images you can only dream of. Amateurs might get lucky with a few nice shots; pros don't rely on chance.

One final team member to recruit is the person who stays home: the spokesperson. Usually a spouse or close friend of someone on the expedition, this individual will be the contact person for families, friends, and associates. In the event of either disaster or great triumph, the team spokesperson will deal with the media so that a consistent and accurate story is presented.

RISK TOLERANCE

Everyone pays lip service to "safety," yet this vague term has different meanings to different people. Before placing your life on the line with new climbing partners, it's a good idea to explore each other's perceptions of acceptable risk. What is reasonable for one person may be reckless to another.

Ask your partners how they would respond to situations that, in your mind, are close calls. Their answers can guide you to an understanding of how you may differ from them in the appraisal of risk and reward.

Following are a few scenarios that should prompt discussion among members of the expedition. You can also make up your own that are relevant to the goals of your team. There are no incorrect answers to the options presented with each scenario. Depending on your risk tolerance, either choice can be acceptable.

1. The government of the country you are visiting suggests placing $4,000 in a special account, to pay for a helicopter in case of emergency. The money is refundable. Not placing the money in the account makes access to helicopters much slower. Other teams who made deposit got the money back, but they told you it's a real hassle doing the paperwork. Do you tie up your money?

2. The approach march goes up the valley of a river that has become swollen by unseasonable runoff and has knocked out the footbridge. It appears that the river can be forded on foot, but it's hard to tell because the water is so muddy. The nearest suspension bridge is a full day's hike in the wrong direction, and the little-used trail on the other side is very rugged. Hiking to the good bridge will result in

continued on page 50

continued from page 49

the loss of two days of climbing time and increase the expedition's costs for porters. Do you attempt to ford the river?

3. It is difficult to find the snow cave that serves as your high camp, which is 70 meters beyond the end of the fixed rope. Two team members are prepared to climb from Camp 2 to that high camp and launch a summit bid. There is concern, however, that if they cannot find the cave, either on the way up or after returning from the summit, they will be stranded in the open at high altitude and might suffer frostbite or worse. The suggestion is made that an extra length of rope be installed from the fixed lines into the cave entrance, and that wands be placed to guide climbers back to the cave from above. The alternative opinion is that since the team has been able to find the cave in the past, its members should be able to do so again. Bringing the extra rope and wands up from base camp would subtract a day from summit attempts. The weather has been variable, with frequent snowstorms inhibiting activity. Do you take the time to enhance safety?

4. You and three teammates have bivouacked on the upper reaches of the mountain of your dreams. Due to unstable conditions lower on the route, it's been agreed that this is your one and only attempt for the top. In the morning, the others are drained by altitude and limited sleep, but you are feeling strong and lead several rope lengths of spectacular climbing. Eventually you reach a bergschrund just a few hours from the summit and wait for the others to catch up. When the third person reaches you, he announces that the fourth has turned back with a spool of rope still in his pack. It's a perfect summit day and the climbing above looks easy enough to solo—you are confident you can reach the top. But you can see glare from ice glinting in the sun and realize that, without a rope for rappelling, down-soloing could be risky. If you decide to go for it, neither of the others is likely to follow—yet the summit is so close, you can almost touch it. Do you go up?

COMMITMENT

Gauging your own level of commitment and that of others is difficult. For yourself, you will likely find that once you make a sincere decision to join an expedition, and the enterprise will draw you in and your energy for the goal will grow. But you cannot see into the hearts of others. Therefore, an expedition must create milestones that maintain and measure commitment during the planning period. These keep the expedition moving forward and serve as a reality check for each member's degree of desire.

Expedition planners should start by requiring everyone to deposit money into an expedition fund to share initial expenses like acquiring a permit and purchasing maps and guidebooks. The required deposit can be any amount, but usually the higher the dollar value, the greater the commitment. It should be made crystal-clear that the deposit is refundable only if there is a valid reason for leaving the trip, such as illness or a death in the family, or a suitable replacement is found.

After the initial cash is in hand, each team member should be given some expedition task to work on. You'll soon find out who can be counted on to do a job and do it well. Both the expedition leader and the other team members need to act as cheerleaders to help keep everyone excited and motivated.

Physical preparation is another measure of commitment. It takes a lot of time and sweat to prepare for the rigors of most expeditions. Everyone should commit to a regimen of aerobic conditioning and resistance training (weight lifting). See *Climbing: Training for Peak Performance* by Clyde Soles (The Mountaineers Books, 2002) for information on getting in shape. If someone is making excuses for not working out, they'll be making a lot more once the real event begins.

A LESSON IN COMMITMENT

My friends and I talk about climbing trips all the time. Dreams, ideas, routes we want to do, and mountains we want to climb fill our campfire discussions. Only a few of these go beyond talk. Turning a dream into reality demands that you cross the threshold into commitment.

While climbing at Smith Rock, Oregon, several friends and I began planning a trip to the French Alps. We named possible routes, judged whether we could afford the airfare, and talked at length about what it would be like to be on the tram taking us to the base of a route on a spectacular peak.

Then came the time to make a decision. I asked each person if they were serious about the trip. They were. I emphasized that I was going to commit to the trip and would be calling the National Outdoor Leadership School (NOLS) where I worked, to tell them I wouldn't be available during the late summer and early fall. I made the call.

By the end of the following week, all my partners had changed their minds, for one reason or another. One of them had a work conflict. He had just called NOLS and learned there would be work available in the late summer and early fall. He was taking the job I had given up.

—*Phil Powers*

LEADERSHIP

Contrary to legend, people are not born as leaders. Instead, they gradually acquire and refine leadership skills, integrating them with their own personality. These lessons are rarely taught in schools, so the "natural leaders" have learned on their own.

Whether you choose to lead or leadership is thrust upon you, it can help to arm yourself with proven techniques. An excellent resource is *Outdoor Leadership,* by John Graham (The Mountaineers Books, 1997)—even for those who are followers, since the book will help any reader better understand group dynamics.

There was a time when most expeditions had single, military-style leaders who organized and coordinated a hierarchy. That model is less common now and quite rare among small teams. Today's situations, as a result, can be more subtle and complicated.

Before the expedition embarks, its members need to discuss leadership, decision-making, and the structure of the group. In general, most conflicts stem from misunderstandings about a group's structure, and controversy continues until a system is developed for guidance. Determining responsibilities in advance helps get things done and reduces conflict.

The advantage of naming a leader is that in a pinch, there is someone designated to make a decision if other strategies fail. A leader who is willing to ask for input, look at all sides of an issue, and then make the decision that is best for the team greatly enhances an expedition. Too often when a team operates by either majority rule or consensus, individuals are mainly concerned with their own opinions, which can be driven by selfishness. A good leader integrates individual considerations into a decision that is best suited to the team and its overall goals.

The expedition leader need not make every decision. The team may choose to make all decisions by consensus, with a single leader as a final arbiter if time prevents full resolution. An expedition can decide to assign its leader anywhere along the leadership spectrum, which extends from the leader who acts in that capacity only when asked to do so, to the leader who makes all major decisions, period.

LEADERSHIP STYLES

There is a great deal of variation within each of the styles of leadership. Give some thought to the following forms of leadership, and before the expedition gets fully under way, decide which of the general styles you plan to use.

Leaderless

With small groups (four people or less) of equally competent climbers heading to countries that don't require permits, the expedition can operate without any form of leader. All decisions are made by simple democracy in which the majority rules, or by consensus (the preferred method). In either case, you should decide in advance how arguments will be settled—because they *will* arise.

The leaderless approach can work well with close-knit groups of friends who have climbed together before. However, it also presents the risk of ruining friendships. It's amazing how silly arguments can escalate into major battles, yet this is often the case. Try to implement a system for resolving issues without hurting feelings. Referring to the mission statement, if one was created, can often settle problems.

Even a leaderless expedition must pick someone to sign the forms when permits are involved. While your form-signer may only have an equal say within the team, as far as the bureaucracy is concerned this person runs the show.

Leader by Consensus

In larger groups, anywhere from five or six people on up, it becomes difficult for everyone's voice to be heard. Some people tend to be more vociferous and domineering; others seek to avoid conflict by staying quiet. The odds are stacked against such an expedition if it tries to operate without an acknowledged leader.

In this situation, what is needed is a leader who will operate by consensus, seeking out the opinions of everyone—even those meek souls who don't normally pipe up. Frequently, this leader will hardly seem to influence the proceedings; at other times, the leader will need to exert gentle persuasion. When consensus cannot be reached, the leader may need to step in to decide a course of action. Only when things are at a critical stage should this leader issue any sort of direct order.

Dictator

Outside of commercial expeditions where the guide is paid to run the entire show, it's now fairly rare for teams to have an autocratic leader. The big nationalistic expeditions, run by a "general," are mostly history, with the exception of some university-outing clubs.

Guided expeditions still need this type of command structure because many of the participants lack the experience to make good decisions on the mountain. While you don't have to ask "How high?" when this expedition leader tells you to jump, you do need to respect the person's authority and question it only when your life may be at risk.

Dual Leaders

Particularly with large expeditions to major peaks, it may be wise to designate both an expedition leader, who handles the logistics of getting to and from the mountain, and a climbing leader, who is responsible for directing the team safely to the summit and back. The climb leader generally is the person with the most experience in the type of climbing involved, though not necessarily the most technically proficient.

The advantage of dual leadership, assuming the lines are clearly drawn, is that it takes a lot of pressure off the expedition leader. This leader can concentrate on the endless demands of organizing and maintaining the operation, confident that the other leader will handle issues of route choices, supplies, and climbing personnel.

TRAITS OF A GOOD LEADER

A number of traits are common among good leaders. These leadership traits can be practiced, and can eventually become second nature.

Noticeably absent from this list is a strong personality; such people *can* be good leaders, but only if they overcome their instinct to dominate. When an expedition ends, a mark of good leadership is that no one has the impression they were led, but everyone feels instead that the team worked together as a whole.

A good leader:

Communicates well. Perhaps the single most important skill of a leader is facilitating open channels of communication. He or she not only is receptive to input but actively seeks it out. A good leader freely shares information so everyone understands a situation and learns from the experience. They never bluff since this invariably undermines authority.

Practices ethical behavior. A good leader demonstrates respect for everyone, including porters, cooks, and residents of the region the expedition is visiting. He or she looks at a situation from all sides and make decisions that are unbiased and fair, something easier said than done.

Cares for others. Hand in hand with a sense of ethics is a sincere concern for others and for their opinions. Even if a leader decides against some team members' ideas or points of view, they will usually continue to support the leader as long as they feel they have received an honest hearing.

Supports people's goals. A good leader supports people's goals as long as they don't conflict with those of the expedition. If a team member expresses a particular interest—in bouldering, local culture, or photography, for instance—the leader encourages the interest as far as is practical.

Exhibits a sense of humor. While it's also true of anyone on an expedition, a leader needs a sense of humor. Both leader and team benefit from the ability to see a lighthearted side to the serious work of an expedition; tension goes down as laughter goes up.

Delegates tasks. A leader cannot, and should not, do it all. A good leader assigns tasks, then lets people do their jobs without micromanaging them. A leader also has the ability to make chores look like fun, more like a game than drudgery.

Works hard. Leading by example is often the best way to get others to follow. A good leader doesn't hesitate to jump in and get his or her hands dirty. Sometimes a leader is also an actor, hiding discomfort or fatigue in order to inspire the team.

Maintains focus. Team members are sometimes distracted from the mission of the expedition, or feel they must push their personal agendas. A good leader keeps everyone focused on the established goals of the team, providing gentle reminders when things become discombobulated.

CHAPTER 3

Alpamayo (19,506 feet, 5,945 meters), Peru

In the Know

One of the keys to a successful expedition is thinking ahead. The more research and legwork you do in advance, the better the odds of having a great experience when you get to your destination. If things don't go quite right, always a distinct possibility, you'll be better prepared to handle the contingencies.

An expedition often needs to educate itself in the intricacies of international travel—the ins and outs of getting to the climbing destination. At the same time, team members will seek out information on their mountain, learning all they can in advance about its challenges.

Some climbers advocate a "going in blind" approach to expeditions as a means to increase the adventure. While there is certainly something to be said for engaging a culture and ascending a route with no prior knowledge, this is best reserved for climbers with a great deal of experience. Stack the odds in your favor by doing the research. What you don't know *can* hurt you.

FACT FINDING

There can be a surprising amount of information available for virtually any destination or peak, but finding it may take some sleuthing. The more obscure the location, the harder it may be to find answers, but don't automatically assume that adventurers have never been there. You might discover that an explorer was in the region a century ago, or that climbers bagged your peak decades earlier but didn't consider it noteworthy (or legal).

The Internet is a good starting point for your quest. Use search engines such as *Google.com* and *Bookfinder.com* to seek out websites and books on the region of interest. The websites of commercial outfitters and of previous expeditions can yield useful tidbits. Many climbers have personal websites that describe their adventures and provide useful links to other sites (for example, *Bonington.com*, *Gdargaud.net*, and *Clydesoles.com*). If you don't mind wading through some manure, posting questions to a newsgroup, such as *rec.climbing*, can turn up worthwhile hints and tips from netizens around the globe.

Even in this age of electronic connectivity, there's no substitute for a good library. Among the most valuable resources are the journals of alpine clubs, which provide annual roundups of the prior year's expeditions. The *American Alpine Journal* offers worldwide coverage but is particularly strong on South America and Alaska. The *Alpine Journal,* from Britain, provides good coverage from around the world. The *Canadian Alpine Journal* is another good source.

Both the *Himalayan Journal* and *Indian Mountaineer* provide excellent information on the great ranges. The Japanese magazine *Iwa to Yuki* (Rock and Snow) ceased publication in 1994, but back issues, with good summaries in English, are still an important resource. The new *Japanese Alpine News* began publication in 2001.

Many of the early expedition accounts and old guidebooks are long out of print; though dated, they sometimes contain gems of knowledge. Back issues of popular magazines (such as *Alpinist, Climbing, Rock & Ice, Mountain,* and *Summit*) may yield useful articles and photos.

A great deal of information is published in languages other than English. The journals of the major European and South American alpine clubs may be helpful if you can translate them. Tales of expeditions from other countries (like Iran, South Korea, or Slovenia) may be harder to obtain, though their climbers have been active for many years.

The headquarters of the various national climbing and exploration clubs usually have detailed reports from sponsored expeditions and a well-stocked library. University or public libraries may not have the books you are looking for but can sometimes acquire them through interlibrary loans.

TRAVEL SMARTS

While the climb is the main event, getting there is half the fun—or it should be. Whether or not everyone enjoys the journey has a lot to do with preparation. No matter the size of your expedition, researching travel logistics will pay off manyfold in reduced stress once you're under way.

Here again, the Internet is an invaluable tool that can save you time and money. By going online, you can find out if you need visas or permits to visit your destination, immunization requirements, and dining recommendations (see the list of travel-related websites in Appendix B, Resources). It's worthwhile to check the website of the U.S. Embassy in the destination country (even if you're a citizen of another nation) because it posts warnings for travelers and will provide useful information about your region of interest.

TRAVEL AGENTS
The importance of travel agents has diminished considerably in this age of the Internet, but they still provide a valuable service. If yours is a small group (six or less) with a relatively straightforward itinerary, you may decide to handle your own bookings. Someone in your group has to be willing to spend a good bit of time looking for the best deals and checking the rules.

Larger groups, and travelers pressed for time, have more to gain by going with a pro. Even though they charge a fee, travel agents can save you money on blocks of seats and find deals that you may not discover on your own. And they can alert you to obscure requirements before they cost you a bundle. For a bunch of team members with conflicting schedules and requirements, a travel agent can sort out the logistics and reduce frustration.

An often-overlooked benefit of a travel agent is that when things go wrong, you have someone who may be able to help. You can try to handle the difficulties of a lost hotel reservation or a canceled flight on your own, but the agent may be able to do it better— even from the other side of the planet.

AIRLINE TICKETS
Sometimes the cheapest tickets aren't the best deals. Many climbers who have taken the lowest price in the past are now willing to pay a bit more for better service. Read the fine print that comes with your airline tickets. Particularly with cheap fares, the restrictions can be deal killers. And don't underestimate the added stress that comes with economy flights.

While you're ticket-shopping, it's worth considering the value of frequent-flyer miles that you may get with one airline but not another (check their alliances); these could help on your next expedition. Also remember that a 7 A.M. departure means arriving at the airport at 5 A.M. (or earlier) and waking a couple hours before that—a rough start on a long travel day.

A major concern for climbers on expeditions is the flexibility of return dates. You would hate to abort a summit bid in order to return on a specific date, chosen months ahead of time, simply because it would cost a few hundred bucks to change flights. Equally bad is getting socked with a hefty fee for returning early if things go well and you're done ahead of time (or if things go badly and you're sick or injured). Spending a few extra days in Rawalpindi might be fun, but two weeks may seem an eternity.

Another huge issue is the baggage allowance. Cash-strapped airlines will hit you hard if you run over the limit; this can run into hundreds of dollars per person. Old tricks, like wearing gear on board or checking one bag with a skycap and another at the ticket counter, no longer work due to enhanced security and computerized information.

Even if you don't exceed the weight allotment, there can be hidden fees that you discover only at the airport. On a recent trip to Canada, a friend discovered that while one pair of skis is free, a second pair costs $75 each way—even when both pairs are in the same bag and are under the weight limit. This extortion works because they have you by the short hairs: the flight is leaving, and there's probably no place to stash gear at the airport.

Typically on international flights with

Piles of luggage can be heaps of trouble at the airport; plan ahead and arrive early.

U.S. carriers, the allowance is two checked bags that weigh no more than 70 pounds (32 kg) each (total of 140 pounds), with the total of the three dimensions of each bag limited to 62 inches (157 cm). However, this may decrease, and many other airlines restrict the checked baggage of passengers in economy class to a total of 44 pounds (20 kg), business class to a total of 66 pounds (30 kg), and first class to a total of 88 pounds (40 kg).

Be cautious about taking a layover for sightseeing in a hub city, particularly if you're switching airlines for the next leg; you may be in for an unpleasant and expensive surprise. The layover prevents you from checking baggage through to the final destination; you must claim it and later check it back in. For example, if you purchase a ticket from United Airlines for travel to Kathmandu, you may fly with United to Bangkok but with Thai Air the rest of the way. Going straight through to Kathmandu presents no problem, but if you stop over in Bangkok for a few days, you have to check in with Thai Air, which may have a lower weight allowance for baggage. Many airlines calculate the excess baggage fee at 1.5 percent of a standard economy ticket per kilogram, so it can be a very costly visit.

In some cases, you will need to book in-country flights independently from international flights (you can't book from Seattle to Lukla or Boston to Skardu). These domestic tickets generally must be purchased locally, so you need to go through your trekking agency or just hope you can get them when you arrive. Should you be traveling during the height of tourist season, it's quite possible you won't be able to get a seat on the day you desire without an advance reservation.

Flights within the region or nation you are visiting will have their own regulations, particularly when they involve propeller-driven planes. In some cases, even the passengers are weighed. Pilots in Alaska are accustomed to carrying climbers, so they generally allow 125 pounds (57 kg) of gear

per person as part of the price. In most other areas of the world, the limit will be more like 44 pounds (20 kg). For an extra charge, you can ask the pilots in Alaska to make a fly-by of your mountain in order to visually check on your safety during the climb. When it's time for the pilot to come pick you up, be aware that if the plane is forced to turn back by bad weather before reaching you, the expedition will still be charged for the flight.

HOTEL RESERVATIONS

A lot of climbers leave the detail of finding a hotel until they arrive at a destination and then just go for the cheapest accommodation available—potentially two big mistakes. Among the perils of an expedition is getting sick before you even arrive at the mountain. This is most likely to happen during the first few days of your trip.

If you have crossed five or more time zones, particularly going from west to east, your body will already be under significant physical stress from jet lag. In many cases, the major city that you'll be flying into has worse air pollution than where you live, so stress is further increased. The city may be hot, humid, and noisy, making sleep hard to come by. And you'll probably be amped up about starting the trip that's been so long in the planning.

All this stress weakens your immune system. Add to this the unusual foods and bugs that are foreign to your body, and you have all the makings for a bout of *turista*. Traveler's diarrhea and infections are no fun under the best of circumstances. For a climber, they produce a weakened condition that makes the trek and acclimatization even harder.

It's worth the extra money for a hotel room with air-conditioning. Request a room that is away from busy streets and that has a window so you can see whether it's day or night, thereby adjusting more quickly to the new time zone. You will breathe cleaner air and sleep infinitely better than in a budget hotel.

To guarantee a good hotel, make reservations before you leave home; you can probably do it by email. The better hotels often provide transportation from the airport, which saves you the headache of negotiating with aggressive baggage handlers and cab drivers. If you need to economize, get a cheap hotel on the way home after the climb.

TREKKING AGENTS

Depending upon where you are going, you may want a local trekking agency or guide service to handle logistics. In some places, like parts of India and Pakistan, you can't get a climbing permit without one. This doesn't mean that you are hiring a guide to hold your hand to the top of the mountain (though that service is likely available). Instead you are getting logistical help, local expertise, and someone to soothe the bureaucratic beast.

Try to get recommendations for agencies from climbers, not just trekkers, who have recently been to the area. It's worth the time to track down members of previous expeditions for advice, since this decision can greatly affect your entire trip. Be sure to let the agency know who sent you their

way; you may get better service or even a price break.

Should you have no luck with word-of-mouth recommendations, your best bet is to stick with one of the older established outfitters, such as Mountain Travel Nepal (founded in 1965; *Tigermountain.com*) and Nazir Sabir Expeditions (founded in 1987; *Nazirsabir.com*) in Pakistan. These companies often charge more than newer, smaller operations, but you are ensured first-class service and peace of mind. Guidebook recommendations are unreliable several years after publication, but they can serve as a starting point for queries.

For most of the last century, it was a significant hassle to communicate with a trekking agency thousands of miles away. But email is now universal, and all reputable agencies have Internet connections; many have websites. This is important because you'll need to do a lot of negotiating prior to your departure.

In general, the agencies will handle the advance paperwork required by their government for your expedition, sending you the necessary forms and documents that need signatures. They can also assist with acquiring fuel for your camp stoves by either purchasing it in advance or acting as a receiving agent for shipments.

Most importantly, the trekking agency will provide any people that you decide to employ for the expedition. This includes a *sirdar* (head guide), cooks for the approach trek and base camp, and porters or other means of transporting expedition supplies and gear. Inquire about the qualifications of the people you are being asked to hire. The sirdar and head cook, two of the most important members of an expedition, often have letters of recommendation from previous employers.

Be sure that the cook is well-versed in Western cuisine; you may not care for local fare or meals preferred by Korean expeditions. The longer your trip, the more important this becomes. Have the agency send you sample menus for the trek and for base camp, and make sure there is plenty of variety in the diet.

Don't take it for granted that the luxuries are included; be sure to verify. At your request, the trekking agency can provide a mess tent, tables, camp stools, kerosene lanterns, thermos bottles, toilet tent, and tents for you to use on the trek and in base camp. Each of these things has a cost, so a low-budget expedition may elect to do without. On the other hand, roughing it gets old by the second week, and in hindsight you may wish you'd coughed up a little extra.

INSURANCE

Every member of an expedition needs to check with his or her health insurance provider to see if the coverage applies in foreign countries. Citizens of Britain and Canada have automatic coverage through their national health systems in many countries of the world; they should check with their national department of health.

U.S. citizens are not so fortunate and must purchase private health insurance. In buying health insurance, be sure to note the disclaimers. A common exclusion is one for preexisting conditions. For

A great cook is worth his weight in gold. Seek him out and treat him well.

instance, if you were treated for pulmonary edema at some point in the past, a new insurance policy might not cover you if it occurs again.

Nobody likes giving money to the insurance companies, thus many climbers decide to go abroad without coverage. However, consider that if it's a struggle to pay for coverage, then it's likely that an actual loss or serious accident could be financially crippling for years to come. Don't make this decision lightly, and remember that indecision is a decision.

It's vital that you read the fine print on any insurance policy you buy. When applying, don't hide the truth under the assumption that what the insurance company doesn't know can't hurt you: this may be just the excuse they need to reject a claim.

An option if you do not have medical coverage is to purchase a travel health insurance plan. For one month of $50,000 in coverage (with a $250 deductible), premiums run about $40 for travelers in their thirties and $64 for people in their forties. The big catch: these plans exclude climbing and skiing, so you'd better have the accident or illness while you're hiking.

Expedition members with dependent children should check the provisions of their life insurance policies. Many policies have exclusions for mountaineering, scuba diving, and other fun activities that actually promote a longer life than comes from being a couch potato.

No matter your health plan, very few provide adequate coverage for rescue operations beyond the trailhead. Although this is one of the benefits offered by some alpine clubs, it may not be sufficient reason to join. The annual dues for the American Alpine Club ($75) includes $5,000 of worldwide rescue coverage for peaks under 6,000 meters (19,685 feet).

If you have higher aspirations, the extra premiums make the alpine club policy a dubious value. For rescue insurance on an 8,000-meter peak, the cost over the course of an expedition will be about $600 per person ($12 a day) for $5,000 of coverage, with a $500 deductible. The British Mountaineering Council offers a much better insurance program, but it's available only to people from the United Kingdom.

It's a good idea to look into travel insurance that covers trip cancellation and baggage loss. Cancellation insurance often has a lot of exclusions—you can't just change your mind about going—but it could save you a heap of cash if you break a leg the week before your trip.

It would possibly be cheaper to lose a duffel stuffed with dollar bills than one that contains all of your mountaineering equipment. The loss-limits established by the airlines barely cover a night on the town. You may have extra loss coverage through your credit-card company if the ticket was purchased with a card (read the microprint), but that often doesn't cover theft or other loss, such as from a burro falling in a river. Many homeowner and renter policies provide coverage for loss of property while traveling, but check with your agent on the details. An additional rider may be necessary, particularly if you have a lot of camera equipment.

MEDICAL INFORMATION

Each member of the expedition should fill out the expedition medical form in Appendix A. If someone has a medical condition that may affect the trip, such as an allergy or a previous case of high-altitude pulmonary edema (HAPE), everyone needs to know about it. It's also important to have emergency contact information for each member, both with the leader and with a friend back home.

Filling out the form prompts expedition members to investigate their immunization status. Tetanus and polio boosters are needed only once every ten years, so it's easy to forget when they're due. For most parts of the developing world, it's also advisable to protect against hepatitis A and typhoid. Depending upon where you are going, other vaccinations may include Japanese encephalitis, meningococcal meningitis, and yellow fever. Check the Internet for updates on outbreaks of disease (see the list of travel-related websites in Appendix B, Resources).

Although you are headed to the mountains, many expeditions pass through lowlands where mosquito-borne diseases are prevalent. A brief stay in a major city and a quick trip to the foothills pose relatively low risk for infection. If you will be spending time below 5,000 feet (1,500 meters), especially in rural areas and the tropics, carry plenty of insect repellent (30 percent DEET). Malaria is a particularly pernicious threat, and prevention requires weekly oral doses of prescription medications while in the risk area and for four weeks afterward.

REGIONAL CULTURE

It is wise to learn the customs of the places you plan to visit so that you don't unknowingly offend those who live there. As a rich Westerner, no matter how little money you possess, you may already be suspect in their eyes. Seemingly minor transgressions can have great significance. Quite simply, there is no excuse for cultural arrogance by visiting expeditions.

There are many do's and don'ts that probably will not occur to you without instruction. For example, in Nepal, when the trail splits at a *mani wall* (wall made of stones carved with prayers) take the left fork so the wall stays on your right; stealing a stone is way bad karma. And you must not touch someone with your left hand, or sit with your feet pointing at another person. Refusing a toast of vodka from a host in Russia, even if you don't drink, is tantamount to a slap in the face. In many parts of the world, when you are a guest in someone's home, turning down a meat dish can be deeply insulting; your hosts will not understand that you are a vegetarian.

Cultural awareness is particularly important for females traveling in Islamic regions. For women accustomed to the freedoms of the West, the Muslim culture is likely to come as a shock. You will have a different, and probably more difficult, experience than men in your group, but you still can have a great time.

In Muslim areas, it will usually be important for women to cover all skin other than their face, hands, and feet. Shorts and sport tops are impermissible—men may even toss pebbles at you. Standard traveling clothes are considered offensive if they reveal the shape of the body. It's best to purchase a *shalwar kameez* (the baggy pant and pretty, long shirt locals wear) upon arrival for town wear. Once out on the trail, you can wear comfortable long-sleeved pants and shirts, but the porters are male so you still can't bare more flesh. It's best to travel with some of the men in your group at all times.

THE ONE-HOUR VOCABULARY

It's always helpful to speak the language of the place you are visiting. If possible, take a course prior to departure; you will ingratiate yourself with local residents. Spanish is invaluable in nearly all of Central and South America, and classes are easy to find at schools in the United States. It will be somewhat harder to find instructors for Hindi

A few words go a long way in making friends.

(India), Nepali (Western Nepal), Tibetan (Eastern Nepal and Tibet), Swahili (East Africa), or Urdu (Pakistan and India). Interactive computer programs, or even language tapes, are a reasonable alternative to classes, but it takes willpower to get through them (*Worldlanguage.com* has learning products for 171 languages).

At the very least, it's worth the time to learn a few words of the native language in order to make communications easier and to demonstrate your interest in the local culture. Following is a short list of common English words that are useful to know in the local tongue. You can research the language enough to find these words, then memorize them during the long flight to your destination.

Hello	Kilometer	Water	Taxi
Thank you	Day	Tea	Bus
Please	Night	Beer	Jeep
Good-bye	Hike or walk	Camp	Airport
How much?	Fast	Toilet	Airplane
1–10	Slow	Mule	Pharmacy
100	Restaurant	Porter	Doctor
1000	Stove	Camel	Police
Kilogram	Food	Horse	Help

KNOW YOUR MOUNTAIN

For a climb up a well-traveled route, there is no shortage of step-by-step information available. If you're heading off the beaten path, however, you may need to base some of your planning decisions upon estimation, and on guesswork based on your own experience.

Sometimes you can anticipate conditions that you will encounter by using information from climbers who have done nearby routes or peaks. But don't be surprised if the rock, for example, is entirely different just one ridge away. You may even find that conditions on the same route differ greatly from those that confronted a previous expedition. Seasonal and annual snowpack fluctuates widely in many places. The popular Southwest Ridge of Ama Dablam has a different character in the spring, when it's dry and rocky, than in the fall after the monsoons have plastered the mountain with snow.

Beware of outdated knowledge. Retreating glaciers can render old information useless in some places, such as Peru and Kenya; a formerly casual approach may now be a nightmare since the freshly exposed terrain is extremely unstable. With rising global temperatures, lakes behind glacial dams are growing rapidly. When, not if, the moraines break, the ensuing flood causes devastation in the valleys below, wiping out entire villages and trail systems. Nepal has

Bridges can be ephemeral so don't rely on decade-old accounts.

identified dozens of these future floods, including one dangerous lake in the Khumbu below Island Peak, and they can be expected in many other mountain countries.

THE REGION

Finding out about your destination involves more than just researching the mountain that is the objective. A full picture of what you're getting into requires an understanding of the physical characteristics of the region as well, such as its weather and topography. Guidebooks often offer generalizations, but it can be helpful to speak directly with people who have local knowledge, such as guides and leaders of previous expeditions.

Weather

To help determine what equipment and clothing to bring on the expedition, you need to research regional weather conditions. You need to know not only the average temperatures and precipitation, but also the extremes that have been recorded during the time of year you'll be there. Find out what direction storms usually blow in from, and the harbingers of their arrival. Many areas have annual weather phenomena, such as Bolivia's powerful *surazo* wind, which usually arrives in August and blows from the south for a week.

In expansive ranges like the Andes and Himalaya, there are dramatic weather differences at opposite ends and in the middle. The side of the range nearer the ocean typically has far greater precipitation, while the opposite side often has wider temperature fluctuations.

Terrain

With every 7.5-minute topographic map in the United States now available on CD, and computer programs that can extrapolate three-dimensional images, Americans are more than a little spoiled these days. In other parts of the world, it can be far more difficult to obtain good maps—if they even exist. Since all maps for outside the United States use metric measurements, Americans should get used to this system ahead of time.

For climbing purposes, only maps with a scale of 1:50,000 (1 cm = 500 meters) or finer are adequate. These have a contour interval of 40 meters (132 feet), so they can still hide a serious cliff between the lines. The standard 7.5-minute maps of the U.S. Geological Survey (USGS) are 1:24,000 (contour interval 40 feet), while the 15-minute maps that are still used in Alaska are 1:63,360. Larger-scale maps such as 1:125,000 or 1:250,000 are useful only for general orientation, such as on the approach march.

Quite often, older maps are seriously inaccurate on the location of trails, villages, and even mountains—so you just might be purchasing an adventure!

Another reason to look at the date of a map is that magnetic declination (the difference between true north and magnetic north) changes over time, called secular variation (see figure 3.1, page 70). If you're navigating by compass and relying on a map over a decade old, the shift can be several degrees, which is enough to throw you off considerably. If depending upon older maps, consult the National Geophysical Data Center's website (see Appendix B) for the current declination.

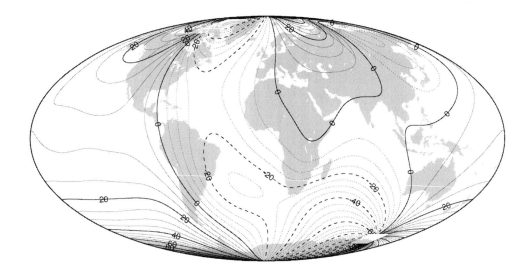

3.1 Magnetic declination. These lines are in a constant state of flux, which can make the corrections on older maps inaccurate.

In many cases, it's harder to find maps in the country you're researching than it is to purchase them before leaving home; don't count on picking them up when you arrive. Good online sources of maps include *Adventuroustraveler.com*, *Chesslerbooks.com*, *Geokatalog.de*, *Maplink.com*, and *Stanfords.co.uk*. Thanks to eyes in the sky, it's now possible to purchase satellite images of almost any location on the planet (*Spaceimaging.com*). While not cheap, the images can provide invaluable information for heading into truly remote areas: you can even have custom topo maps printed.

Some maps are works of art, with marvelous coloring and shading. If you plan to present slide shows after your trip, you may wish to photograph the maps before they get messed up on the trip, with your route drawn in to orient your audience.

THE APPROACH

Undoubtedly you're mostly interested in the "real climbing," but the climb actually starts where public transportation ends. This is where you need to begin your planning. Thus you may start climbing, and acclimatizing, in the Cordillera Blanca at Yungay, Peru, in the Karakoram at Skardu, Pakistan, and in the Khumbu at Lukla, Nepal. The questions you must answer: how will you transport the team and a mountain of gear to base camp, and how long will it take?

For some places, this is a simple matter. In the Alaska Range, a Cessna 185 can fly two climbers and their gear right to the

BEASTS OF BURDEN

Pack animals can be significantly cheaper than porters, though they offer their own set of issues and are not practical or allowed in many regions. Be sure the negotiations include handlers and fodder (if needed) and try to get it in writing before leaving. Unless everyone rides, which is rare, don't expect to cover more ground than a standard day's hike.

Typical Loads:

Burros (small donkeys)	60 lbs (27 kg)
Llamas	65 lbs (30 kg)
Horses and mules (horse/donkey hybrids)	100 lbs (45 kg)
Yaks and zopkios (yak/cow hybrids)	110 lbs (50 kg)
Bactrian camels (two humps)	175 lbs (80 kg)

Give yaks a wide berth.

base of many climbs. Many of the peaks in the Cordillera Blanca can be reached in a day's hike with the aid of a *collectivo* (hired minivan) and *arriero* (burro driver). Both Shishapangma and Cho Oyu, two popular 8,000-meter peaks in Tibet, have truck access right to their base. This rapid access has its drawbacks too, since it allows you to move up in altitude far faster than your body can adjust; pounding headaches and other symptoms of acute mountain sickness (AMS) are common.

Fortunately, there are still many places that can be reached only by a long approach trek. Most of the major peaks in the Karakoram require at least a week to reach them, more if crossing Tibet. While the recently paved airstrip in Lukla makes access easier to the Everest region, most travelers still require ten days to reach base camp. Although it adds another five days, expeditions to the Khumbu (Everest, Pumori, Ama Dablam, etc.) would do well to begin the approach in Jiri, the traditional start, since you will be better acclimatized and conditioned when you reach your goal—plus it's a delightful trek without the hordes encountered above Lukla.

While examining the approach options, also consider the means of transportation.

Where mechanized vehicles (four-wheel drive vehicles, snowmobiles, helicopters) are available, the load is primarily limited by what will fit. In Nepal, a standard porter load is 65 pounds (30 kilograms) while in Pakistan it's 55 pounds (25 kilograms) and rigidly enforced; check in advance for other countries. Sometimes strong porters will carry double loads for double the pay but you may find it embarrassing when you pass them on the trail while wearing your day pack.

ROUTE EVALUATION

After the initial lust has worn off, it's time to critically appraise the object of your desire. While you won't be able to determine some things until you see her up close and personal in all her naked glory, a careful study ahead of time can indicate what kind of trouble you may be getting into. Forewarned is forearmed.

Although a detailed route description may diminish some of the adventure, most climbers will still find that their cup runneth over on a high peak far from civilization. If somebody from a previous expedition went to the trouble to prepare a topo or a good verbal description of your route, this information can save you massive headaches.

The prospective first ascensionist will be more reliant upon studying photographs which, ideally, were made in the same season as your visit and at different angles and times of day. If you aren't used to the scale of things in the greater ranges, it's easy to underestimate the difficulties and risks. What appears as a small, easy obstacle may in fact be a major cliff that requires a full day's effort.

Using whatever maps, photos, and route descriptions you can assemble, study your potential line and envision scenarios at critical junctures. Look for alternatives in case you arrive to find that what appeared as a hand crack was actually a black streak in a blank face. Consider that the most obvious way may not in fact be the best route in less than ideal conditions.

When evaluating the technical difficulties of a route, also think about what

The Gasherbrum Icefall

equipment you will need. This early planning stage isn't the time to get into the minutiae of what to bring, but you do want to get a handle on the basics: number of campsites, amount of technical rock protection (minimal or full aid rack?), quantity of snow anchors, distance of fixed rope (if any).

Sometimes the route is less problematic than getting to it. Hiking up fresh glacial moraine can be slow and treacherous due to routefinding difficulties and loose rock. Long talus slopes can transform into time-consuming, knee-twisting terrain with a few inches of snow. Icefalls occassionaly block the path to the upper mountain; they are almost always difficult and occasionally impenetrable.

Clyde's Gasherbrum II expedition was the first to arrive that season, so they had the task of establishing a route through the icefall—a massive frozen cascade that drops about 1,200 feet in a mile. With many crevasses still hidden by snow, it was a nerve-wracking five days on the sharp end—punctuated by unexpected plummets into bottomless black holes—until a safe path was established. It took the team two full weeks to reach advanced base camp at the start of the real climbing. Subsequent expeditions used the trail and fixed lines to reach advanced base camp in one day—but they missed out on the fun of exploration!

Route Hazards

As you study maps, expedition reports, and route descriptions, learn all you can about the likely objective hazards of your intended climb. Alpine face climbs have a propensity for dropping rocks and large blocks of ice from great heights. Gullies can be either shortcuts or death traps, depending on the time of day and luck.

Ridges offer less rockfall danger. Instead, you may have to cope with horrendous cornices and unconsolidated snow. A complicated route that wanders between towers can turn into an irreversible epic; read the account of Pete Athans, Peter Metcalf, and Glenn Randall on the Southeast Spur of Alaska's Mount Hunter in *Breaking Point* (Chockstone Press, 1984).

Gentle to moderate snow slopes can offer fast going or they can become major avalanche hazards waiting for a climber to trigger them. When located high on the mountain, a snow-loaded plateau can block progress—waist-deep wallowing at altitude requires superhuman strength—or it may prevent retreat unless it was carefully marked with wands.

Perhaps you've seen an avalanche in the Alps, Cascades, or Rockies, but they are no comparison with the power and size of those in the Himalaya; a *much* wider berth is required. Immediately following a storm is certainly the most dangerous time for powder avalanches. Often you must wait a day or two for conditions to settle. But wind-loaded snow slabs can lurk for many days or weeks; look for clues such as prevailing winds and direction of cornices.

Guessing when one of the glacial towers of ice (known as seracs) will collapse is like playing Russian roulette without knowing how many chambers are loaded. Some climbers argue that major serac and cornice collapses occur most frequently in the early

An avalanche plummeting thousands of feet has no mercy—avoid at all costs.

morning and late afternoon during the freeze-thaw cycle. Others claim that midday, when it's hottest, and predawn, when it's coldest, are the most dangerous times. Certain parts of icefalls will be more active than others, so there is no substitute for firsthand knowledge. One issue is clear: the less time you spend below big things that fall, the better.

Glaciers take on a distinct flavor in different parts of the world. This isn't just a matter of size, though bigger glaciers have bigger crevasses, because climate also plays a role. Climbers in the Pacific Northwest and the western Alps may be used to relatively stable snow bridges thanks to heavy snow and temperate weather. But the extreme cold of the Alaska Range produces less stable snow and thick but weak bridges. And the mid-latitudes and high altitudes of the Karakoram mean extreme daily temperature swings and less predictable bridges.

Although glaciers are not inherently dangerous, complacency is: climbers tend to let their guard down when on relatively flat terrain. One of the world's premier climbers, Renato Casarotto, died from a fall as he returned to base camp following a solo summit bid on K2; the lip of a small crevasse collapsed as he tried to jump across.

Route Options

Concurrent with planning your way to the summit, you need to prepare the escape. Often this is just a matter of descending your route, so on the way up, the wise climber will prevent problems in advance by wanding tricky descents, leaving fixed lines at tough spots, and caching extra food and fuel. A safe retreat is more important than style.

At some point during the initial planning process, you should come to grips with a turnaround time. This doesn't have to be a carved-in-stone number based upon armchair analysis. But you should make a rough approximation based upon elevation gain and expected terrain. Without this vaccine, summit fever can get you into a world of hurt. When you're actually up there, hopefully enjoying the summit view, the top question on your mind should always be, "How long will it take to get down?"

For more technical climbs, it may be significantly faster and safer to descend another route instead of the line of ascent. In some cases, the only way down is up and over the top. These situations demand extra attention in planning, particularly if none of you have been on the descent route before. Many trip reports are written from a ground-up viewpoint, and things have a way of looking very different from the top down, especially in a storm.

If there is any doubt about finding your way off the mountain, you may want to prepare a description and topo of the descent. Don't count on an infallible memory after you've been climbing for days at high altitude. Include all the relevant information, such as compass bearings, elevations for traverses, key points to look for, and map coordinates for GPS. Make copies for everyone, laminate them in clear plastic, and attach a keeper cord to each one.

While you're at home researching your mountain, it makes sense to investigate other climbing options in the vicinity. You may need to budget extra time, but it can be well worth the effort to warm up on a nearby trekking peak or perhaps a moderate line on your chosen mountain. Just don't let the minor goal subvert the real prize (read: don't get hurt and don't waste too much time).

HIGHER GOING

Everything takes longer at high altitude—the higher you go, the more things slow down. A 5.7 pitch is easily dispatched at 6,000 feet; it's an entirely different matter at 26,000 feet. This reality must be accounted for during the planning of your expedition.

Indeed, the higher you go, the less technical the climbing should be, or you may never see the summit. If your goal is hard free-climbing or dicey aid on alpine rock, it's best to aim for spectacular peaks with the crux sections below 20,000 feet.

"Easy climbing" takes on new meaning with one-third of sea-level oxygen.

Climb Time

For routes that have had multiple ascents, it's reasonable to base your time estimate upon the others. If your climb will be a second ascent, you can probably plan on a few days less than the original; third ascents tend to be slightly faster yet. Naturally, if you're going alpine style and the first team used expedition style, you're likely to be much faster on the climb. But the total expedition length will be about the same for taller mountains, because you always need time before the main climb for acclimatization.

When examining photographs of a potential new route from the comfort of your living room, it can be difficult to gauge how long the climb will take. This is even harder if you have never been to high altitude or attempted a peak with 10,000 feet (3,000 meters) of vertical rise, since you lack a sense of perspective.

Using a top-down approach based upon campsites is a good method for estimating times. At higher elevations, the average climber will find that 3,300 feet (1,000 meters) of vertical gain on summit day is a serious challenge. Those who are hyper-fit, thoroughly acclimated, and very experienced may be able to make a 6,600-foot summit push—but everything must go exactly right.

These estimates assume you're carrying a lightweight pack over fairly easy technical terrain, without long traverses through deep snow. If the summit day will involve significant horizontal ground, then the upper camp may need to be higher. From the South Col, it's a relatively straight shot to the summit of Everest, with a gain of about 2,950 feet (900 meters). But on the North Ridge route (next most popular), which involves a lot of low-angle climbing, the high camp is more than 1,000 feet higher, for a summit-day gain of 1,830 feet (560 meters).

Lower camps on the mountain generally need to be closer together—perhaps only 2,000 feet (600 meters) of vertical gain apart—because you will be carrying significant loads in these areas. Obviously, terrain and conditions play a huge role in determining camp locations. If you have decent photographs, what appear as potential sites should be suitable. Maps, on the other hand, are rarely accurate or detailed enough to be reliable for predicting campsites.

Beware the tendency to overestimate how far you think you can travel in a day, particularly if it's a little-known route or you are inexperienced at high altitude. Climbers are often surprised by how long everything takes up there. While climbing at moderate elevations (Cascades, Rockies, Alps), you can probably prepare a meal and break camp in under two hours, but up high it will likely take twice as long to get moving—boiling water is slower, cooking is slower, *you* are slower. Likewise, setting up camp and preparing meals can easily take four hours unless you are fully dialed for maximum efficiency.

It may be tempting to think, "We're tough, we'll just bivy." Unless you've practiced bivouacs often, think again. While there is much to be said for climbing fast

Photo by Jack Roberts

Bivouac is French for "long night of suffering."

and light, there's also a lot of value in getting a good rest. Most climbers in the United States, Canada, and the Alps have probably spent only a couple of bivy nights in a row. After several nonstop days of climbing on a big peak, the mental and physical wear take a cumulative toll that drains everyone. Planning four or five bivouacs in a row is begging for punishment: such climbs have a way of lasting longer than anyone thought possible. (But if you survive, they make great reading for the saner of us.)

Once you have figured out the minimum number of climbing days based upon location of the camps, you need to estimate how long it will *really* take. The descent will take about half as long, depending on route and conditions. As a rough approximation for an alpine-style ascent at moderate altitudes, double the climbing time; if you think it will take six days (four up, two down), budget twelve. This gives you leeway for storms and other setbacks. If

you will be stocking camps or going to extreme altitude, you may need to double that figure again (planning for up to twenty-four days above base camp).

With luck, you'll be down with plenty of time to spare—nothin' wrong with that! To cut yourself short is to deny yourself the summit in most cases. Face it, high-altitude mountaineering is always a gamble. There's little point in going to great effort and expense and then stacking the odds against yourself with a tight timeline. There are infinite ways to use up extra time afterward, but nothing can buy you more.

Climbing High

Given sufficient time, the vast majority of climbers should have few problems due to altitude for peaks up to about 23,000 feet (7,000 meters). Above that, personal factors (genetics, health, appetite) become much more significant. Even if you are doing everything "right" and have been high before, there's no guarantee that you won't become afflicted by altitude illness.

Big, very fit men (high aerobic capacity and lean body mass) tend to have the most performance loss at altitude. Women and smaller men have less muscle that requires oxygenation so they feel the effects less. While raising your aerobic capacity won't help much unless you are really out of shape, increasing your lactate threshold (essentially your tolerance for sustained hard work) improves your muscles' ability to use oxygen. Anyone who wants to climb their best up high will benefit by interval training (see *Climbing: Training for Peak Performance*,

77

by Clyde Soles, The Mountaineers Books, 2002), though this won't necessarily help you in the early days of an expedition. Everyone acclimatizes at a different rate, so don't expect your entire expedition to be in their prime on the same day.

The rule of thumb has long been to limit the ascent rate to 1,000 feet (300 meters) of gain per day for altitudes above 10,000 feet (3,000 meters). Many climbers find this too conservative, but a few will suffer even at this rate. A recent study of 262 climbers on Monte Rosa (15,204 feet; 4,634 meters), on the border of Italy and Switzerland, found that 75 percent had indications of subclinical high-altitude pulmonary edema (HAPE). While this fluid buildup in the lungs didn't cause obvious symptoms, the study indicates many climbers are closer to HAPE than they realize.

Both expedition- and capsule-style climbs tend to be self-limiting in their ascent rate since it takes time to move supplies up the mountain, and storms frequently mandate rest days. For peaks over 6,000 meters, however, it's wise to budget extra time for bodies to adjust. A prolonged spell of good weather can be a prelude to disaster: everyone rushes upward before they're physiologically adapted, somebody gets edema of the lungs or brain, and a storm closes the back door to retreat while the victim deteriorates.

Alpine-style expeditions must plan to acclimatize either by rehearsing the lower portion of the route or by climbing nearby peaks (possibly a safer alternative). Once you reach base camp, it will take your body two to four weeks to reach full aerobic potential. Excursions to higher altitudes while sleeping low, where you get better rest and nutrition, will best prepare you for the main event.

Some climbers claim fast ascents by going from one expedition straight to the next, but they actually are away from home for a very long time. It's possible to climb in Nepal during the pre-monsoon season in the spring, quickly travel to the Karakoram for the summer season, and return to Nepal for the fall's post-monsoon season. Although the red blood cell percentage stays high (cells have a 120-day life span), climbers appear to lose resistance to HAPE upon even a brief descent to low elevations such as Kathmandu at 4,430 feet (1,350 meters), and Islamabad at 1,750 feet (530 meters).

Where high peaks are clustered—as in the Karakoram, which has four 8,000-meter peaks near one another—moving from one to the next is feasible if you are fit, recuperate well, and can afford the permit fees. Anatoli Boukreev used this tactic by climbing Broad Peak (mostly) and then making the short trek over to Gasherbrum II for a "one-day, solo" ascent. He started at advanced base camp and used the established trail to climb and descend over 6,600 feet in a day: certainly an impressive feat, but it should be admired in context. (Sadly, Toli was killed by an avalanche a few months later on Annapurna.)

So what about the risks of climbing where the air is so thin? When Reinhold Messner and Peter Habeler made the first ascent of Everest without supplementary oxygen in 1977, it was theorized that, if they survived, the climb would result in permanent brain damage. Such was not the case. Although scientists have documented short-term cognitive deficits and damage to nerve cells from hypoxia (reduced oxygen), there is no evidence of significant lasting drain bramage in high-altitude climbers.

A Faster High?

The obvious question for anyone with a busy life: is there anything I can do or take that will shorten the time needed to adjust to high altitude? Perhaps.

Many herbal supplements are touted for alleviating mountain sickness. Advocates out to make a buck hype the altitude benefits of astragalus, or Huang qi (*Astragalus membranaceus*); coca leaves (*Erythroxylum coca*); cordyceps fungus (*Cordyceps sinensis*); golden root (*Rhodiola rosea*); Korean ginseng, or Ren Shen (*Panax ginseng*); Siberian ginseng, or Ciwujia (*Eleutherococcus senticosus*); reishi mushroom, or Ling-zhi (*Ganoderma lucidum*); stinging nettles (*Urtica dioica*); ashwagandha (*Withania somnifera*); milk thistle (*Silybum marianum*); and schizandra (*Schizandra chinensis*)—among others.

While the claims are great, the science is minimal. No independent peer-reviewed, well-controlled studies have been published that support the propaganda for these herbs. Just because they are natural ancient remedies doesn't mean they are effective or safe, particularly when combined. Eventually, some compounds from these plants are likely to prove

Anatoli Boukreev going strong at 24,000 feet on Gasherbrum II.

helpful, but whether they are better than known options is another matter. Anecdotal evidence makes for good advertising copy but is totally useless for deciding if a product is worth the money and potential risks. In many cases, it's supposed to take four to six weeks of large daily doses before anything is even noticed.

This is not to condemn all herbal products, however, since some have credible evidence for providing benefit at high altitude. Standardized extract of ginkgo biloba, made from the leaves of this ancient tree, has been shown to significantly reduce the symptoms of acute mountain sickness (AMS). The usual amount is two 120-milligram doses per day, starting five days prior to ascent and continuing through the climb. Garlic also helps open the airways in the lungs, in addition to its other documented health benefits (2 grams of powder or four large raw cloves per day). Originally derived from white willow bark, aspirin has long been used to relieve altitude headaches.

Although ginkgo, garlic, and aspirin can be beneficial to climbers, all three are anticoagulants that thin the blood. They should not be taken together, or with acetazolamide (or by themselves prior to surgery). Some of the other herbs mentioned above may also cause problems with excessive bleeding.

Recent research indicates that antioxidants are effective at preventing AMS (possibly why ginkgo works, since it too is an antioxidant). When going high, supplementing your diet with 1,000 milligrams vitamin C and 400 IU vitamin E per day may be prudent. Other antioxidants (such as alpha-lipoic acid, selenium, and green tea extract) may also be helpful, but the research is lacking and the media hysteria overblown.

Avoid megadose multivitamin/mineral supplements, because they can cause more problems than they correct. It can't hurt to take a standard daily pill with about 100 percent of the recommended daily allowance, though it's unlikely to help your performance; deficiencies take many months of inadequate diet to become a problem.

Since excess iron can cause serious complications, men should not supplement this mineral unless a blood test shows it to be deficient; a normal diet has abundant iron. However, women often do not have adequate iron intake, particularly if they are vegetarians, and may benefit from supplementation. If taking iron supplements, avoid high doses of vitamin C.

Glutamine is normally the most abundant amino acid in the body, but supplies are depleted following stress and endurance exercise. Supplementing with 5 to 10 grams of glutamine per day may improve recovery and boost immune protection against ailments. Another possible aid for high-altitude climbers is branched chain amino acids (BCAAs; leucine, isoleucine, and valine), which account for a third of muscle protein. Taking 10 to 20 grams per day may help reduce fatigue and prevent muscle loss. Both glutamine and BCAAs are adequately supplied in a normal diet, but the combined effects of hard work and high altitude tend to shortchange us. There appear to be good reasons for mountaineers to add these to the expedition diet.

Probably the best-known prescription drug for altitude is acetazolamide (Diamox), which is very effective at preventing AMS but not at stopping it once symptoms appear. This medicine works by increasing your ventilation rate, thus improving oxygenation, and is particularly useful for improving sleep quality at extreme elevations (by eliminating periodic breathing).

If you are forced to make a rapid ascent to 10,000 feet or higher, or if moving to a camp that is 3,000 feet higher than the previous night's, 250 milligrams of acetazolamide (half a tablet in the morning, the rest in the evening) starting the day before can save you from misery. But most climbers will be better off taking their time instead of relying on this pill. The drug has numerous drawbacks, not the least of which are that it increases urination (dehydration is already a problem at altitude) and can ruin the taste of beer.

It's important to realize that none of the above supplements speed the production of oxygen-carrying red blood cells, one of the major adaptations to altitude. Reduced oxygen in the air stimulates the body to release a hormone called EPO (erythropoietin), which causes bone marrow to produce more red blood cells than normal. But this process takes about three days and it takes an additional three days for the

blood cells to mature; your hematocrit (percentage of red blood cells in the blood) doesn't peak for about two to four weeks. Until your body catches up, you will not be able to perform to your full potential.

The only way to safely shortcut this is by sleeping in an altitude chamber (a $7,000 to $20,000 gadget) for several weeks. A special filtration system reduces the oxygen content of the air to give you a head start on acclimatizing. Some elite endurance athletes use these to enhance performance without taking banned substances (though the distinction is debatable).

A few climbers advocate spending a couple of nights up high, say on the summit of a 14,000-foot mountain, prior to a trip, yet this is impractical and unlikely to have a significant effect. Taking blood-boosters such as EPO would be most unwise because your blood could become too thick, making it difficult for the heart to pump blood into your muscle tissue; your performance would suffer.

Bottom line: you can't just take a bunch of pills and plan on a shorter expedition that has a good chance of success. However, supplementing antioxidants, including ginkgo biloba, can decrease your risk of illness from altitude. In addition, amino acid supplements may stave off infection (a major concern), keep you from tiring as quickly, and prevent muscle loss.

CHAPTER 4

Uli Biaho Tower (20,042 feet, 6,109 meters), Pakistan

Time and Money

Budgeting is a necessary evil for all expeditions. There is only so much time and money available—usually you are short on both—so you must make the most of what you have. When you don't plan ahead, the shortfall at the end of the trip is always painful.

TIME FLIES

You can change plans, find more money, replace partners who drop out—but you can't create more time. While planning your expedition, it's vital that you budget your time to avoid nasty surprises. Although you yourself may be flexible, that is seldom the case with the companies and bureaucracies you will be dealing with.

In general, the bigger the goal, the more lead time you will need to prepare. While you might be able to put a trip to Alaska together in just a few months, it's likely to take two years of gestation after the seed of an 8,000-meter peak climb has been planted. This seems like a lot, but all too often climbers planning an expedition end up in a final frenzy asking, "Where did the time go?!"

Here are time-eaters to consider (see figure 4.1. page 87):

Permits. It used to take ages to get a permit for the more desirable Himalayan peaks (very few mountains elsewhere require them). Now, partly due to an effort to encourage tourism, most countries have streamlined the process and eliminated the requirement for sponsorship by alpine clubs. Nonetheless, you should start working on obtaining a permit as soon as the idea for an expedition solidifies. Typically, this means that one person will pay the application fee and become the de facto leader (at least as far as the government is concerned). The more popular the route, the more lead time is needed—perhaps two or three years for peaks like Ama Dablam and Everest.

Grants. If you decide to pursue grants or sponsorships, you will be facing application deadlines. Committees that oversee grants often meet just once a year and do not have a support staff, so either you make the deadline or wait till the following year. Be aware that companies plan budgets for fiscal rather than calendar years, so the dates when they will consider your sponsorship proposal may be far earlier than you would expect.

Publicity and promotion. Before you get to the step of applying for dollars, you may need to put a presentation together. Although an expedition's goal must be merit-worthy to receive funding, a professional look—logo, letterhead, brochure—can help convince the powers-that-be of your commitment to following

through with your plans and promises. Allow a couple of weeks to do the job right since amateurish work reflects poorly upon everyone involved.

Passport. It takes six to eight weeks for issuance or renewal of a U.S. passport, or two weeks if you pay an extra $60. Only in a life-or-death emergency will the government expedite issuance of a passport; put this off to the last minute and you may not be going anywhere.

Visas. Many countries require a tourist visa: some will issue the visa when you arrive, while others require you to obtain it from their embassy in your home country (check *Lonelyplanet.com*). This process can take several months and requires a valid passport number on the application. If you are renewing your passport, it will be issued with a new number, so be sure to use the new passport number on your visa application or you might be turned away at the border.

Immunizations. Start your immunizations six to eight weeks prior to departure. You will need to visit a travel clinic, local health department, or your doctor once or twice for the necessary shots (see the section "Medical Information" in chapter 3).

Medical checkups. If you have any medical condition that might affect you during the expedition, let your regular doctor know what you're up to and act on any advice you receive. At least six months before heading off on the trip, schedule an appointment with your dentist (you'll be lucky to get in two weeks before you leave). Don't underestimate the debilitating effects of a cracked tooth, broken filling, or lost crown—you won't be thinking about climbing or much else besides pain.

Fitness and conditioning. Fitness doesn't happen overnight. Depending upon your current level of conditioning and your goal, it can take four to six months of aerobic and resistance training to adequately prepare for the mountains. Some people will need a year or more to lose sufficient weight and improve cardiovascular health enough to have a reasonable chance of reaching the top without being a liability to others. See the book *Climbing: Training for Peak Performance* for suggested programs.

Stove fuel. The days when you could smuggle butane cartridges by hiding them in your luggage are gone—never a good idea in the first place. (Note that some airlines even prohibit stoves that have been used.) If you are lucky, you'll be able to purchase stove fuel when you arrive, but this is something you can't leave to chance—the climb is over without it. Shipping fuel by land or air cargo can take ages, so make queries with trekking agencies at least nine months before departure.

Personal equipment. Most climbers considering an expedition already have the bulk of required equipment: clothing, packs, camping and climbing gear. However, if you need any specialty items (such as double boots, expedition parkas, down pants), be prepared for a long lead time, possibly six months, since few retailers stock them year-round, if at all. If you buy boots through mail order, it may take several go-rounds before you get the right fit, and then you need time to break them in. Don't wait till the last minute to buy an essential item.

Group supplies. If your team will be fixing ropes in place on the mountain, you will likely need to order spools of rope and snow pickets a couple months in advance, since few stores will stock enough. Shopping for mountain food also must be done far ahead of time to allow testing.

Shakedown trips. At least one short shakedown trip can be invaluable for testing gear and personalities. Try out the proposed menu to find out if it's actually edible. If you will be using unfamiliar equipment (such as ascenders), working out all their peculiarities in advance is

4.1 A year in the life before an expedition. This time scale will expand or contract depending on the size and remoteness of the goal. ▶

WEEKS

WEEKS	Permit	Research	Assemble team	Shakedown trips	Funding/grants	Gear/food lists	Shopping	Publicity	Fuel	Plane ticket	Training	Medical/dental exams	Hotel reservations	Immunizations	Passport/visa	Pack
48	▓	▓														
46	▓	▓														
44	▓	▓														
42	▓	▓	▓													
40	▓		▓													
38	▓				▓											
36			▓		▓	▓			▓		▓					
34			▓						▓		▓					
32			▓		▓				▓	▓						
30						▓				▓						
28				▓		▓	▓		▓							
26				▓			▓	▓	▓							
24						▓	▓	▓								
22					▓		▓	▓								
20					▓		▓	▓				▓				
18				▓			▓	▓								
16				▓			▓	▓								
14							▓	▓			▓		▓			
12								▓			▓		▓			
10														▓	▓	
8				▓			▓				▓			▓	▓	
6				▓							▓					
4							▓	▓				▓				
2							▓	▓								▓
0					**Go to Airport!**											

————— Normal Life: job, spouse, kids, etc. —————

vital. Every member should know how to set up all the tents during a windstorm with numb fingers; this is also the time to make sure guylines are rigged properly and there are no blatant manufacturing defects in a new product (these typically show up in first use or not at all). Stoves can be remarkably finicky, no matter how simple their design, and aren't compatible with all pots; you need to have your entire cooking system dialed in. Remember, nothing gets easier at high altitude.

Getting to know the other members of your team is the other function of shakedown trips. This can help build camaraderie and alert team members to potential issues that may arise later. Coordinating everybody's schedules to make a weekend excursion happen can be tough, but it's well worth the effort.

Arrival tasks. While you are budgeting time, if this is your first expedition to a country, plan on needing three to five days once you arrive to get squared away. If your climb requires permits, allow an entire day or more to deal with the paperwork.

Many countries have different business days from those you may be used to, so banks and government offices may be closed when you assumed they would be open. In Latin countries, it's common for everything to shut down for several hours in the middle of the day for siesta, but to be open later in the evening. Religious festivals can hamper your departure for the trailhead; the exact dates often change from year to year, so be sure to research these events before you book your flights.

MONEY MATTERS

For many people, the crux of an expedition is pulling sufficient funds together to make it a reality. While raising money may be a daunting task, it is usually manageable if you are committed. Don't let finances be your excuse for not making a dream come true.

Although a guided climb up Everest can cost wealthy clients up to $70,000, the highest summit can be reached for about a third of that by unguided climbers (even less if you find the right sponsor or other financial support). None of the other 8,000-meter peaks are anywhere near as expensive as Everest; costs generally run around $8,000 to $12,000 per person as long as the expedition operates without guides, Sherpas, or supplementary oxygen. The world's second-priciest summit is Antarctica's Mount Vinson (16,076 feet; 4,900 meters), which runs about $26,000 per person largely due to exorbitant travel costs.

Going for a peak that is lower than 8,000 meters drops the costs dramatically since the permits are cheaper and less time is needed. Regions throughout the world offer spectacular peaks and big walls, many of them still unclimbed, that can be tackled on a shoestring budget.

No matter the size of your expedition, one person should be designated as the treasurer. This is an important role that often gets treated too lightly. The treasurer keeps a notebook detailing all expedition income and expenses and keeps all receipts for a final accounting.

MONEY: SOURCES

Reality check: it's extremely rare, even for famous climbers, to have all expedition expenses paid by sponsors. In fact, it's unlikely that you will get any money at all from most companies. And if you do get cash, it always comes with a hefty price tag.

Forget the illusions of grandeur. Whatever you are doing is unlikely to be remembered a decade later—or even next week by most people. Sadly, what makes the history books and general public interest are the screwups, not the successes. Do well and nobody cares. Kill a bunch of people and barely survive, you're golden.

Self-financing

The best answer for any expedition is to pay your own way. After all, this is *your* recreation. Sure, it may be a struggle to raise the funds, but you won't have to answer to anyone but yourself. There may even be a greater sense of accomplishment since you did everything.

Going public by enlisting sponsors, contributors, and media places an expedition under a big microscope that increases expectations and obligations. Climbers who have been involved with the circus-like atmosphere of a big-budget expedition often express regret. It just isn't the same as heading off with a couple of friends.

Should you decide to do it yourself but don't have deep pockets, then be creative about fund-raising. Just a few possibilities: Organize a gear swap and charge sellers and buyers a small fee. Put

together a slide show and give it in a wide range of venues (stores, clubs, schools, senior centers). Perhaps you can convince a celebrity to give a slide show on behalf of your expedition. Hold a raffle or silent auction at these events (make sure people know to bring cash or checkbooks). If you are bold, perhaps sell a nude calendar of team members.

The old standby of selling T-shirts is no longer a good bet since it's a lot of work (design, ordering, distribution), few stores will carry them, few people need more T-shirts, and there's a risk of getting stuck with boxes of extras. Always calculate the potential payback for your efforts; it may be better to just put in some overtime at your paid job instead.

Grants for expeditions (see Appendix B, Resources) often require a lot of paperwork for relatively little reward. Still, these may be worth your while, since a small award may convince others to contribute as well.

Obviously, try reducing costs wherever possible. If you have been a loyal customer of your local climbing shop, the manager may offer a discount to team members. Purchase food, batteries, and other sundries at a discount warehouse. Shop around for cheap flights, but beware of possible problems (see "Airline Tickets" in chapter 3).

It may be tempting, but avoid funding the expedition with your credit cards or a bank loan. If your trip ends in failure or disaster, paying off the debt will just add insult to injury. Better to take an extra job now than to suffer financially for years afterward.

Sponsorship

If you insist on seeking outside support, the key to winning sponsorship is professionalism. Realize that you are but one of hundreds of "worthy causes" looking for a handout. Many of these petitioners seem to think that potential sponsors somehow owe them, and some even get miffed when nothing is forthcoming. The question to ask yourselves is "What can we do for the sponsor better than anyone else?"

Put together a brief presentation on what you are doing, who is going and their qualifications, and what you can offer in return for support. A cover letter and concise background information is usually sufficient to get your message across. While a logo is a nice touch, it isn't absolutely necessary. A simple brochure on recycled paper can help, but a glossy four-color prospectus may tell prospective sponsors that you already have plenty of money.

Whether approaching a company or an organization, find out specifically who makes the decisions and address the material to them. Letters that start "To Whom It May Concern" go straight to the trash can. It's generally better to send printed information first and then follow that up with a phone call, rather than ringing them up out of the blue.

Be specific, and realistic, about what you are requesting. Outdoor companies seldom provide cash but may loan gear or offer discounts. Corporations might have funds available, but you may be getting in bed with the devil.

Among the main concerns of any potential sponsor is your commitment to follow through on promises. This is a legitimate issue, because climbers often return from trips and fail to deliver photos, expedition reports, product feedback, and publicity. It's a significant post-expedition time commitment, so plan accordingly. All too often, life gets in the way after the luster of the expedition has worn off.

Unless you have a unique project, it will be very difficult to get a magazine assignment prior to departure. Most editors take a wait-and-see approach to expeditions; few queries make it to print. Thus you can't promise great media coverage to sponsors unless you have a signed contract.

While free schwag may sound appealing, there can be some serious pitfalls as well. Often, manufacturers use expeditions for testing prototype equipment that is not ready for prime time. They may send clothing that fits and performs poorly or is too fragile to survive the trip, packs that are uncomfortable, and boots that shred your feet. Preproduction single-wall tents might be nicely designed but have lousy fabric that leaks. Cases of engineered food that nobody can stomach are just dead weight.

Despite these inconveniences, sponsors will probably expect your entire team to use their products to the exclusion of everything else—even if some of you already own gear that's better. Do you really want to risk your summit bid, or your life, with substandard products?

Another drawback to sponsorship is they

often expect you to sew gaudy labels on everything. Aside from the tacky appearance, these logos can prevent photos from being used later on in other catalogs and even magazines.

One financial issue that should be agreed upon from the start is how to deal with loaned or donated equipment after the expedition is over. If team members provide gear (tents, ropes, hardware) for use by the whole group, a system must be in place to value it and share the cost of replacement equally. If a company donates a piece of gear but one person ends up keeping it afterward, it's only fair that the new owner pay into the expedition fund once everyone agrees upon its value.

Charity Climbs

If everyone is sincere about the effort, using an expedition to raise money and awareness for a charity is a noble cause. This is not, however, a ticket for a free ride. Although you might get some discounts on airfare and equipment, members of charity climbs are still expected to pay their way.

Organizing a fund-raiser of this sort adds a great deal of complexity to an expedition. Somebody must work closely with the charitable organization to ensure you meet their guidelines for use of their name; the last thing a nonprofit needs is bad press due to your actions. Try to select one, or at most two, charities that have a significant meaning to team members; don't divide the pie too thin.

When contacting potential donors, it must be very clear what portion of their contribution will go to the expedition and what portion will go to the charity. It is vital that bookkeeping be thorough and accurate. Since charity climbs attract media attention, which is one of the goals, there will be greater scrutiny than usual.

Overall, the benefits of mounting a charity expedition can outweigh the drawbacks. Clyde's Gasherbrum II expedition raised $10,000 for the University of Colorado Cancer Research Foundation and the Islamic Cancer Foundation in Pakistan. All team members paid for their share of the trip, while saving some money and supporting a cause that affects everybody.

MONEY: WHERE IT GOES

When planning a budget for an expedition, consider everything from start (when you come up with the idea) to finish (several weeks after your return). If you don't look at the big picture, your bank account may be in for a serious hit because the incidentals add up fast. Should your expedition extend longer than your accrued vacation time, you will also need to factor in lost wages.

Preparation Costs

To apply for a Himalayan permit usually requires a 10 percent nonrefundable deposit; additional payments are due before departure. Applications for Denali are due sixty days before the climb and must be accompanied by a deposit of $25 per person; each person pays the remaining $125 in Talkeetna.

Expeditions may be required to make a substantial cash deposit (up to $5,000) for

The scenic flight to Lukla, Nepal saves time but bypasses wonderful country.

environmental cleanup and helicopter rescue. If you've been good and things go well, this money will be returned afterward. There may also be nonrefundable fees for environmental protection ($200 to $400), a radio permit ($50 to $250), a satellite phone permit ($2,000 to $5,000), and a film permit ($2,000 to $7,000).

If you will be seeking outside financial support, plan on some public-relations expenses. These may include creating a letterhead, mailing press releases, printing brochures, phoning potential benefactors, and hosting a website.

The cost of maps and guidebooks can add up, too, though this usually isn't considered a group expense. Vaccinations probably won't be covered by health insurance, and some shots can be quite pricey ($50 or more).

Travel

For the majority of expeditions, the biggest expense is getting there. Overseas flights cost a pretty penny—$1,000 to $5,000 depending upon many factors—unless you have plenty of frequent-flyer miles saved up. On top of this, you may get hit with a substantial excess baggage fee unless you have researched and packed carefully.

Flights within your destination country won't be so bad—perhaps $100 to $300—but baggage fees could double the initial price that is quoted. Trains and buses are much cheaper, but the extra time and stress may negate the savings.

Before the hiking begins, and upon your return, you will need to spend at least a few days in a hotel. This need not be extravagant, but going one-star at the beginning of a trip can be false economy (see "Hotel

Reservations" in chapter 3). Many hotels include breakfast in the price, so you just need to budget extra for lunch and dinner. If sightseeing is on the agenda, you'll need cash for taxis and to enter some museums and temples. Consult a recent guidebook to anticipate these costs.

The approach and return trek is also a significant expense, though of course the amount depends on where you are going and how much gear must be transported. Be sure to ask explicit questions about every aspect of the trek; it's common to hear stories of climbers finding out about unexpected charges when they are no longer in a position to negotiate. Try to get everything in writing to avoid hassles.

Paid Staff

For arduous treks where there are no villages, such as up Pakistan's Baltoro Glacier, you may be required to provide shoes and sunglasses for the porters. Nothing fancy (purchase them at a local market), but it's an expense you should prepare for.

It's customary to give porters a small tip (about 10 percent of the total wage) once their services are no longer needed. This is a minor drain on your finances but a huge reward to someone who may earn less in a year than you do in a week. Be sure to include this in your budget.

By the end of an expedition, your sirdar is likely to be a good friend and you will hopefully recognize the value of the cook and his staff. These people deserve a significant bonus, preferably a combination of cash and gear that can be used (fleece jacket, down parka, good glacier glasses) or sold (rope, pitons, fuel).

You may be required to bring a liaison officer (LO) with you from the host country, usually a government official. You will be required to provide food, shelter, and transportation, and may even have to pay his salary. In some countries, you must

Payday at the end of the trail in the Karakoram.

The sirdar organizes porters and ensures everything reaches base camp.

Whether carried by two legs or four, duffels are needed for gear.

also outfit him from head to toe with appropriate boots and clothing that you will not get back (India allows you to pay $500 instead). Don't think you can just give him cheap stuff, since LOs often get together and compare notes, and an unhappy LO can make your trip miserable. Although the LO will dine with the climbers, his religion may not allow him to eat the same meals (for example, Hindis cannot eat beef and Muslims cannot eat pork), so extra food may be required.

All staff on an expedition, including the LO, must be covered by insurance. This may cost a couple hundred dollars depending upon duration and the number of porters hired.

Supplies

Aside from personal equipment that you may need to acquire, group gear can be a significant budget item. This may include rope (both for climbing and fixing lines), rock pitons, ice screws, snow pickets, tents, and hanging stoves. Some members may be able to provide these out of their closet, but it's only fair that everyone share the expense of lost or damaged goods.

Once you get to the mountain, the major expense (unless you've hired high-altitude porters) is food and fuel, though you will pay for this in advance.

To keep gear organized and prevent pilfering, it's wise to purchase (or have made) cheap duffel bags (about $5 each) and small locks (all with the same combination or key). Fragile items and things that must stay dry should be transported in large (100 liter) plastic drums with secure lids. Some expeditions purchase these at

Photo by Greg Collins

Anticipate the cost of processing film.

home and use them for shipping, but they are rather heavy and expensive (about $30 each). Others buy used barrels at their destination and resell them at the end of the trip.

Post-Expedition Spending

Be prepared for some power-shopping after you return to Islamabad, Kathmandu, or other craft centers of the world. There will be shops aplenty with fine rugs, beautiful *tankas* (religious paintings), wonderful jewelry, and countless other temptations. When you discover how incredible the deals are, it's a drag not having two rupees to rub together!

Some people take extra jackets to Kathmandu just for the purpose of having them embroidered with intricate designs. If you think you might want a rug ($100 to $500, depending on size and quality), bring measurements from home for the place where you think it will reside. Try to have your sirdar accompany you when shopping, to get the best prices and avoid being cheated.

Depending on how serious you were about photography, film processing can be a significant expense when you get home. If you shot a lot of slide film, the $8 per roll can add up to several hundred dollars.

CHAPTER 5

Paiju Peak (21,686 feet, 6,610 meters), Pakistan

Supply Line: Home to Base Camp

Many climbers obsess about gear; often, the less experienced they are, the more catalog specs they can recite. Despite celebrity endorsements and magazine reviews, no summit success can be attributed to specific products. Which is not to say equipment is unimportant—far from it—just that the latest widget won't get you to the top.

Before plunking down your credit card for another high-tech "must-have," it's worth remembering that Mallory, Norton, and Somervell reached 26,640 feet on Everest without supplemental oxygen in 1922 (for which they earned Olympic gold medals). Prior to the outbreak of World War I in 1914, people had already been above 23,000 feet on several occasions—the first documented high ascent was in 1860 (Shilla Peak in the Spiti region of India). And the Incas buried mummies at 22,000 feet on a volcano around the year Columbus rediscovered America.

When selecting gear for an expedition, reliability should be the determining factor on what goes. While many are tempted by ultralight products for venturing to high altitudes, it's generally better to choose slightly sturdier items that will get you to the top and back. A trick tent that can't survive storms is dangerous, and a fantastically light pack is a sad joke if it rips open partway up the climb.

A major, multimonth expedition has several distinct stages, each with its own gear requirements. While in transit and staying in hotels, you're in the casual travel stage. Once you leave the towns behind and until you reach base camp, you're in the approach stage. Since you spend so much time in base camp, it is actually a stage in and of itself as far as equipment is concerned. Then, of course, there's the actual climbing, which often breaks down into the lower and upper mountain phases.

Shorter trips also go through these same stages, though they are greatly compressed and often allow you to get by with less equipment. It's relatively fast and easy to reach Talkeetna on your way to Denali, so travel gear isn't a major concern. If your approach is two days versus two weeks, you may not need to plan for this stage independently from the climb. Still, even for a quick trip, there's potential for an unpleasant foul-up to your vacation if you don't anticipate pre- and post-climb supplies.

Wherever possible, select equipment that can do double, triple, or quadruple duty. Sometimes, though, this multifunctionality just isn't practical: running shoes may be fine in town and base camp but can leave you miserable on a long, rugged hike with deep mud and snow; a winter sleeping bag can be insufferable on a long approach march with balmy nights.

ON THE MOVE

The travel stage of an expedition begins the moment you walk out your front door and ends when you walk back through it. Traveling can be surprisingly tiring despite the relative lack of physical activity. You can make your life easier, and arrive at the mountain fresher, by giving consideration to what you bring for the cities.

DOCUMENTS AND FUNDS

Before heading to the airport, be certain everyone has their passport, visas, and inoculation information. Clyde almost missed a flight to the Caicos Islands in the West Indies, which would have literally meant missing the boat, because he forgot to check the expiration date on his passport. A frantic flurry of phone calls and faxes saved that trip, but it's a mistake he will never make again!

In some countries it seems that every time you turn around, there will be another official document that requires a passport photo. Take at least a half-dozen extras (black and white are fine) since getting new ones abroad can be a serious hassle.

Back yourself up by being ready to speedily replace any lost or stolen documents. The extra passport photos and a photocopy of the first four pages of your passport should be kept in your luggage. Make a record of credit card numbers and the international phone numbers you will need to cancel them if necessary. Photocopy your plane tickets and hotel reservations. Also bring a list with the serial numbers of all camera bodies, lenses, and other expensive electronic equipment.

Protect yourself further by leaving copies of all of this with a trustworthy friend back home. If you lose everything, the friend can call your credit card companies for you, fax you copies of your passport, even wire you money if necessary.

How to carry your funds is a matter of convenience and comfort level. In most major cities, paying for hotels and other major expenses with a credit card is the norm (MasterCard seems to be more readily accepted abroad than Visa or American Express). Throughout practically all of North America and Europe, and in many surprising locations elsewhere, ATMs may be found for quick cash withdrawals. While convenient, be aware that many card companies are now charging 2 percent extra on currency conversions plus an ATM fee.

Traveler's checks (American Express are the most universal) offer greater comfort in case of theft or loss. But you may pay twice—a fee for getting them (free in some places) and a higher exchange rate for cashing them—and they're a hassle since traveler's checks often require bank visits and a lot of signatures. When carrying big chunks of money, such as to pay the trekking agency, large-denomination ($50 or $100) traveler's checks do offer peace of mind.

For all the incidental expenses, it's hard to beat good ol' cashola; some people don't bother with traveler's checks at all. No offense to other countries, but the U.S. $20 and $100 bill are probably the most universal forms of currency that can be converted almost anywhere. A hundred miles from the nearest road, local merchants will know the current exchange rate to the fourth decimal. The caveat here is that the new-style U.S. bills may not be recognized in very remote places, so it may be smart to keep a reserve of the older bills for certain portions of your trip.

Keep the most important items (passport, cash, credit cards) on your person at all times. A traveler's wallet worn inside your clothing or a small fanny pack worn in front of you are excellent for carrying the necessities around town and on public transport. If you elect to use the pockets of your clothing, be certain that they have snaps or zippers to deter pickpockets. Leave the bigger documents (climbing permits, plane tickets, backup info) at the hotel, preferably in the safe or at least hidden deep inside your luggage.

HARD LESSON LEARNED

Learning about vigilance is best done vicariously. It had been a fantastic trip and this was our final celebration. John, Richard, and I had spent three weeks living out of our antique VW van while climbing near Chamonix and then at the Calanques in the south of France. My time was up and they were dropping me off at the train station in Marseilles so I could head back to Paris for my flight. We got there early and there was still time for one last beer.

Returning to the van, something was amiss. It quickly became apparent that my duffel, with all my gear and clothes, was gone! In less than an hour, thieves had broken in during the middle of the day and grabbed what was in easy reach: my conveniently packed bag with a small fortune in climbing equipment.

Things quickly went from bad to worse. Throughout that trip, I had been careful to keep my passport, plane ticket, and cash with me at all times. But during the packing frenzy at the station, I'd let my guard down and stashed them where they'd be handy—for the thieves. When the reality of just how screwed I was sank in, my frustration turned to anger. Not being a man of violence, I vented my frustration by punching a plexiglass bus stop. Wrong answer. Broke my knuckle.

So after hours of filling out reports for the unsympathetic French police, I got to experience the emergency room of a busy city hospital at midnight. Then the joy of calling home to tell my parents and beg for money, the fun of proving who I was to obtain a new passport, and the mirth of purchasing a one-way plane ticket. Of course, all the gear has now been replaced and most of the ugliness forgotten. But I have a permanently flattened knuckle as a reminder, and the loss of fourteen rolls of film still hurts.

Never let your guard down.

— *Clyde Soles*

TRAVEL CLOTHING

Sometimes this is the hardest part for climbers: we are so used to camping conditions and situations that do not demand good grooming that we often overlook the importance of decent travel clothes. You will be especially thankful for some nice cotton duds on the return trip.

Think seriously about everyone you will encounter during the portion of your trip in which you are in street clothes. Ticket agents at airports, security guards, customs agents, and government officials are just some of the people you may encounter who can influence the success of your trip—or make your life hell. Nobody likes to dress different from their personality, but it's smart to adopt a clean-cut, conservative look for meetings with people who have power over the cost of extra baggage, the time you have to spend at an airport, or finding the correct forms.

There's no doubt you'll get better service if you wear neat khakis instead of tattered jeans. Don't wear T-shirts or baseball caps that shout "rich American" or "dumb foreigner"; leave the flags, corporate logos, NFL team shirts, and insulting designs at home. It's better to blend in and look generic while walking down a street than to look like a target.

Clothing for travel should be comfortable, neat, and not easily wrinkled. Travel-specific shirts and pants are made from low-care fabrics that breathe well and have extra zippered pockets (sized to carry a passport) and vents for hot weather. While rather pricey, these products do work well and are great for long trips.

Certainly you'll want to keep the volume of your travel clothing to a minimum. Take just enough clothing to get you from laundry to laundry. Carefully chosen clothing can also be worn on the approach trek and when lounging in base camp.

Wear comfortable shoes or sandals that won't blister you after many miles of walking and allow a quick dash to the opposite end of a concourse to catch a flight. Footwear that is used on an approach may be trashed by the time you return to civilization, so town shoes may be a good idea. If you are returning to the same hotel, they often will store unneeded luggage while you are away.

Photo by Phil Powers

The approach is often its own adventure.

TRAVEL ACCESSORIES

Some of the little things can make traveling less stressful and more comfortable. Much as with an alpine climb, however, evaluate every item that you pack and leave behind what you don't really need.

Travel duffels. For getting your valuable equipment halfway around the world and to the base of the mountain intact, it's wise to use heavy-duty travel duffels. Even though airlines offer large plastic bags, it's a bad idea to use your pack for air travel because it looks as if it holds valuable goodies, it can't be locked, and it invites uncomfortable questions about whether you're carrying a stove (some airlines confiscate used stoves even if they don't contain fuel).

The bigger travel duffels (roughly 9,000 cubic inches, 150 liters) can hold an expedition-size pack with room to spare. Burly material and construction is required to hold up to the abuses of baggage handlers, porters, and yaks; better ones are expensive but will last many expeditions. Select a plain-looking model without flashy logos that scream "valuable stuff inside" and be sure it has the new-style zipper pulls that cannot be pulled open when locked. Pick a lighter color that's easy to write on with a black marking pen.

Among the greatest inventions of recent times for frequent adventure travelers is the wheeled duffel bag. When it's just you and a mountain of gear, these make life *so* much easier that they are well worth the additional cost (baggage carts are never around when you need them). The only drawback is the extra 5 pounds of deadweight, particularly if you're cutting it close on the baggage allowance.

Cable lock. If you will be traveling alone or in a small group, it's handy to bring a small combination lock with retractable cable (sold in ski shops). When all your luggage is heaped up in a pile, run the cable through the handles to prevent a snatch-and-run robbery. One person cannot effectively guard everything, because they face the dilemma of chasing the thief or watching what's left.

Since locks on checked luggage may be cut by security screeners, some use heavy duty zip-ties to deter unauthorized access. Small combination luggage locks are still useful for hotel rooms and trains.

Film shield. Anyone who is serious about photography must anticipate greater problems clearing airport security. Under no circumstances should unprocessed film be placed in checked luggage; it *will* be ruined by high-intensity X-rays. While the uniforms with guns will claim that the carry-on scanners aren't supposed to fog film slower than ISO 800, the effects of X-rays are cumulative and not all machines are properly calibrated. By the time you travel to a different continent and return, it's likely you'll go through at least a half-dozen inspections, and there is a slight risk of losing all the images of your trip.

Unfortunately, hand inspection of film is rarely an option anymore, so it's best to carry film in lead-lined bags (sold in camera stores) to reduce exposure, though this is likely to trigger a search. To minimize hassles, discard film boxes before leaving home, be sure all the film containers are transparent, and place them all in clear, resealable plastic bags that then go in the lead bags. And arrive early.

Sleep aids. The hardened may scoff, at first, but there's a lot to be said for catching some decent Z's on long flights, train trips, or bus rides; better to arrive rested than wasted. A U-shaped inflatable pillow, sleep mask, and earplugs take up almost no carry-on space and allow you to rest peacefully. Take the sleep mask and earplugs on the expedition as well.

Electronic gadgetry. By no means a necessity, a personal digital assistant (PDA) that runs on disposable batteries can be handy while traveling. This device can serve as your address book (for postcards and emails), exchange rate and tip calculator, alarm clock, to-do reminder, and language dictionary. When you're faced with a long delay, a few games on a PDA can help pass the time, and it's a lot smaller than a paperback.

If shooting video, carry a voltage converter and plug adapters so you can recharge batteries. An inexpensive Polaroid camera is a great way to make friends with locals in remote regions; a print of themselves will be a much-appreciated gift.

Pleasantries. Pick up some postcards of your hometown to show people who may never have the opportunity to visit. Bring some photos of your parents, spouse, and children; these will be of great interest in many cultures.

Bear protection. Climbers heading to the Arctic should understand that polar bears consider you good eatin'. Guns are ineffective—it took one expert hunter six rounds from an elephant rifle (.416 with 400-grain bullets) to stop a charging grizzly . . . and polar bears are one-third larger. The best protection is bear spray with 30-foot range and 2 percent capsaicin (*counterassault.com*, *udap.com*). Bullets and shotgun slugs just piss bears off, but bear spray makes them turn tail. (Note that they do not allow this stuff on airlines, so plan ahead.)

THE APPROACH TREK

On larger expeditions, the approach trek is an expedition of its own. Many of the world's high peaks tower over desert or jungle environments with climates and terrain completely different from the world of snow and ice above.

The proper equipment on your approach will help you arrive at base camp healthy and with plenty of energy for your climb. Approaches are often sweaty, dusty endeavors, and it's nice to have some proper clothing for this portion of the trip. The travel clothes one needs for long, hot hikes are unsuitable for use in town or on the mountain.

Make sure your clothing provides adequate sun protection. Long, loose-fitting pants and shirts offer more coverage than shorts and reduce the volume of sun cream and insect repellent that is slathered on. Synthetic fabrics dry faster and tend to be more comfortable than cotton, particularly after several days of hard work wearing the same outfit. In equatorial zones, sun may penetrate thin clothing unless it is designed to block UV light.

A highly breathable hat with a full brim to block the sun is essential; select one that can be stuffed in a pocket. While perhaps fashionable, a baseball cap is inadequate for protecting the ears and neck unless it has a cape. If you'll be in bug country, a mosquito-net hat can preserve sanity and blood volume. Be sure to wear good sunglasses; wraparound sport styles are comfortable and seal out wind and sun.

For relief from the unrelenting sun on the long trek up the Baltoro Glacier and other treeless areas, some carry a travel umbrella as portable shade. During monsoon approaches in Nepal and elsewhere, all-day light rain and warmer temperatures are common. Many find that an umbrella is more pleasant than wearing the hood on their shell. For rain and wet snow at lower elevations, it's worth bringing a waterproof/breathable jacket and pants.

Give serious thought to your footwear. It must be comfortable, durable, and offer adequate protection for the anticipated conditions. Playing tough by wearing running or approach shoes can be a silly mistake, even if the porters get by with far less. Messing up your feet with blisters, stone bruises, or a twisted ankle before you reach the mountain is a bad deal. An otherwise easy hike can leave you miserable if there is a few inches of snow on the ground or the hillside turns so muddy that you must cling from tree to tree.

The best option is generally a pair of lightweight, over-the-ankle hiking boots with a Gore-Tex lining. These are fairly inexpensive, are imperceptibly heavier than shoes, and require no break-in if fitted properly. If you have a smaller foot (under size 9), the boots might make a much-appreciated gift to one of your local helpers at the end of the trip. Those who use leather boots should bring extra wax to keep them from leaking. You may wish to wear somewhat lighter socks than you'll use with your mountaineering boots up on the hill.

If there will be crossings of glacier-fed rivers, bring sandals and neoprene socks (or dive booties with a walking sole) so your boots and camp shoes stay dry. It's a bad idea to cross barefoot since the water is barely above freezing and rocks tend to be slick and rounded so they roll on top of your feet, kinda like walking on slippery marbles the size of grapefuit.

Trekking poles can relieve significant stress from your knees, especially if there are long sections of downhill, and they help keep your upper body in shape. A pair of poles also provides extra traction and stability on tricky talus or mud slopes, snowfields, and river crossings. The better poles have a comfortable grip and strap for bare hands, shock-absorbing springs, and small baskets that won't snag. Use them as in cross-country skiing so that the strap supports your weight, not the grip of your hand.

PACKING FOR THE TREK

Some climbers prefer to let the porters or pack animals do most of the work, so they'll march with just a light day pack (around 15 pounds; 7 kg). Others like to use the approach as a training exercise and will carry a moderate load (up to about 45 pounds; 20 kg).

In either case, it's a good idea to bring

Porter loads often dwarf those of climbers and trekkers.

enough clothing for severe weather since the rest of your supplies may be on the back of a porter who is hours away. There generally is no access to anything you don't personally carry until the end of that day's stage. For approaches during the monsoon, bring a pack cover to keep things dry.

Some climbers take a chalk bag and slippers for those trailside boulder problems; just don't make a mistake that ends your trip early. Listening to tunes while hiking is another personal decision. Digital MP3 players like the Apple iPod let you bring a huge music collection.

Try to keep the gear you'll need for the approach in a single bag so it's readily accessible and requires less rummaging. It may be prudent, however, to divide your critical personal gear into two or three separate porter loads if you'll be fording rivers. Prominently mark your private bags so they're easy to spot in the heap. Everyone will be happier if you padlock all of the expedition's duffel bags; select a common key or combination for all group gear so all team members have access. Number every porter load so they can be checked out and in each day.

During the approach trek is a good time to start a journal, since afternoons are often free. Even if you don't normally write in a diary at home, years later you may appreciate looking back. Carry a small, bound book with lined pages and a couple of pens in a resealable plastic bag. Since you can send mail out with a porter once you reach base camp, bring a bunch of postcards and the necessary stamps.

AT BASE CAMP

Base camp survival is a cornerstone of expedition success. It goes without saying that an expedition must bring the correct climbing equipment and food, but the details of base camp living can make or break an expedition's attitude. The easier one's existence at this home-away-from

Private tents make base camp life more comfortable.

home, the longer a team will be able to work together with high spirits.

Some argue that too much comfort makes it easy to lounge rather than climb. At crowded mountain bases, however, you'll often find members of the Spartan teams over at the camps of the styled expeditions.

Consider your sleeping arrangements. Would the extra expense and transportation cost of having a tent for each individual be worth the privacy and personal space? On a short trip, probably not. If you are planning to be at a base camp for more than a few weeks, perhaps.

KITCHEN

Whether or not you hire a cook for base camp, bring kitchen gear to allow easy food preparation. A two-burner, high-output (50,000 BTU) propane stove with adjustable legs, like the Camp Chef River Runner, is the ideal way to cook for a large group,

though obtaining bulk fuel tanks (with the correct fittings) may be difficult abroad. Big, single-burner kerosene stoves are the norm in the Himalaya, but they are ornery beasts that sputter and spew vile smoke; bring a backup and a filter funnel.

For groups larger than four people, you will need some big pots and a fry pan (or griddle), which can be purchased at a bazaar or hardware store in the capital city of your destination country. Select aluminum pots with thick walls to spread the heat, riveted handles on both sides for control, and lids; pots in the sizes of 20, 10, 6, 4, and 2 liters can nest inside each other. Avoid enameled pots (fragile) and cast-iron pots (too heavy). An 8-liter pressure cooker reduces fuel consumption and allows for faster rice and potatoes (mainstays of the diet) and even some amazing breads and desserts.

Be sure to bring large, high-quality knives, a sharpening stone, and a large cutting board. If you are using plastic barrels to transport gear, one can become a handy table. Make a circular cutting board and bolt it to the inside of a barrel lid so that it can be easily packed and found for use during the approach march.

A strainer is helpful to prevent dumping the spaghetti on the ground and for removing food bits from dishwater. Several 5-gallon (20-liter) jugs are needed for hauling water from the nearest source (sometimes a considerable distance). An insulated water cooler, with a spigot at the bottom, and a few hand towels (cleaned frequently) make it easy for everyone to wash their hands with hot water—vital for staying healthy!

Other useful kitchen supplies include a ladle, spatula, serving spoons, tongs, can opener, pot holders, pot scrubbers, three plastic basins for washing dishes and laundry, biodegradable soap, and sterilizing bleach. Serving plates and bowls should be plastic; metal cools your food too fast in frigid camps. A supply of paper towels or napkins is also nice.

Bring at least two large thermos bottles for milk, tea, and other hot drinks; they're glass, so you want a backup. These should be kept full whenever climbers are at base camp to encourage hydration.

Climbers descend to base camp to rest and recover or because of storms. A tarp or well-ventilated cook tent makes kitchen chores during poor weather easier and more pleasant. Although this is a warm

Glacial moraines make good camps once the rocks are cleared.

place to congregate, understand that it is the domain of the cook and he may not appreciate your intrusion; respect his space. Even on smaller trips, it's sometimes nice to bring a small tarp or single-pole fly (such as a Black Diamond Megamid) for cooking.

A good mess tent becomes the meeting, eating, and gaming place; it should be sturdy, spacious, and cheerful. Trekking agencies can usually provide a mess tent; however, they sometimes aren't in the best condition and dark canvas makes them dreary inside. The fancy geodesic domes are deluxe accommodations that hold up well to storms but are hyper-expensive ($2,000 to $5,000). Large family camping tents are more affordable ($400 to $800) but less sturdy (use a double set of poles and a lot of guylines). Weeks of high-altitude UV light zaps the fabric, so the tent may not have much life left after an

The mess tent/meeting space/gambling hall is the heart of base camp.

expedition unless you rig a tarp over it.

If base camp will be located on a glacial moraine, bring a pickax (or at least a heavy, beefy ice ax) and a sturdy shovel. It can take a lot of hacking into rock-covered ice to clear away suitable tent platforms, and proper tools make a big difference.

LATRINE

Each person deposits about a pound of solid waste every day. In the past, this was not a significant problem since few people visited the mountains. Now, however, at the base camps of major peaks, it is common for hundreds of climbers and support staff to share the same area for a couple months each year.

Do the math: 10 expeditions with 10 members for 30 days equals 3,000 pounds (1,400 kg) of shit in a climbing season—and it's five times that at either of the Everest base camps. Due to the high altitude (frozen most of the year and limited biological activity), the stuff doesn't break down either.

The old policy of "out of sight, out of mind"—that is, crevasse disposal—is becoming less acceptable as well. Mountain glaciers in many regions are retreating at a faster rate than two decades ago: 25 feet (7.5 meters) per year in some cases. What emerges at the snout will be essentially unchanged from what was deposited, and will contaminate downstream water supplies.

It is becoming increasingly common for the "pack it out" directive to include *everything,* just as on the Colorado River in the Grand Canyon. Rainier and Denali National Parks have already implemented human waste disposal regulations, and other parks around the world are sure to follow.

Expeditions in remote areas should build a pit toilet for all human and food waste (no trash!). In sensitive areas, expeditions may need to bring enough 5-gallon food buckets (good for forty poops) and have them hauled out to where the waste can be incinerated or used as fertilizer. Also bring a toilet seat for comfort and lime to quench the stench. Understand, however, that the porters will not use your sit-down toilet; in their culture, everybody squats. No matter the waste disposal method, toilet paper and tampons are collected into a trash bag and burned later.

From high camps, it is often impractical to carry down human waste, so on-the-mountain disposal is required. This is usually done in a designated area, away from camps. But even this is a problem on popular routes with exposed camps since winds scour away snow. It may be necessary for everyone to defecate into gallon-size resealable plastic bags—it isn't as bad as it sounds—which are gathered into a trash bag for proper disposal. Purchase an adequate supply of bags and toilet paper; running out of the latter is most unpleasant.

LUXURIES

The longer you'll be in base camp, the more the luxuries become necessities. While toting them along does add to the cost, it's generally a minor blip in the overall budget.

Table and chairs. For any trip over a

couple of days, some sort of back rest is essential. Each member should bring a folding chair (such as a Crazy Creek, a sleeping pad conversion kit, or even a lawn chair) in order to read and write comfortably; many carry theirs on the approach. If you have a large party or will be spending a lot of time in base camp, it's advisable to bring folding tables and stools for eating and game playing. Most trekking agencies have these for rent, or include them in the package, but you do need to consider porter costs. Tablecloths offer a nice touch of ambiance.

Light. Base camp time in stormy weather can be tedious. Consider a method for providing reading and gaming light. This is essential on winter trips when the nights are long. For a breezy mess tent, kerosene lanterns provided by the trekking agency are standard, though they are finicky and smoky. Bring one for the cook, one for the mess tent, and a backup lantern. Also pack plenty of extra mantles and a filter funnel to remove gunk from the fuel. If fuel is available, consider butane or propane lanterns, which are much more convenient and reliable. Try to get frosted globes to soften the harsh light.

Library. Consult one another so that each brings books that can be shared. It's easy to go through a dozen books in the course of a major expedition, but that's too many for one person to pack. The situation is grim when you're stormbound and the only thing left is schlock or books you've already read.

Extra sleeping bag. Some climbers bring a three-season bag (0 to 20° F; −18 to −5° C) for the approach and base camp. The most versatile option is a semirectangular design that can be opened up like a quilt when it's hot and is roomy enough to let you wear down clothing when it's really cold. On expedition-style climbs, using a second bag saves about 4 pounds off your back when making trips down to base camp and allows more room for carrying loads upward. For the trek/base camp bag, a cotton or silk sleeping-bag liner is comfy and keeps the bag clean from body oils and dirt.

Extra pads. Bring a thick, wide mattress for sleeping comfort while in base camp. A nice luxury is to insulate the entire floor area of the tent from the cold ground below. Purchase large sheets of thin (one-eighth inch; 3 mm) closed cell foam at a hardware store, tape them together, and cut to shape. The resulting pad is cheap, lightweight, and fairly compact when rolled.

Coffee. Serious aficionados and addicts are unpleasant people to be around when they don't get their fix of the good stuff. Bringing your own beans (preground in small, airtight containers) and a nonbreakable French press is the best solution. Packing a grinder and cappuccino maker is getting a bit decadent.

Libations. Somehow a fine single-malt whiskey just makes harsh wilderness life a bit more civilized. Those who imbibe might want to bring some to enjoy in base camp, but keep a bit in reserve for the post-climb celebration (or commiseration). Note that alcohol is frowned upon or completely banned in Islamic countries; smuggling is illegal, but breweries in Pakistan produce beer and spirits for infidels.

Binoculars. Since you're traveling through spectacular country on most expeditions, it's nice to get a good view. A pair of 8X compact binoculars (size of a deck of cards), and possibly a 25X spotting scope, can be useful for viewing climbs, vistas, and wildlife.

Portable shower. While a sponge bath is okay, a nice hot shower after a few weeks on the trail is a sweet luxury that should not be missed. A solar shower sitting on a rock can heat up in a couple of hours on a sunny day. Bring some biodegradable soap and an absorbent camp towel.

Camp clothes. It's nice to have some comfortable, nonclimbing clothes for lounging around camp. This will probably be what you wore on the trek, but you may want some running shoes or sandals for walking around.

Clothespins. On a long expedition, hand-washing clothes every now and then is mandatory. Drying clothes on a rock is slow, so it's worth stringing a clothesline of parachute cord (3 mm). Clothespins keep things spread out for faster drying and save you from chasing wind-blown socks.

DIVERSIONS

It's important to have a variety of diversions for the down times in base camp; these are not luxuries. Otherwise people begin to go stir-crazy and start having thoughts of getting the hell out of there. When several teams are sharing a base camp, there's often a lot of social interaction and sharing of treats.

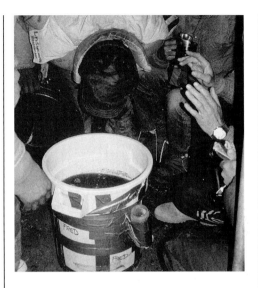

Breaking into the freshly-brewed beer is a fun way to end the expedition.

Bring several decks of cards, since they wear out, and a rule book of card games to settle arguments. Backgammon and chess are popular board games. Trivia games are good only if everyone is from the same culture. But games that force players to act things out or draw pictures can be very entertaining for all. Bring plenty of popcorn, too.

Games and activities that let you interact with the porters—Frisbee, football, kite flying—are a great laugh. While trekking up the Baltoro Glacier in 1997, expedition member Gary Neptune removed horse-shoes from the skeletons of ponies the army formerly used for transport of supplies. The team taught the Balti porters how to play horseshoes.

At base camp on Ama Dablam in 1989, Freddie Snalam made beer for the final celebration—a tradition started by Brits many years earlier. All it requires is a very clean 5-gallon food bucket, a dark-beer kit (from a home-brew supply or large liquor store), and insulation to prevent freezing (store in the cook tent). After about two to three weeks of fermentation, you can pour off a flat, yet tasty, alcoholic beverage (don't stir up the muck on the bottom) and have a party.

ELECTRONICS

Base camp radio. While climbers on the mountain use small handheld radios, the base radio should have far more power (5 watts or more) and a serious antenna. The most common bands are 2-meter VHF-FM (144 to 148 MHz) and 70-centimeter UHF-FM (420 to 450 MHz). It helps to expand the range with a CAPS/MARS modification to extend transmission (140 to 174 MHz and 420 to 470 MHz) since FRS (Family Radio Service) radios and European expeditions will be on those frequencies. There are several antenna options, but plan to erect a mast (20-foot poles are rare above treeline).

Since this is specialized ham-radio equipment, few expeditions want to purchase a brand-new rig. It may be possible, however, to purchase radios from past expeditions so you might contact leaders through your alpine club. Be aware that higher-powered units consume a lot of battery power.

In Alaska, CB radios (27 MHz) are the main method of communication (channel 19). These are comparatively heavy, bulky, and have limited range but are the standard in Denali National Park and elsewhere; Kahiltna Base Camp broadcasts the weather at 8 P.M.

Shortwave radio. After a few weeks, it's nice to know what's going on in the outside world. Plus you can get weather forecasts. On the south side of Denali, FM radio stations come in quite well at the higher camps.

Portable stereo. A huge matter of personal taste. It seems the more expeditions a climber has been on, the fancier his or her sound system; Some bring boom boxes to base camp; others use battery-powered speakers off their portable CD or digital player (cassette tapes are too bulky). Be cognizant of the people around you and don't let your noise intrude on their experience.

Computers and satellite phones. Those who cannot live without their electronic umbilical cord have ample opportunity to take technogeekdom to new heights. Most major expeditions with corporate sponsors are now expected to bring a laptop computer, digital cameras (still and video), and a satellite phone for Internet access. Plan on bringing somebody who knows how to make it all work, too. Since this technology changes weekly and each expedition has unique demands, this book will not cover computers or satellite phones. One good source of information is *Humanedgetech.com*. Satellite phones (Iridium is one option) may be rented from many sources for around $300 per month, and calls cost about $4 per minute.

ELECTRICITY

With our increasing reliance on electronic gadgetry, reliable power is a significant concern on extended expeditions. Even on shorter trips, a team can burn through a serious quantity of batteries just from using headlamps.

Personal Power

Sadly, the base camps of major destinations around the world are littered with decaying alkaline batteries. This disregard for the environment is inexcusable. Any disposable batteries *must* be packed out when you leave and disposed of properly.

A better solution is to use solar-panel chargers and rechargeable batteries. The inexpensive solar chargers can handle four to eight AA batteries and are a great way for each member to power their headlamp and personal stereo. The cheap units are often rather fragile and can discharge batteries left in when the sun goes away. Better compact solar chargers are of a flexible material that is quite durable and have a diode that provides reverse-current protection.

The standard nicad batteries found in stores hold only 500 milliampere hours (mAh) of power, while high-capacity nicad AAs hold 700 mAh (about the same as AA alkaline batteries). The new, second-generation nickel–metal hydride (NiMH) AA batteries store about 1,700 mAh, do not suffer from memory effect, are nontoxic, and don't cost much more than nicads; the main drawback is that they offer little warning when running low. When at home, it's best to use NiMH batteries with a special "smart" charger to get the full capacity, but they should work fine with most solar chargers.

For use in critical electronics—namely headlamps and radios—up high on the mountain, lithium batteries are the best choice. They're expensive ($3 per AA battery) but provide juice down to –40° and are half the weight of alkalines or rechargeables (13 grams each versus 25 grams). (These were not yet available in the AAA size, and the rechargeable lithiums are 3.6-volt, so they are not compatible.)

Professional videographers rely on the Expedition Battery, a lithium-based power source made by Automated Media Systems (*Automatedmedia.com*). These are light-weight, environmentally safe, and very reliable, but cost around $100 each.

Base Camp Power

To handle the needs of a base camp radio, computers, scientific equipment, and video cameras, a larger solar array is required. Calculate your needs based upon 12 volts and add up the ampere hours (Ah) of all the appliances that will be in daily use.

Many options exist, though size and cost depend upon your power needs. Expect to spend several hundred dollars at a minimum. High-output portable solar cells typically deliver 8.5 to 25 watts and can be arranged in series to increase voltage or in parallel to increase milliamps. Sources for a variety of photovoltaic options include *Automatedmedia.com* and *Realgoods.com*.

Since high-altitude sun increases output, you may need a voltage regulator to prevent melting electronics. Many well-financed expeditions use a 12-volt master battery (from a 10-amp motorcycle battery all the way up to a 210-amp truck battery) that can charge smaller batteries when the sun isn't available. If you need to operate higher-voltage gizmos, you'll also need a power inverter to provide the necessary output. Be sure you test all of this before you leave home!

It's increasingly common for large expeditions to bring portable generators; some even run electric lights to each tent. These run on gasoline or diesel, deliver 2,000 watts or more, and may be purchased in Kathmandu or Islamabad. Be advised that this level of decadence puts out a lot of noise that is intrusive to nearby camps; you might find pancake syrup in the gas tank. Even if solar is your main power source, if your expedition's financial success depends upon electricity, it's wise to have a backup system.

MEDICINE CABINET

Grizzled veteran alpinists sometimes scoff at a first-aid kit and spew about how they've been out a thousand days and never needed more than aspirin and duct tape. As with a hundred-year flood, the odds never get better—and the more time spent in the danger zone, the greater your risk. Being caught unprepared is foolish.

The farther your expedition ventures from good emergency care, the better you should be able to handle whatever comes up. Even if helicopters can theoretically reach the victim, there is no guarantee that one will be available when needed; weather and politics may intervene. Unprepared expeditions have become such a problem that a health clinic is being set up at Everest Base Camp.

Every extended climbing trip has slightly different demands, and the first-aid kit must be adjusted accordingly; there is no single kit ideal for everything. Even the different stages of an expedition (approach, lower mountain, upper mountain) have their own requirements, so it's best to assemble a modular kit that can easily be adjusted. A minimal kit with altitude meds is lightweight, so it's worth carrying even on a summit bid.

For a comprehensive list of medications and supplies that a medical doctor might bring on a large expedition to a remote area, see Appendix D, Medical Supplies. For information on use of the Gamow Bag and similar air-pressure chambers, see the section "Hyperbaric Chamber" in chapter 6. Use *Medicine for Mountaineering* (The Mountaineers Books, 2001) and *Wilderness Medicine: Beyond First Aid* (Globe Pequot Press, 2000) for advice on building and using your expedition kit.

While not a necessity, a portable pulse oximeter, which measures the oxygen saturation of blood, is useful for checking how people are acclimatizing. The little Nonin Sportstat (about $400) just clips onto a fingertip and gives the percentage of oxygen and pulse to confirm other signs of acute mountain sickness (AMS).

Although some newer medications are shockingly expensive, the faster action and greater punch than older, cheaper drugs can make them worth it. Some of the common drugs, such as Diamox and Valium, may be available in the destination country without a prescription; just don't try to bring them home.

If possible, select a local health clinic in the area you will be traveling and designate it as a recipient of unused medical supplies (check *medicinesfornepal.org* for one example). With this prearrangement, you may be able to get medicines donated to your expedition by drug companies. Even if you must purchase your drugs, giving the leftovers to a clinic is good karma—and many of the drugs will expire before your next trip anyway. Include the consumer information sheet for each medication to assist the clinic staff.

Be warned that some of the medicines in a well-stocked kit are controlled drugs in many countries. Doctors will understandably be reluctant to provide prescriptions, since screw-ups on your part can haunt them (and the victim). Learn all the indications and, especially, the contraindications before you approach an MD.

Transporting controlled drugs across borders can land you in serious trouble, and every country has different regulations. Be certain that each drug is clearly labeled and that you have a copy of the prescription. It may be wise to make a list of all prescription drugs and have the doctor and team leader sign it. If medical oxygen is planned,

try to obtain it at your destination, since transport is an extreme hassle.

REPAIR KIT

The repair kit is like the first-aid kit: an essential item that varies in size with the nature of the trip. For an extended expedition, you need to be able to repair just about anything—remember, Murphy was an optimist.

Among the essentials are duct tape (at least one big roll), epoxy adhesive, baling wire, an assortment of safety pins, a bundle of zip-ties, and a few hose clamps. Perhaps the most useful product is Seam Grip, a clear, flexible liquid urethane that can patch holes and fix tears; bring several tubes. Barge Cement can hold a pair of boots together after they start to fall apart. Include an assortment of plastic buckles, since these break at inconvenient times.

At the very least, bring a multitool that has pliers and screwdrivers. Needle-nose vise grips often come in handy and a file has many uses, including sharpening ice tools and crampons. If the trip includes skiing, bring a posi-drive screwdriver, some extra screws, and a bit of steel wool (mix with epoxy to plug stripped-out holes). A sewing kit should include needle, thread, and thimble for light repairs, an awl and waxed thread for heavy repairs, as well as extra buttons. Include some normal fabric swatches as well as adhesive-backed fabric repair tape.

CHAPTER 6

Pumori (23,494 feet, 7,161 meters), Nepal

Supply Line: Base Camp to Summit

Many peaks present a moderate section of climbing between base camp and the serious business. In some cases, this lower part of the mountain is long enough to require its own gear. Obviously the expedition needs to bring climbing equipment for the technical difficulties higher up. On the 8,000-meter peaks, you may need specialized products for the upper mountain.

THE LOWER MOUNTAIN

Finding your way through the minefield of a snow-covered glacier can be mentally draining, but exciting. Rope teams of three or four people work best since there's a good likelihood that somebody will take the plunge into a crevasse. During the exploratory stage, it can be faster if everyone travels with light packs. For easier detection, the lead person should carry a trekking pole without a basket to use as a probe.

WANDS

When climbing on large glaciers, mark the way, since a storm may bury your tracks. The standard method is to use bamboo wands with fluorescent-colored flagging (buy two or three rolls at a hardware store) tied to one end. Try to find bamboo about one-half to three-quarters of an inch (1 to 2 cm) in diameter (thinner ones break too easily when trying to insert them in hard snow) and about 4 feet (1.25 meters) long; a few thicker, longer ones are useful for marking caches. Since wands should not be spaced farther than a rope length apart, you may need anywhere from 20 to 200 depending on your route.

An Iranian expedition in the Karakoram made some very nice wands from half-inch plastic pipe, with triangular red flags that bore their silk-screened logo. This artistic touch backfired on the expedition, because the flags soon became souvenirs for other climbers. The remaining white wands weren't visible in a storm. But the flags looked marvelous while they lasted.

FIXED LINES

Icefalls and steep rock sections commonly require fixing with ropes so that climbers can move up and down at their own speed with minimal fear of falling. This takes a lot of static rope about 9 millimeters in diameter (smaller than that and ascenders won't grip, particularly when the rope is icy). Although twisted polypropylene rope is probably the least expensive, it's nasty stuff that kinks and handles horribly. Spools of static kernmantle cost more but are much easier to work with.

Snow pickets are the most common anchor for fixing ropes on a glacier; ice screws are too expensive and melt out too fast, and snow flukes are a hassle. Generally you'll want 3-foot-long pickets made of 3-inch aluminum angle stock or T-stock with some holes drilled for carabiners. These can be purchased commercially (MSR or SMC) or made at home; don't get carried away with drilling, since too many holes can severely weaken the picket. Estimate the number you'll need based on how much fixed rope you're bringing: approximately one picket every 50 feet.

TENTS

On the lower part of the mountain, you'll likely want roomy two- or three-person tents that can hold up to heavy snowfall and high wind. Poles need to be a larger diameter than usual for extra strength and rigidity (some climbers even double up the main support poles). There should be plenty of guy points to increase support;

Complex routes must be marked with wands to allow escape.

for maximum strength, the fly should fasten to the poles at the guy points.

Yellow is a popular choice for the color of the tent fly since it's visible in poor light and transmits a pleasant hue; tan and light blue are also common. No matter the fly color, the tent should have reflective patches on all sides to speed finding it by headlamp; attach your own if necessary. Reflective guylines are also a good addition that helps prevent tripping at night.

Since you may be spending a lot of time inside, it's important that the tents have a bright, cheerful interior. Dark tents are depressing at best, and intense color (red or bright yellow) is unnerving. An off-white inner canopy will let light in and reflect light from a headlamp or candle.

A vestibule (or two) for storing gear makes the tent much more livable, and it's pretty much essential if you're using liquid-fueled stoves. A door on the opposite side allows easy egress while somebody is cooking, and it improves ventilation. It's handy to have a lot of pockets in the tent, and a mesh gear-loft helps dry things. Each tent should include a small, stiff brush in the stuff sack to help remove snow from clothes and to sweep out the floor; a little diligence minimizes moisture inside the tent.

The best option for tent stakes are 12-inch squares of fabric with two loops of strong cord attached to the corners like little parachutes. Girth hitch one to each stake loop on the tent and tie one to the end of each guyline. These soft stakes can be piled up with rocks for camping on a moraine, or filled with snow and buried. Just leave them attached to the tent when it's time to move on.

Another option for fixed camps is to carry an igloo-maker (Grand Shelters IceBox; *www.grandshelters.com*), which allows construction of a solid structure for two (8-foot diameter) to five people (11-foot). This simple device weighs about 5 pounds, and its use is easier than cutting and

Good mountaineering tents are havens from a sometimes harsh world.

trimming blocks: just shovel loose snow into the mold. It's faster and drier to build an igloo with the IceBox than to dig a snow cave, often a tedious, backbreaking endeavor. The dome is far warmer at night, cooler in the day, and quieter in a storm than any tent. Be sure to mark an igloo with wands, since it's hard to spot white on white.

SHOVELS

Each tent team should carry a shovel for digging out a ledge, building snow walls, or excavating a snow cave. Aluminum blades have the best bite in hard snow, but be careful not to pry or they will break. Plastic shovels are good for collecting snow to melt since they won't chip off paint into your water; keep this separate from the latrine shovel.

An extendable handle with a D-grip gives the best performance, but when going light, try to find a blade that will accept an ice tool for a handle. Some shovels have a saw blade inside the handle, which can be helpful when building windbreaks.

COMMUNICATIONS

Climbers once had to carry absurdly heavy and bulky radios, which of course were very unpopular. Now we have the compact FRS radios that weigh only 6 ounces (170 grams) and are very compact and relatively inexpensive (less than $100 each), making it feasible for each team member to carry one if desired.

The FRS radios are limited by U.S. law to 0.5 watt of output, must have built-in antennas, and can broadcast only on fourteen frequencies between 462 and 467 MHz. Since these frequencies are allocated differently in Europe and elsewhere, FRS radios may technically be illegal, though it's unlikely to be an issue in remote mountains.

Normally an FRS radio has a range of only about a mile (1.6 km), due to obstructions. But several thousand feet of elevation gain tends to give them greater range, and 10 miles (16 km) or more is possible with line of sight. If you want a better guarantee for communication, choose 1- or 2-watt GMRS (General Mobile Radio Service) radios. These require an FCC license in the United States ($75 but no test) but have greater power, and some allow antenna upgrades.

For maximum flexibility, select 2-meter/70 cm ham radios, which aren't much bigger or heavier but are more expensive and complicated. When "opened up" with a CAPS/MARS modification, often just a simple bit of desoldering, these become compatible with FRS/GMRS radios.

Whichever radios you select, be sure that they use AA batteries, because that gives you the option of using lithium batteries to reduce weight and improve cold-weather performance (many FRS/GMRS radios use only AAA batteries).

THE MOUNTAIN KITCHEN

It's difficult to overemphasize the importance of properly functioning stoves on an expedition: your choice can make or break the climb. For higher altitudes (above

15,000 feet; 4,600 meters), the most popular options are stoves that take screw-in cartridges. In cold weather at lower elevations, however, the fuel does not vaporize well and the stove doesn't put out enough heat unless a heat exchanger is used. Butane/propane blends suffer this effect the most (the propane burns off first); an isobutane/propane blend (MSR) is relatively immune to this problem but may be difficult to find overseas.

Butane stoves are lightweight and simple to operate—open the valve and light—and require no maintenance; you just have to bring the empty canisters back for disposal. For igniting the fuel, a piezo lighter is a worthwhile feature, but still bring plenty of reliable butane lighters. Bic disposable lighters are far better than market cheapies or the expensive refillables (some don't work at altitude).

Particularly when camping above 23,000 feet (7,000 meters), it's helpful for a two-person tent team to carry a second stove to speed the process of melting snow for water—stay hydrated! A titanium butane stove with a 1-liter titanium pot weighs only 10 ounces (285 grams) and takes up minimal space; the stove and a fuel cartridge fit inside the pot.

As a cartridge nears empty, it loses efficiency and needs external heat. Merely insulating the fuel actually makes matters worse, and using your hands is not particularly pleasant. You might consider the Primus Heatpad, which fits into the cavity on the bottom of the cartridge. It provides heat for 15 minutes, is recharged by 5 minutes of boiling,

Cooking inside is a standard procedure made easier with a hanging stove.

and weighs 3.2 ounces (90 grams). If you're using hanging stoves, use a butane lighter's flame on the cartridge while the stove is running—scary but effective.

In some areas of the world, such as Baffin Island, butane cartridges may not be available for purchase. Shipping fuel in advance by cargo transport may be an option, but allow a lot of lead time (at least several months).

By choice or necessity, you may want to bring a multifuel stove (such as the

Optimus Nova or Primus OmniFuel) that can burn kerosene (paraffin) and white gas. In North America and parts of South America (such as Peru), white gas (benzene) is easily obtained, making it the fuel of choice since it's clean burning and easy to use. When white gas isn't an option, use the best grade of kerosene that you can find and run it through a filter to remove impurities (avoid automobile and aviation gas). Take note that the same fuel has many

Photo by Jack Roberts

The roar of a multifuel stove is comforting when far from home.

names around the world (see the Fuel Name FAQ at *www.ultralight-hiking.com/ fuelnames.html*) and may be found in unlikely places (paint stores, pharmacies). Bring priming paste to help get reluctant fuels going, and spare parts for anything that can wear out or break.

A good windscreen channels heat up the sides of the pot and hangs the stove with three cables from a central point. In a crowded tent, this is a much easier system than cooking on the floor, where pots get knocked over, and it's essential when living in a portaledge on a big wall. The most popular hanging stove systems (Bibler and Markhill) use butane fuel. At present, only Primus offers a hanging kit for their liquid-fuel stoves, though it may work with other brands.

It's nice to have the option of using a stove on the ground as well, but choose only a model that has teeth on the pot supports to minimize slipping on an uneven floor. Ideally, the pots should also have ridges on the bottom for greater friction. When cooking on snow, you'll need a stove platform to keep from melting in. The MSR Trillium Base weighs only 3 ounces (80 grams) and works with many stoves, but you can also make one from a square of masonite or a non-plastic clipboard.

The weight savings and durability of titanium pots make them a good, albeit expensive, choice for mountaineering. Thin-walled aluminum pots are also light, and a lot cheaper, but are easily dented. Stainless steel pots are indestructible but too heavy, as are most Teflon-coated aluminum pots (great for normal use, though). If you're just rehydrating freeze-dried food, you only need a single pot for melting snow and boiling water. However, you generally want a second pot if you'll be cooking meals.

Keep the stove and pots together in a stuff sack. Also include a fuel cartridge, lighters, pot grips, a spice kit, spare parts, soap, and a pot scrubber/sponge. This way you have the entire kitchen in one bag, ready to go. A plastic measuring cup is handy for dipping and pouring fluid into narrow-mouth bottles.

STOVE HELL

Our Gasherbrum II expedition purchased a half-dozen Bibler hanging stoves, since many of us had used them before and knew them to be reliable and efficient. It's really just a basic Primus butane stove with a cheap but effective windscreen, so the Bibler is about as simple as can be. We had tested them that winter in the Colorado Rockies, and there were no problems. Enter Murphy's Law.

It took us eight days of hard effort to find a safe route through the icefall. By then we were all antsy to get on with the real climbing, so half of our team established a temporary camp at 18,200 feet near the base of Gasherbrum I. That evening the advance team radioed down with the distressing news that half of their fuel cartridges were inoperable—they were full but nothing was coming out.

After a frantic round of testing, including cutting open an empty cartridge to look inside, we confirmed that the problem affected all of our stoves. But none of us could figure out a solution. Ultimately we had to test each of the 200 Primus cartridges on each of the six stoves to weed out the apparently defective fuel. It would have taken nearly two weeks and a lot of cash to have more fuel brought to us, but another expedition saved the day by trading for our "bad" fuel, which worked fine on their stoves.

This little episode cost us probably 50 person-hours accented by much cursing. There was a brief time when we weren't even sure we would be able to do the climb—no stoves mean no water. Happily, the stoves and fuel that made it to high camp at 23,850 feet (7,270 meters) worked fine.

Only when we got home did we find out that the stoves were defective, because the center pin wasn't quite as long as it was designed to be. Differences in thread length on the cartridges were enough to keep half of the cartridges from working because they couldn't mate properly with the shortened pin. Ever since, I've brought along a multifuel stove (that I hope to never use) as a backup.

— *Clyde Soles*

HIGH ON THE PEAK

Once you reach the technical climbing, things get more exciting and you need to break out the special equipment. Just existing at altitudes above 23,000 feet (7,000 meters) requires gear you may need nowhere else.

The nature of the mountain will dictate what climbing equipment you bring: Patagonian towers are certainly different from Himalayan giants. This topic fills more than a hundred pages of Clyde's book *Rock & Ice Gear* (The Mountaineers Books, 2000), so it's impractical to go into great detail here. One safe rule of thumb—the higher you go, the less you want to take.

ROPE

For glacier travel, something like a 50-meter, 8.5-millimeter dynamic rope with a tight weave and a water-repellent treatment works well since it isn't too long for two or three people. If the climb entails a lot of moderate snow slopes, a 100- to 120-meter rope is a good choice. This allows for full-length rappels and a rapid retreat down snow slopes when used with a 3-millimeter pull cord (use an 8 mm haul line on rock).

If a glacier route has a lot of fixed lines, such as in the Khumbu Icefall on Everest, it's not a bad idea to carry a short (about 15 meter) piece of half rope for quick belays on dicey sections of crevasse crossings. As the ice melts, fixed anchors get sketchy and aren't always maintained.

On routes with technical rock climbing,

Rock that is easy when dry becomes a nightmare when snow-covered.

it's best to go with a cut-resistant 10- to 10.5-millimeter single rope (Edelweiss, Mammut, and Roca). While the reduced weight of thinner single ropes (9.4 to 9.8 mm) is attractive, they can cut with frightening ease, and the rock in high mountains often has sharp edges. Avoid using a dynamic rope for a weight-bearing fixed rope; use static rope instead. The stretch in dynamic ropes, especially skinny ones, can cause a sawing action over an edge.

Some alpine climbers who are pushing the limits use cut-resistant 9-millimeter ropes (Edelweiss, Roca) as single ropes for demanding mixed climbs—but this is a calculated risk since these are tested as half ropes (55 kg versus 80 kg on drop tests), intended for alternating use with a second rope the same size. While not as light, a pair of twin ropes (about 7.4 to 8 mm), which are used in tandem, offers better cut protection and longer rappels.

If the expedition will be fixing lines, you'll need to estimate how much static rope to bring based on prior expeditions (if any) and best guess. Some of the major towers in Pakistan and India can use up 1,000 meters of fixed ropes. For routes on the south side of K2 and the north side of Everest, it's common to fix 2,500 to 3,000 meters of line. Both the north ridge of K2 and the south side of Everest (not including the Khumbu) take about 5,000 meters—more than 3 miles—of rope to protect clients and porters.

The smallest practical rope diameter for use with ascenders is 8 millimeters, which typically comes in 100-meter spools that weigh about 10 pounds (4.5 kg). Mammut offers 200-meter spools of 9-millimeter static line that weigh 22 pounds (10 kg). Most companies will make any length you want, given sufficient time. For vertical jugging and hauling on walls, larger-diameter (10 to 11 mm) static line is required to minimize stretch and increase cut resistance.

ROCK PROTECTION

Although camming units are often faster to place, chocks are still the lightest and most compact option for rock protection. If your route will involve a lot of cracks, Wild Country Forged Friends and Zero Friends offer the best weight-to-performance ratio.

When you're hundreds of miles from the nearest hospital, the solid feel of a well-placed piton is reassuring. For a lot of big-wall use, the super-durable chromoly steel pins are the way to go. But for occasional alpine placements, titanium knife blades save a significant chunk of weight.

Hand-drilling bolts is a slow, tedious process in most mountain regions where hard rock is the norm. If there is no other option, be sure to bring plenty of spare drill bits that have been presharpened, plus a diamond sharpening stone. In alpine environments without much traffic, quarter-inch compression bolts are a reasonable compromise between speed and safety; use $^3/_8$-inch expansion bolts if more parties will follow.

The advent of wire-gate carabiners has allowed climbers to easily reduce a half-pound (quarter-kilo) from the rack without compromising safety or usability. These are also glove-friendly (in the larger sizes) and less prone to icing up than conventional gate designs. Wire-gate ovals are excellent for big wall climbs.

SNOW AND ICE PROTECTION

Snow pickets offer the best protection on steep snow slopes since one can be pounded in if conditions are hard, or buried

Gasherbrum IV (26,000 feet, 7,925 meters), Pakistan

as a deadman if less consolidated. While 3-foot pickets are commonly used for fixed lines, the shorter 2-foot pickets (like the Yates Cable Picket) are easier to carry when leading. Snow flukes are an alternative to pickets; however, they don't rack well.

If you will encounter significant amounts of hard ice, the clear choice for protection is steel ice screws with coffee-grinder handles; the security and speed of placement is unbeatable. The main drawback is their hefty price (about $50

each) and weight (about 6 ounces). The better titanium ice screws cost about the same but are about 1.5 ounces (40 grams) lighter, which can really add up. Cheap titanium screws are best used as "leavers" for rappels since they aren't very strong.

A better option for rap anchors in hard ice is a V-thread, made by intersecting two screw holes and threading with a runner. This requires a tool to push the sling in one hole and snag it to pull out the other; make your own from a wire coat hanger or buy a commercial one. Another alternative is to chop out a bollard, creating a knob of ice for an anchor, though this takes much longer.

TENTS

Alpine assault tents all share one common feature: they are made for performance, not comfort. Tents for high altitude need to be as light and compact as possible, hence they are tiny, while remaining bombproof in hideous conditions. Ideally, a two-person tent should weigh less than 6 pounds (2.7 kg) and be easy to set up in a strong wind.

Although single-wall tents have long been the favorite, the new generation of double-wall tents are beginning to rival them. Single-wall tents (such as those by Bibler and Integral Designs) are made with waterproof/breathable fabric so they don't need a fly, but they aren't well-suited to warm, humid approaches. Double-wall alpine tents (for example, models by Kelty and Marmot) will be warmer up high and have fewer condensation problems down low.

Some may be tempted to skip the weight of a tent and use snow caves instead. However, do not underestimate how much you will be slowed by high altitude. It can take hours of hard work to dig even a small cave, while you would already be out of the storm and brewing up tea with a tent.

For big-wall climbs, two-person portaledges are the "tents" of choice. Most of these have flies that are better suited to Yosemite or Zion than to the extremes of Baffin Island or Baltoro towers. Only ACE (formerly A5) makes a serious mountain ledge with a fly that fully encloses every-

thing; the ACE Cliff Cabana can snugly sleep three climbers in the most outrageous locations.

The drawback of ledges is that their weight (about 22 pounds; 10 kg) and bulk (almost 4 feet long when packed) make them difficult to carry. This could prove awkward if you must go over a summit and descend a different route. Some single-wall alpine tents (Bibler and Integral Designs) were designed to fit on a portaledge to replace the fly, though availability is scarce. These ledge tents can be pitched on the ground too, making for a versatile system.

HYPERBARIC CHAMBER

Since Igor Gamow (GAM-off) patented his eponymous air-pressure chamber, the Gamow Bag, in 1990, numerous lives have been saved from high-altitude cerebral edema and high-altitude pulmonary edema (HACE and HAPE). Placing the stricken person inside the bag and inflating it with an air pump quickly lowers them, in effect, about 7,000 feet (2,150 meters) so their body can recover enough for descent. A comatose patient often pops back after about 15 minutes in the bag.

There are three portable hyperbaric chambers that operate on the same principle. The Gamow Bag is well-proven, weighs about 15 pounds (7 kg), and costs $2,500. The Certec Mam'out caisson from France is about the same weight and price but goes to a higher pressure (3.2 versus 2 PSI), hence lower altitude. The Portable Altitude Chamber made in Australia is a bit heavier, also goes to 2 PSI, and is half the price of the others ($1,200). Differences between the brands are of real concern only to frequent users such as clinics and rescue services; any of these is better than none.

Fortunately, these hyperbaric chambers are available for rent, either in the United States or from trekking agencies in India, Nepal, and Pakistan, for less than $500. (Believe it or not, you need a prescription to buy or rent one in the United States.) They may also be available used from previous expeditions; check with your alpine club.

Given their excellent track record and reasonable expense, hyperbaric chambers are worthwhile insurance for expeditions to 6,000-meter peaks and above. The lives you save may not be your own; porters and climbers on other expeditions have been saved too. Many guided treks to Kala Patar, the classic tourist's viewpoint of Everest, now carry hyperbaric chambers.

Usually, the victim is placed inside for about an hour, during which the pumping must continue to provide oxygen, and then they are reassessed. To avoid ear pain from the pressure change, patients should do valsalva maneuvers (hold nose, close mouth, and blow). It often takes somebody with HAPE about 2 to 4 hours for significant improvement, while HACE takes about 4 to 6 hours. Depending on severity and at what point during the expedition a person experiences problems, a bout of AMS or HAPE may not necessarily spell the end of the trip for the stricken climber; HACE probably means go home.

As with many other safety procedures

you hope you never use, everyone on the expedition should be familiar with operation of the bag. It's a good idea to test it at the beginning of the trip so you aren't patching holes when it's needed.

OXYGEN

In general, peaks under 8,500 meters (28,000 feet) are routinely climbed without oxygen. Since 1,000 meters is about the usual maximum elevation gain for a summit day, the high camp is typically under 7,300 meters (24,000 feet) and is visited for only a few days. For these "lower" peaks, the difficult logistics of using oxygen outweigh the benefits.

On the highest peaks (Everest, K2, Lhotse, and Kangchenjunga), the use of oxygen is still common (all were first climbed with it). Although they have been climbed without oxygen, the odds of success (defined as coming back alive after reaching the summit) improve dramatically with this supplement. An analysis published in the *Journal of the American Medical Association* in 2000 showed that the death rate for Everest summiters increased from one in twenty-nine with oxygen to one in twelve without. On K2, the situation was even worse, increasing from a grim one in seven with oxygen to a grimmer one in five without.

Many different oxygen systems have been developed for mountaineering since 1922, when the British first used oxygen on Everest. Until the 1950s, the tanks were made of steel and contained a limited amount of oxygen at relatively low pressure (500 liters at 122 bar at room temperature).

Hillary and Norgay reached the top with aluminum bottles that held 800 liters at 228 bar and weighed 11.5 pounds (5.2 kg) apiece; their oxygen rigs (two bottles plus regulator and frame) weighed 30 pounds (13.6 kg).

Since then, oxygen systems have evolved to using aluminum bottles wrapped with Kevlar or carbon fiber, which weigh less and can hold higher pressure (hence more gas). The systems made by Poisk and Zvedsa in Russia are the most common, which also means they are the most easily pilfered from high camp on crowded routes. Each 3-liter Poisk cylinder is 19 inches (48 cm) long, 4.25 inches (11 cm) in diameter, and weighs 5.8 pounds (2.6 kg) when full and 3.5 pounds (1.6 kg) when empty. The bottles contain 720 liters of oxygen at 260 bar (the new 4-liter cylinders are about 25 percent more) and cost roughly $360 apiece (not including transport to high camp).

Unhappy with the existing systems, Eric Simonson of International Mountain Guides assembled better technology. The American cylinders, made by Structural Composites Industries, are much larger and heavier (15 pounds, or 6.8 kg, when filled; 12 pounds, or 5.5 kg, empty), with 1,850 liters of oxygen at 207 bar. This system reduces the number of bottle changes on summit day (one may suffice), there's no risk of theft (different regulator), and reliable fills are assured (done back home in the United States).

With the Russian system, you can cache the smaller bottles as they are drained, in order to significantly lighten your load, but you must pick them up when heading down. Using a rate of consumption of 3 liters per minute, a bottle will last 4 hours; at 4 liters per minute, it lasts 3 hours. Three Poisk bottles are typically used for an Everest summit bid, plus two more for sleeping, and most climbers will want to be prepared for two summit bids. So prepare to spend $3,600 for gas and another $400 for mask and regulator, though you can sell the gear afterward. In addition, there is a hefty deposit required for oxygen bottles and a stiff penalty if you don't bring down as many as you take up.

With any oxygen system, you must increase the flow rate as you go higher to compensate for the change in pressure. To check whether bottles are full, you need a reasonably accurate scale; a pressure gauge doesn't work, since tank pressure is affected by temperature.

Be sure that the masks are close fitting and are comfortable to wear all day long, and that they work with your clothing system. Try several brands, since facial structures vary and some masks are uncomfortable or will cause sunglasses and goggles to fog. The tubing between bottle and mask should be light and flexible yet kink-resistant.

Although used oxygen systems can be rented in Kathmandu, considering that you've already spent a year getting ready and a small fortune to reach high camp, it makes sense to purchase a new system and sell it afterward. Whether you rent or buy, it's very important to test your system early (use a partially full bottle) so you are completely familiar with its operation; failing to do so has cost several people their summit.

CHAPTER 7

Gasherbrum IV (26,000 feet, 7,925 meters), Pakistan

Mountain Living: Personal Gear

It's essential to refine your personal climbing gear and clothing far in advance of the expedition. As a general rule, the closer a product arrives to your departure deadline, the more likely that something will go wrong with it. If you will be testing prototype equipment that is mission critical, bring a complete backup that has proven reliability. All your careful preparation will pay off once you leave base camp and head up for the true climbing.

CLOTHING

When assembling your clothing system, start next to the skin and work outward to include your harness and pack. Be certain that all vents and zippers are compatible and that freedom of movement is unimpaired. The energy costs of overcoming friction between layers can be significant (a couple hundred calories wasted per day), so you don't want to fight your clothing.

Women no longer must contend with ill-fitting "unisex" clothing. Accept no compromise regarding performance and comfort, ladies, and support companies that recognize your needs.

When it's well below freezing and the wind is howling, answering nature's call must not be a chore, no matter your gender. Through-the-crotch zippers are the easiest to use while wearing a climbing harness, though some prefer drop seats since there is less chafing of the inner thighs. The systems are not interchangeable, so commit to one style for all your lower-body clothing, including underwear.

It's worth considering the colors of your clothing and packing so you don't clash: there's nothing wrong with fashion as long as you aren't giving up any performance! No need to ruin the photographs of your friends with a dreadfully boring or hideously ugly outfit; reds and yellows provide nice contrast to blue sky and white snow. From a practical standpoint, dark or very light colors are difficult to spot in stormy weather. Some reflective patches make spotting your partner easier by headlamp at night.

INNER LAYER

Midweight synthetic long underwear is the best option. Lightweight has only minimal warmth, and heavyweight is poor at wicking moisture. Some people still prefer wool; it isn't as scratchy as in days of old. Zip T-necks work well for keeping your neck warm and for cooling off when working hard. Bring at least two sets of underwear since you'll be living in this stuff for days on end and washing isn't always convenient.

No matter the underwear's material or style, if you'll be on a glacier be sure to choose a light color (white is best) because you need sun protection and don't want to bake. Wear nylon shorts over them when it's too warm for layers.

Heavyweight, knitted wool socks work well and don't require liner socks unless you have tender feet. Depending on the length of your trip, you may want three or four pairs. Avoid neoprene socks since they tend to impede circulation more than they add warmth.

MID LAYER

Keeping warm in the wide range of conditions encountered in the mountains is something of an art that each climber must work out on his or her own. Your metabolism and level of conditioning makes a huge difference. In the ugliest conditions, the new technologies offer numerous options that are superior to the wool and cotton of yore.

Packing for the mountain often calls for tough decisions: what goes, what stays.

Among the most popular as a first line of defense is a windproof shirt with a wicking lining (à la Marmot DriClime Windshirt). This breaks the wind, provides a bit of warmth, and makes a good sliding layer. Stretch woven fabric (such as Schoeller DrySkin) is a fantastic pants material that is rugged and breathes well yet is wind and water resistant; a thigh pocket is handy for sunscreen and snacks.

For chilly to cold temperatures, midweight fleece jackets offer a lot of versatility; the new generations are even reasonably light and compact. Windproof fleece is less breathable and a bit heavier, but it's nice not having to wear a shell in a breeze. A sleeveless stretch fleece bib is great when it's consistently cold, since it eliminates bulk around your midsection. For variable conditions, fleece pants with full-length side zippers are easily donned while wearing crampons or skis.

When climbing in temps that drop from rather cold to downright bitter, Primaloft-filled jackets and pants give the best protection with the least bulk. For technical routes with potential for cold, wet conditions, this synthetic clothing is a great choice. Two-person teams doing one-push climbs sometimes carry a single synthetic parka for belays because it can help dry the inner layers that get damp while climbing.

OUTER LAYER

Whether you choose a "hard shell," which is windproof and waterproof and fairly breathable, or a "soft shell" that is wind- and water-resistant and very breathable, depends on when and where you are going. The 2.5- or 3-ply (no lining) versions of the high-end waterproof breathables, like Gore-Tex XCR and eVENT, give the best performance if you will be working hard and encounter rain and melting snow. For winter and high-altitude climbs, jackets made of stretch fabrics, like Polartec Power Shield and Schoeller Dynamic, are very comfortable when climbing and are trim-fitting so they can layered over.

When wearing a climbing harness, bibs and a shorter jacket are the most convenient. A hip-length parka and pants can work adequately with a harness and are fine without. One-piece climbing shells can be hard, soft, or a combination; they are certainly comfortable but you do give up some versatility, so they are best for one-day pushes.

If you will be climbing in extreme cold where dampness is less of a concern, high-quality down-filled clothing still offers the best warmth-to-weight ratio. Opt for a windproof fabric (such as DryLoft) for best efficiency. A one-piece down suit is about 10 ounces (300 grams) lighter and $100 to $200 less expensive than a separate down parka and pants. But the ability to wear the parka alone at base camp makes the two-piece system a better choice for many, and fit is less of an issue.

HATS AND GLOVES

Headwear is a matter of preference, but a lightweight balaclava and a warmer wool or fleece hat make a good combination. The hat should cover the ears (ski hats often leave the lobes exposed) without blocking hearing (avoid windproof fleece). When wearing a helmet, skullcap liners are warm and comfortable.

If you'll experience extreme cold (below

A clothing system includes your pack and climbing harness.

0° F; –18° C) and high winds, a balaclava or face mask makes life tolerable. Better designs fully protect the face, ears, and neck without restricting breathing or icing up; be sure they work well with your goggles. Masks with heat exchangers built in, such as the PolarWrap or Psolar.EX, prewarm each inhalation to minimize heat loss and possibly prevent the "Khumbu cough" (a nagging hack aggravated by cold, dry air).

Finding a suitable glove system is often a matter of trial and error that is affected by your cold tolerance, sweat output, and tastes. Insulated gauntlet gloves work well for many and offer reasonable dexterity. The better gloves can be remarkably expensive (more than $100), but the cheap ones tend to leak and fall apart quickly. Wrist leashes (a.k.a idiot straps) are a good idea, but always bring a spare pair of warm handwear on an expedition.

Lightweight, windproof fleece gloves with reinforced fingers and palms are excellent for a wide range of conditions and dry quickly. Some climbers like wool gloves instead because they can be warmer when wet and won't melt. If you'll spend much time on a hot glacier, a pair of very thin white gloves can protect your hands from the sun (sunscreen doesn't last); these liners are also good inside mittens when it's especially frigid.

Mittens are the obvious choice for use in extreme cold, and for people with Raynaud's Syndrome (a circulation problem that affects up to 10 percent of the population, women more than men). Chemical

heat packs can help warm fingers, but they need oxygen to work and are less effective up high (or inside boots).

FOOTWEAR

For routes where you are climbing only a couple of days at a time, insulated single boots are lightweight and offer superb ankle flexibility. Combined with supergaiters, these can provide adequate warmth for all but Arctic or high Himalayan conditions. However, if sized for technical climbing performance (relatively snug), the boots may restrict circulation and increase the risk of frostbite. Women have limited selection in this category of insulated technical boots because demand is fairly low.

On longer expeditions to the greater peaks, moisture buildup within single boots becomes a concern. Each foot generates about a liter of sweat in one week. This water dramatically reduces the insulative value of boots and is difficult to remove. Using antiperspirant and changing socks religiously can help, since wool absorbs much of the moisture. Vapor barrier socks (essentially waterproof bags) are another option, but many climbers don't like the feel and trench foot is a possibility.

Double boots have an outer shell of plastic, leather, or synthetic that protects a removable insulating inner boot. This allows the inner to be dried more easily, and they can be worn as camp shoes for doing chores. You can also replace the stock liners with custom-molded models, such as Garmont or Intuitions that are lighter, warmer, and more comfortable (add some antislip material for walking on snow); they are vapor barriers, though, your socks will get wet.

Beware of boots that leak water through the tongue; check for a gusset to ankle height. Since glaciers often course with icy streams in the afternoon on warm days, partial immersion is common while hopping over them. A boot that is passable in wet snow may leave you soggy after a plunge that leaves others dry.

When climbing a lot of snow, a pair of rugged gaiters is useful even if your shells have built-in gaiters or your stretch pants fit over boot tops. As you make a high step, the heel points of crampons often graze the upper calf of your opposite leg, and gaiters with protection to the knee can save your pants. Look for a pair with a trim, snug fit, waterproof/breathable uppers, and replaceable instep straps.

The warmest double boots have an integrated gaiter, but adding a supergaiter, which extends from the knee to the sole leaving the tread exposed, to an expedition double boot is equally warm and offers more versatility. Overboots that cover everything are even warmer, but they are terrible for walking on snow or climbing rock. Use overboots only with strap-on crampons since toe bails are insecure.

Those who have real problems with cold toes might consider using heated footbeds (such as the Hotronic FootWarmer). The battery packs last about 8 hours but need to be charged in base camp with a solar panel, so these would best be used on summit day.

If you aren't wearing double boots with removable liners that have walking soles, a pair of Primaloft booties can be a nice luxury at lower camps; synthetic is better than down for drying damp socks. Traction is important, as climbers have died by slipping while going to the latrine.

EYE PROTECTION

Blinding sun, reflective snow, and drying winds can play havoc on your eyes at high altitude. Unless you like the thought of hot sand poured into your eyes—a common description of snow blindness—give serious consideration to eyewear. This is so critical that you should bring two pairs on most expeditions.

While glacier glasses were once the norm for most mountain endeavors, the new sport sunglasses with interchangeable lenses have a lot to offer. If you shop carefully, the sculpted designs can hug your face better than all but the best glacier glasses with leather side-shields; very little light should sneak up from below. With either style, however, the inexpensive models tend to fog badly when you're working hard, rendering them useless. Antifog products are a temporary fix, but it's better to find a quality pair of glasses that ventilate and protect.

The best tint for the widest range of lighting conditions is a dark brown or amber with about 10 percent light transmission. Some glacier glasses are darker (5 percent transmission), but they don't block any more UV and are too dark when clouds pass over. Gray lenses are good when it's contrasty but are poor in flat light, so they're less versatile. Either an orange or yellow lens tint with about 60 percent transmission is great in flat light. Blue-tinted lenses are a fashion trend, but they decrease your acuity.

Multilayer antireflective coatings inside the lenses reduce internal reflections and enhance contrast. Avoid mirrored lenses since they place your nose in a solar oven. Many climbers buy or fashion a removable nose shield for greater sun protection; baked noses are ugly and painful.

High-quality goggles with double lenses, good ventilation, and adequate peripheral vision are essential; cheap goggles will permafog at the worst time, guaranteed. Select a model with a flexible lens, since rigid ones break easily, and bring a spare lens anyway.

Those with vision problems have many options nowadays, but plan for contingencies. If you can wear them, the latest extended-wear contact lenses (silicone-hydrogel) have excellent oxygen permeability and work well at altitude (when very high, you may wish to take them out for sleeping). Bring prescription glasses and goggles that fit over them, plus sunglasses, in case an irritation or infection prevents wearing contacts. Be aware that CR-39 plastic lenses can fall out of metal frames in very cold weather.

Laser eye surgery (LASIK is the most common, LASEK is a newer alternative) is increasingly popular, but it's best to have this done at least a year prior to going to extreme altitude (it takes six months for the flap to bond and two years for complete healing). Compared with contact lenses, this is still a risky procedure with unknown long-term consequences and only half of patients achieving 20/20 vision—beware the hype.

Photo by Jack Roberts

Wearing a pack while frontpointing at altitude is a serious workout.

PACKS

Because your pack must coexist with your clothing system and climbing harness, it's wise to shop accordingly. Sometimes pack straps interfere with shell vents and pockets, or a pressure point is created under the hip belt by parka doodads. Pockets attached to the hip belt or shoulder straps make an excellent place to carry sunscreen, camera, hat, and crevasse rescue gear. A few packs offer well-designed gear racks and tool holsters, useful since gear loops on a harness are covered by the pack's hip belt.

Unfortunately, few if any companies build packs for glacier travel. It's common for climbers to clip the rope to a carabiner on their shoulder strap to keep from stepping on it and prevent flipping upside down after a crevasse fall. Yet packs are poorly designed for use as a quasi-chest harness, so if you jettison the pack, a cheap plastic buckle is all that keeps it from disappearing (consider replacing the buckle with an aluminum cam-lock).

Since weight is the enemy, less is more—as long as the pack doesn't fall apart midclimb. Even a pack as large as 6,000 cubic inches (100 liters) should weigh less than 5 pounds (2.3 kg) and comfortably carry 50 pounds (23 kg). Loads above that are impractical for moving quickly through mountainous terrain at altitude, no matter how fit the climber.

Smaller, fighting-size packs around 3,000 to 4,000 cubic inches (50 to 65 liters) are a better choice for lean, mean alpine climbs than for load-slogging routes. Because you really can't climb technical terrain with more than about 35 pounds (15 kg) on your back, an alpine pack doesn't need much of a frame. If the climbing is very difficult, your pack needs to be burly enough to withstand hauling.

Bladders with drinking tubes are a fantastic aid for staying hydrated while climbing, which can really boost your performance. Be sure your pack is designed for a hydration system, though you may want to upgrade the one provided (many are lame). An insulated tube and nipple cover can minimize freezing problems in 10° F (−12° C) temperatures. For extreme cold, it's best to carry fluid inside your down parka in collapsible plastic containers (such as Platypus) to prevent freezing. Consider carrying a small, lightweight thermos, too; it won't physically warm you, but the morale boost of hot fluids can offset the weight.

If you must haul a lot of gear over relatively flat terrain, sleds are the best alternative. You can make your own quite cheaply from a kid's plastic sled for one-time use (common on Denali) or purchase a standard-length (about 42 inches; one meter), commercial sled for better performance (integrated covers to protect gear, superior traces and harness for much more control, and brakes for resting while going uphill). For trips that require skiing while hiking, the sled should allow you to strap the pack inside in such a way that permits you to wear the pack with the sled attached. Extended polar expeditions typically use double-length fiberglass sleds that can hold 400 pounds of gear.

For only a few ounces more, a no-frills summit pack (about 1,500 cubic inches; 25 liters) can double as a sleeping bag stuff sack. Using this small day pack instead of your climbing pack can save 2 pounds when you're going for the top and is more convenient than just using pockets.

Keep your gear organized in the new stuff sacks made of silicone-coated fabric. These are half the weight of regular sacks and easier to stuff due to the slippery material. Bring a couple of large stuff sacks or plastic trash compactor bags (garbage bags tear too easily) for caching gear. Compression stuff sacks are useful for reducing the volume of a sleeping bag and down clothing.

SLEEPING SYSTEMS

There are two schools of thought on sleeping bag systems: carry a lighter synthetic bag (around 20° F; –7° C) and wear all your clothing in the bag, or bring a warmer down bag (about –20° F; –30° C) and remove some layers at night. Both concepts are valid and each has its pros and cons.

Using a synthetic bag will dry your clothing without risk of losing loft. It's also about 20 ounces (0.6 kg) lighter than the warm down bag, though the bulk is the same. This system requires experimentation before you put yourself on the line; even sleeping in a meat locker to test everything is not unreasonable.

The down bag tends to be more comfortable, so you sleep better, and provides a better safety margin since you can still add clothes if necessary. After multiple days of hard work in thin, cold air, often with inadequate nutrition, your body has a harder time generating heat, so extra warmth may be appreciated. However,

down bags may lose loft over time from moisture accumulation.

For winter bags, the insulation should be equal on top and bottom so you can roll onto your side without exposing a cold spot; a bag with 60 percent of the insulation on top means a cold night's sleep. Women should select a bag that is the appropriate length, but "female-specific" sleeping bags are just hype.

A water-repellent shell (for example, DryLoft) greatly helps protect from external moisture such as frost. With this shell fabric, a bivy sack is neither needed nor desirable; the use of two layers of waterproof/breathable fabric reduces overall breathability, so moisture builds up faster in the insulation. Replace the locking slider with a dual-pull, non-locker for a fast exit in an emergency.

If you will use a bivy sack, choose one that is entirely waterproof/breathable (not just on top) and a sleeping bag with a microfiber shell (such as Pertex) to minimize condensation. Select a bivy that has easy entrance, with a stormproof closure and a built-in runner for tying into the mountain; rolling off in the night would suck. Should bivouacs be likely, a two-person sack (sometimes called a bothy bag), such as an Ortovox, offers greater warmth for minimal weight.

Mountaineering expeditions often provide an opportunity to dry sleeping bags when you drop to lower camps; choose a model with a black lining to speed solar drying. Yet polar explorers may experience intense cold for weeks, which makes moisture buildup a problem. If drying may not be possible for many days, consider using a vapor barrier liner inside your bag. This waterproof sack keeps the insulation dry, but you must remove all clothes except underwear.

No matter the bag system that is used, good sleeping pads are important to prevent heat loss. Sleeping on snow and frozen ground requires a pad with an insulation R-value greater than 3. A full-length pad is desirable but, when minimal weight and bulk are critical, a three-quarter pad (plus the foam from a pack) will suffice.

The safest and lightest, but bulkiest, option is a closed-cell foam pad about three-eighths of an inch (10 mm) thick. Look for dense EVA foam with a nonslip surface that is smooth (no bumps or ridges, so that snow can be easily brushed off), and attach a tie-off loop at each end. Rather than rolling up the pad for carrying, some alpinists cut the pad into pack-width sections that are taped together to fold out flat; this is carried inside the pack.

Closed-cell pads leave a lot to be desired in the comfort department, so many climbers bring a self-inflating air mattress instead, or as a supplement, at least as far as base camp. These are roughly twice as heavy but the most compact, and they allow better sleep due to more padding and higher R-value when fully inflated. With reasonable care (carried inside the pack, ground prepared), Thermarests and such can work fine on expeditions, but they don't hold up to rough handling. Always carry a patch kit. An equally heavy option is an open-cell/closed-cell laminate that is comfortable and durable but far bulkier.

CLIMBING GEAR

An alpine harness needs to be lightweight, be adjustable enough to handle a wide range of clothing (two waist buckles help keep the tie-in point centered), and fit comfortably underneath the hip belt of a pack (gear loops sometimes hurt). It should

The climbing harness must be comfortable under a heavy pack's hipbelt.

also allow you to easily go to the latrine without having to untie from the rope (a drawback of the Bod/Whillans-style harnesses). Some of the skimpiest harnesses don't weigh much but are painful to hang in, particularly when wearing a pack, so wider waist and leg loops are desirable.

Though some European climbers favor a full-body harness for glacier travel, these are a nuisance for layering. A commercial or self-made chest harness will keep you from flipping upside down after falling with a pack. But many climbers do without and use the pack itself as a chest harness (clip a biner to the strap and run the rope through it); this works, but packs could be better designed for this feature.

Since you may end up using a variety of ropes (sometimes not your own) on an expedition, bring a belay/rappel device that can handle both skinny and fat ropes. If you anticipate very long rappels or lowers involving a knot pass, a figure-8 device prevents having to unclip; it's also easier to use while wearing gloves and can't be dropped accidentally (clip the large hole with the belay biner when storing). It's important to know how to use a Munter hitch, too, but it's terrible for rappelling.

Select locking carabiners that are easily operated one-handed while wearing heavy gloves. Auto-lockers are convenient and can be lighter than screw locks, though some models tend to ice up (spray with WD-40 before the trip). Each climber should carry at least two lockers: one for the belay device and the other for anchoring.

For glacier travel, a pair of prusik slings (6 mm cord tied into 12-inch loops) is the lightest option for ascent, and one of these may be used as a rappel backup (attach to a leg loop and extend the rap device with a runner so the knot is below it). Mini-ascenders also work, but are not suitable for rappel backup if the ropes are doubled for retrieval. Each person's glacier kit should include at least one racheting mini-pulley (two is better) for assembling a Z-rig to haul somebody out of a hole; doing this without pulleys is dramatically harder. Keep all of this emergency gear where it is easily accessible; some climbers pre-rig the prusiks on the rope.

If your climb will include fixed lines, bring at least one full-size ascender (two if the route will be steep). These are heavier than compact models but much easier to use, particularly at knot passes. Be sure the handle is large enough for your hand wearing gloves or mittens. The cam should have aggressive teeth and clearing slots to bite on icy ropes. It's important that the ascender cannot twist off the rope accidentally when on low-angle traverses (sometimes an extra biner is necessary).

Connect to the ascender with a short sling (no longer than arm length) girth-hitched to your sit harness's anchor point. For passing anchors on fixed ropes, girth a sling or daisy chain to the harness and clip it with a locking carabiner to the rope, allowing it to slide freely as you climb. This runner is also useful for clipping into anchors on steep ground.

Hard-shell helmets (either plastic or carbon fiber) offer the best protection from falling rocks and are the most durable. The soft-shell helmets use foam to absorb shock; these are lighter and offer better protection against side impact (common in swinging falls on rock). But soft-shell helmets can break if sat upon, so they are not suited to expeditions where rough handling is the norm.

If there are significant sections of technical rock, it may be worth bringing a pair of climbing slippers with a Velcro closure for fast on and off (size them large to fit over socks). For major rock climbs in the cold, consider using insulated rock shoes with an integrated gaiter (Boreal and Five.Ten).

SNOW AND ICE GEAR

Hard technical alpine climbs call for a pair of 50-centimeter ice tools, usually a hammer for pounding pins and an ax for chopping. The better designs offer good clearance, yet the gently curved shaft doesn't interfere with hammering or plunging. Select a thicker (4 mm) pick that won't break; thinner picks penetrate hard ice better but aren't as durable. Leash design can generate endless debate, so it's best to experiment while wearing the gloves you'll use on the mountain. Some alpine climbers enjoy the freedom of the new leashless designs; carry a backup tool.

Lower-angle ice and snow slopes predominately between 30 degrees and 60 degrees are best climbed with a straight-shafted 70-centimeter ice ax (give or take 5 cm). This is a good length for use on the uphill side of a slope when angling upward,

Photo by Jack Roberts

Crampons and technical ice tools must be versatile and reliable.

chopping steps, and self-arresting. Make sure the ax head is comfortable in your bare hands (file sharp edges if necessary), the shaft is smooth for easy plunging (avoid rubber grips), and the spike is a symmetrical point. If climbing in bitter cold, purchase an insulated head cover (Grivel) to keep your hand warm, or make your own with foam and duct tape.

A few companies have tried making shorter ice tools with extendable or modular shafts for use on lower angles, but so far they leave a lot to be desired. If the terrain will be wildly varied, you may want to bring a technical hammer and a standard ice ax.

Most climbers seem to prefer a long wrist loop on a mountaineering ice ax— one that is attached at the head and is the length of the tool. Other alternatives include a short sliding wrist leash or an over-the-shoulder sling attached to the head. If the risk of dropping the ax is low (easy climbing with no hidden crevasses), you can do without a leash, but be prepared for the consequences if you screw up.

For gentler slopes (less than 30 degrees), many climbers forgo a long (80 to 90 cm) glacier ax in favor of ski poles. A pair of poles is lighter and more supportive than an ice ax, and you can still stop a slip if the poles have self-arrest grips. They can't be used as an anchor, however, so carry a snow picket where it can be reached for crevasse rescue.

The distinction between technical and mountaineering crampons has blurred so much that one good pair (such as the Black Diamond Bionic, Cassin C14, and Grivel G14) can suffice for most climbing. Vertical front points with a T-shaped cross section work well in hard ice and soft snow, and most crampons allow either a mono- or dual-point configuration.

Do not even consider a pair of crampons without anti-balling plates to prevent the dangerous clumping of snow; better designs have plates built in. These plastic (preferable) or rubber plates add a few ounces but save you energy since you aren't lifting big snowballs on each step.

Most climbers will want 11- or 12-point crampons with clip-on bindings that have a toe bail, a heel lever, and an ankle safety strap. These are easy to operate, secure, and do not impede circulation. If you will be wearing overboots, however, pick a model with toe straps instead of a bail, or you risk losing a crampon at an inopportune moment.

Steel crampons certainly offer the best durability, but they are a tad heavy. If all the climbing will be on snow, then aluminum crampons save about 7 ounces (200 grams) per foot—a substantial difference at 8,000 meters. Unfortunately, the points tend to bounce off ice, and rocks wear them down quickly; points can even snap off. So far, titanium crampons have not proven economically viable, but the material is ideal for the application (with steel front-points).

Given the massive size of avalanches in the greater mountain ranges, avalanche beacons may be useful only for body recovery. These lightweight (9 ounces; 250 grams) radio transceivers are most valuable in relatively small avalanches triggered by climbers or skiers, where there is less chance of fatal trauma. Since beacons are an all-or-nothing proposition, and they are basically useless without a shovel, everyone on the expedition must decide whether to carry them.

SKIS AND SNOWSHOES

After a heavy snowfall, it's always smart to wait for avalanche conditions to settle. If the route is a moderate snow climb and dangerous slopes can be avoided, it can be safe to proceed on skis or snowshoes before the snow has compacted enough for walking. While fun, don't consider skiing unless everyone on the expedition is an advanced skier. Remote backcountry is not the place to learn. What's more, glacier skiing with a heavy pack while roped is very demanding.

For mountaineering purposes, alpine touring (AT, or randonnée) is the only ski equipment that makes sense. These are lightweight, shorter skis (160 to 180 cm) designed for easy parallel turns in backcountry snow conditions by somebody wearing a pack. Newer, shaped designs have more sidecut depth (about 14 mm) for effortless turning. Some of the lightest racing AT skis (it's a sport in Europe) are probably too fragile for an expedition and don't perform well in funky snow.

The AT bindings allow free-heel touring and fixed-heel turning with release functions. Some, such as the Silvretta 500, are compatible with mountaineering boots as well as AT and alpine boots. Although your climbing boots may fit and are fine for touring, due to their flexibility they lack control on downhill runs and may not release when you fall. If the route doesn't require much technical climbing, such as the West Buttress of Denali, then AT boots can be a better alternative. They are light, warm, crampon compatible, comfortable for walking, and allow you to enjoy the descent.

Though you may not need them most of the time, self-arrest grips on ski poles can be real lifesavers. The better poles are modular, so you can use a standard grip on the approach. Adjustable length and a probe feature are nice but not really necessary; graphite shafts have a better swing weight than aluminum shafts.

In addition to skis, bindings, poles, and possibly boots, you will need runaway straps to prevent ski loss (don't use brakes on glaciers or in deep powder), climbing skins (full length, shaped to fit) to ascend steep slopes, and ski crampons for traversing icy slopes. For long ski trips, you may also want cross-country kick wax, rub-on glide wax, extra skin adhesive, spray-on skin waterproofing, and spare binding screws.

For those without an extensive ski background, snowshoes are the way to go. Even expert skiers are better off with snowshoes in many situations. Mountaineering snowshoes often have sturdy construction, clip-on bindings, and aggressive crampons underfoot; recreational and running snowshoes need not apply. Snowshoes are about 8 pounds (3.4 kg) lighter than a ski package and compact enough to lash onto a pack. Even just one or two pairs of snowshoes can be helpful for breaking trails on an expedition.

THE OTHER STUFF

Never underestimate how the little things can stop your expedition cold! They can make life more pleasant—and at times some of these items are critical. On any expedition, no matter how large or small, there are a number of accessories that should pretty much always be on your person.

Knife and lighter. Everyone should

carry a small pocket knife, though it needn't include the kitchen sink. Probably the most used features are scissors, tweezers, and a straight blade (back home, the can opener and corkscrew come in handy). Another indispensable item is a Bic lighter; carry your own and make sure there are lighters with each stove. Some climbers even wear the knife on a neck lanyard and tape a lighter and lip balm to the cord so they are readily accessible.

Sunscreen. Even if skin cancer weren't a concern, frying your face is no fun. Bring plenty of broad-spectrum (blocks both UV-A and UV-B) sport sunscreen with an SPF of 15 (minimum) or 30+ (preferred). Test new sunscreens at home to make sure they don't sting your eyes when you sweat; this can be debilitating at inconvenient times. Also stash several lip-balm sticks or tins throughout your gear, since they often vanish.

Eye protection. Sunglasses and sun hats were discussed earlier, but it's worth reiterating that they are essentials at high altitude. Don't forget a lens-cleaning cloth, since synthetic shirttails do a poor job. If you wear contact lenses or prescription glasses, be sure that you have backup eyewear for both day and night vision. Contact wearers should have rewetting drops and plenty of cleaning fluid; eye drops in single-use containers are convenient. Individually packed towelettes allow hand washing prior to handling contacts.

Headlamp. Woe be to he or she who is caught after sunset without a headlamp! With the introduction of the miniature LED lights that run on a pair of AAA batteries (such as the Black Diamond Starlight and Petzl Tikka), there's no reason that even the most minimalist climbers can't carry an emergency light.

If you are planning to climb in the dark, the tiny lights don't have enough reach, so a more powerful headlamp is called for. The best of these use seven or eight high-quality white LEDs for a bright, even light pattern and have several power settings. Some have a halogen spot that is helpful for brief moments of searching. Most headlamps operate on two to four rechargeable AA batteries worn in a pack on the head, though some find the weight uncomfortable. If lithium batteries are used in the cold, there's no need for a remote pack worn inside clothing.

Wristwatch. At a minimum, everyone should wear a basic wristwatch with a loud alarm, backlight, and a fresh battery. The band should be easy to remove and don so you can put it near your head at night; you'll rarely hear the alarm from inside the sleeping bag. An altimeter is a very useful feature for determining location, though it tends to make the wristwatch bulky. Some watches offer a rudimentary compass— better than nothing, and all that many climbers take. You probably don't want to know your heart rate while chugging uphill, and the chest straps are uncomfortable, so don't bother with a heart rate monitor (helpful for training, though).

Navigation tools. For some routes, navigation is easy—up or down—but others may require finding your way through a vast expanse, sometimes in a whiteout. If you will be atop an ice cap or need to find a buried cache, a small GPS unit (like the Garmin Etrex Summit; about 5 ounces, or 150 grams) can be a blessing. However, at least one person should carry a decent compass that has a sighting mirror and declination adjustment, and also a globally balanced needle (Suunto) if you are traveling to the other hemisphere.

Wind meter. Here is one of those things that isn't needed but makes for more accurate reports and better bragging rights. The digital models are the size of two lighters and some provide temperature, humidity, and wind chill factor.

First aid. Although the expedition may bring an extensive medical kit, each person should carry a minimal first-aid kit. This should contain a good supply of a nonsteroidal anti-inflammatory drug (NSAID), such as ibuprofen, along with throat lozenges, some adhesive bandages in different sizes, a blister kit, a whistle, and any personal medications (including altitude drugs) required. This all can fit in a tiny waterproof pouch.

Eating utensils. A large insulated mug that holds at least a pint (half-liter), with a lid, can serve as both bowl and drinking vessel. Some people put a leash on the lid. Another option is a plastic bowl with a snap-on lid, which allows rehydrating meals inside a sleeping bag. For versatility, it's hard to beat a titanium spork (spoon with fork tines), but a plastic (Lexan) soup spoon is also popular.

Water bottle. Though you may use a hydration system, it's also helpful to carry

Navigating during a whiteout is far easier with a GPS receiver.

a 1-liter plastic wide-mouth bottle for mixing energy drinks and bringing inside your sleeping bag at night. Use an insulated cover over this to help prevent freezing. The bottle cover also is a great place to store a freeze-dried meal while you're waiting for it to hydrate.

Pee bottle. Find a 1-liter wide-mouth, collapsible bottle, with a different shape than water bottles, for answering nature's call during the night. Women may need to practice a bit—and everyone must overcome modesty—but this is essential for winter camping.

Sleep aids. When climbing on snow,

there are days when the heat of the sun shuts you down by noon, and you'll try to get some sleep while it's still daylight. Near the North and South Poles during their summers, going to bed with the sun still up is a certainty. Since quality rest is vital and light disturbs this, a virtually weightless sleep mask is worth packing. To tame flapping tents and snoring partners, don't forget your earplugs.

Hygiene. Basic grooming needn't go out the door on an expedition. Bring a tooth-brush, small tube of paste, comb, nail clippers, and antiperspirant at least to base camp and possibly higher; you'll look and feel better. Foot powder is helpful for absorbing sweating and reducing vile odors. Women should bring an adequate supply of tampons or pads unless they decide to delay menstruation with the Pill, which has no known altitude problems.

PHOTO GEAR

Most expeditions are the trip of a lifetime, even if you have to go back for another attempt. Since these trips often include some of the most fantastic scenery in the world and encounter fascinating cultures, it's worth the effort to bring back some memories on film.

As of mid-2003, there was little contest between film and digital—the latter still had a long way to go, even for nonprofessionals. With 35 mm color slide film, you have the option of making quality prints, giving slide shows, and making submissions to maga-zines and catalogs. Digital is great for its immediacy, and the 4- to 5-megabyte

cameras can generate decent prints and good Internet images. However, there are many problems during an expedition with image storage, cold weather, short battery life, and fragile construction.

If your interest in photography is casual, the best option is a compact point-and-shoot camera with a moderate zoom lens (about 35 to 105 mm). Avoid zooms that go longer unless you like lousy photos. Though larger than the cute APS (Advanced Photo System) cameras, a 35 mm point-and-shoot is more versatile and you can find film almost anywhere.

When you really want to bring home more than snapshots, lens quality is the primary concern. If compactness is critical, select a fixed-lens point-and-shoot (28 or 35 mm) such as the Ricoh GR1v. What you give up in not having a zoom is made up for with better images.

Many climbers are tempted by a budget 35 mm auto-everything camera body with a single zoom lens, thinking it will do all they need. In truth, they would be better off putting the same amount of money into a decent point-and-shoot. No matter the brand, the entry-level camera bodies and lenses are poorly built and of inferior quality; they are little more than cheap toys. As a rule of thumb, if the camera body has a pop-up flash, it isn't suitable for an expedition unless you bring a spare body.

If you are going to the effort of carrying a 35 mm camera with interchangeable lenses, it's best to pick a model made for serious use. When shopping, keep in mind that all the bells and whistles are purely for the amateur market; pros seldom use the gimmickry. In fact, high-end manual focus cameras still have many advantages for serious photographers: better longevity and cold-weather reliability, more accurate focus, smaller size.

If you must have autofocus, the best choices are semi-pro models (such as the Canon EOS 3, Contax N1, and Nikon F100). With any of the SLR (single-lens reflex) cameras, you will want a dedicated flash for portraits and interior shots; built-in flash has many drawbacks.

When choosing a camera, it's best to start with the lens system. Pick your lenses first and then find an appropriate body to hang on them. If money is the main issue, the best bang for the buck comes from a set of fixed focal-length lenses such as 28 mm/f2.8, 50 mm/f1.4, and 100 mm/f2.8 macro. To get this level of performance from a zoom lens requires a fixed 2.8 f-stop (most decrease from 3.5 to 5.6 when zoomed out) that generally costs around $1,000 and tends to be huge (77 mm filter or larger). Cheaper zooms make many compromises, including optical quality and speed; they're okay if you want amateur results. For telephoto, an 80–200 mm/f2.8 zoom is the way to go.

Filter quality should be the equal of your lenses; multicoatings eliminate glare so that contrast is not degraded. Attach a leash from the lens to the cap so it doesn't disappear. Get in the habit of using a lens hood whenever possible, even if it's cloudy; better photos result. If you decide to bring a tripod, be sure that it has a quick-release

head with platforms for each camera.

The most versatile and affordable films are the amateur 100 ASA color transparencies (Fuji Sensia; Kodak Elite Chrome); equivalent pro films just cost more. If you have a spare body and are using a tripod, then Fuji Velvia is a good choice for nature images (otherwise don't bother).

Bring film from home since the age and storage conditions in distant lands can be uncertain. Do your best to protect film from high temperatures and X-rays. Never store film in checked luggage, where it is certain to be destroyed. A film shield can reduce the cumulative effects of X-rays but is likely to result in security personnel taking your carry-on luggage apart for a hand search.

Ideally at least one person will bring a video camera and all members can get a copy of the resulting tape. It may even be worth sharing the expense. The most compact digital mini DV (or micro MV) camcorders weigh around one pound, cost about $1,000, and can take still images, too. While not pro quality, the results are acceptable for home viewing. Try to find a model that has a AA battery pack available so recharging is less of a hassle. If it will go to the top, consider using an Expedition Battery, which is a lithium battery made for many camcorders (about $80).

Protect all your expensive equipment with a modular camera bag system (such as the LowePro S&F series). This gives you the most flexibility for deciding what gear goes when and where. Some bags have an optional harness that holds the bag securely on your chest for easy access while on the trail.

CHAPTER 8

K2 (28,251 feet, 8,611 meters), Pakistan/Tibet

Mealtime: Power Eating

Nobody summits without eating well, which in the case of climbing expeditions means eating a lot! If you are a fairly active person with a normal diet, you probably consume around 2,000 to 3,000 calories per day when at home. On an expedition, each climber needs about 4,000 to 6,000 calories every day for adequate energy.

To put this in perspective, cyclists in the three-week-long Tour de France—possibly the toughest of all sporting events—average 6,000 calories per day, and some pack in 9,000 for hard stages. Unlike climbers, however, each team has its own chef to prepare all the meals.

Equally important is the absolute necessity for adequate hydration. During each hour that you are working hard, you sweat about a half liter to a liter of water; three liters per hour is possible in heat and humidity. In the dry air of high altitude, you lose another 1.5 liters per day just from breathing. You will likely need to drink 4 to 7 liters of fluid every day to keep even.

Consuming this much food and liquid can be a real challenge, made all the harder by altitude, fatigue, and illness. On an expedition, eating and drinking commence soon after you wake up and cease only when you go to sleep—and middle-of-the-night snacking and sipping are also encouraged! Every rest break is an opportunity to ingest more calories, either from snacks or energy drinks.

Even with all this power fueling, you may still lose weight. It's no easy task putting together a food supply on which every expedition member can thrive. Simply meeting daily requirements is insufficient if even one person has a hard time stomaching the selection.

As soon as possible upon joining the team, each member should fill out a Diet Questionnaire (see Appendix A). While it may be tempting to say "Speak now or forever hold your peace," the reality is that there will be much bitching and moaning unless you account for all tastes.

Although someone may be on a doctor-ordered diet to reduce cholesterol and fat, this should be suspended on an expedition (after consulting with the doctor). Consumption of the "forbidden foods" during the few weeks away from home, with everyone working hard and probably losing weight, will likely do less harm than inadequate fueling. Diabetics, on the other hand, have no choice and must continue to pay attention to their blood sugar levels. Likewise, those with food allergies could find themselves in a life-threatening situation if they aren't vigilant.

DINING UP TO BASE

For major expeditions, the food on the approach and in base camp will likely be handled by a trekking agency. This is great, since it allows you to concentrate on food for the mountain, but you still need to work closely with the agency to ensure that all needs are met. It's wise to go over the menus far in advance, and it still may be a good idea to accompany the sirdar and cook on their

trip to the market. It's worth bringing some treats (such as canned hams and smoked salmon) for this portion of the trip as well.

If you don't have the luxury of a full-service trekking agency, the "cupboard method" of provisioning works well for groups. This basically means stocking the kitchen with a lot of carbohydrates (rice, beans, potatoes, flour) and building meals around them with fresh vegetables, eggs, meat, garlic, and imagination.

Although this is basic camp cooking, what is served should be tasty and bountiful. With the most rudimentary equipment, a good cook can produce a remarkably delicious pizza at 15,000 feet. But without an assortment of provisions, the meals can get dreadfully repetitive after a while. Bring plenty of spices, herbs, and condiments to enliven things; salsa and hot sauce are very popular. Brush up on your Spam haikus (one website lists nearly 20,000), because the ever-popular mystery meat has a multitude of uses.

While some advocate "living off the land"

by purchasing supplies locally, this isn't possible in areas like the Baltoro Glacier, where there are no villages. In areas that don't receive much tourist traffic, small villages often do not have adequate reserves for themselves, let alone rich outsiders. Ancient customs about helping travelers may make them generous to a fault; your expedition could place the village at risk months later.

Thus it is better to acquire everything you need in the capital or the last city before the trailhead. Consult in advance with locals about availability. For the trek up the Baltoro, it is common for an ox, some goats, and chickens to make a one-way trip to feed expedition members and porters.

In the heavily touristed Everest and Annapurna regions, a small expedition can easily dine at the countless teahouses along the way; large teams will overwhelm the kitchen. Eating at these businesses is usually safe if you frequent the larger establishments that receive a lot of traffic and if you apply common sense to what you order (stick with bottled or boiled drinks, peeled fruit, cooked meals). However, there is a risk of getting sick before you reach the mountain, particularly if you imbibe *chang* (a local fermented rice drink). Save the riskier menu options until after the expedition.

MOUNTAIN FOOD

The first step in planning for the foods you'll need above base camp is guesstimating how many days each expedition member will spend on the mountain. This

All calories are good calories on an expedition; variety and quantity are important.

total number of person-days serves as the basis for later calculations. For example, a two-person team spending 12 days climbing in Patagonia represents 24 person-days of food. A group of four people climbing for 3 weeks in Peru is 84 person-days, and a six-person expedition working for 6 weeks on an 8,000-meter peak is 252 person-days. Due to weather and illness, these numbers will be a bit on the high side, but this gives you a bit of cushion for the unexpected.

Many factors affect daily calorie requirements, including climate, level of exertion, fitness, and metabolism. For high-altitude climbing, plan on 5,000 to 6,000 calories per person per day—less if the expedition is going to a warmer region. Each person's needs are different based upon their lean muscle mass. A bantamweight climber simply requires fewer calories than a heavyweight.

Breakfast really is an important meal—you need the energy for optimal climbing performance—and should total about 1,000 calories. Among the popular options are whole grain cereals and instant oatmeal, which are fast to prepare and provide long-lasting energy.

Since lunch is more of an all-day grazing process, it should total at least 2,000 calories spread out over the course of the day. That's six energy bars (250 calories) plus five energy gels (100 calories), if you rely on the engineered stuff.

Another 1,000 to 1,500 calories should be consumed at dinner. If you're relying on freeze-dried meals, take into account that most have a minuscule serving size and inadequate calories. These often need to be augmented with olive oil (120 calories per tablespoon), salami, or nuts.

That daily 4 to 7 liters of fluid should also contain 1,000 calories or more. Hot chocolate, tea with milk, apple cider, soup, and energy drink are all sources of carbohydrate and water. While standard sport drinks like Gatorade offer about 80 calories per cup (an optimal amount for fastest hydration), the high-carb recovery drinks contain more than 200 calories per cup.

LABEL POWER

Once armed with the number of days and the calories per meal, you can begin to prepare the menu plan. This is when you must read the labels on all possible food sources to determine the number of "servings" per package. (The first chapter of *Climbing: Training for Peak Performance* offers an overview of nutrition and understanding labels.)

Any hungry climber who has eaten freeze-dried glop knows that the suggested quantities are pathetically small. A so-called two-person meal typically contains three 8-ounce servings with about 250 calories each, for a total of 750 calories per package (some only have 400), not even enough for one person.

To ensure that everyone has enough energy throughout the climb, the person in charge of food needs to do the servings and calories math on all the food sources. Then, for each day, add up the number of calories actually consumed. When you start doing this, you'll likely notice that the standard diet we rely on during short excursions often comes up short on fuel: there just aren't enough calories.

Preferably, about two-thirds of your calorie intake should come from carbohydrates (starches and sugars), with the rest about evenly split between fat and protein. An approximate 65-20-15 (carbohydrate-fat-protein) ratio has been shown to aid performance at altitude, in part because burning carbs uses about 10 percent less oxygen than burning fats.

When reading labels for calorie content, don't stress too much on the ratios—just avoid the severely flawed 40-30-30 fad diet. The main challenge is finding foods that everyone will eat while up on the mountain. The "ideal" food combination is garbage if it repulses all who go near.

If you have the proclivity, it's a simple matter to input the information on nutrition labels into a database. This data could be useful for future expeditions, particularly if you keep track of what did and didn't get eaten.

MENU PLANNER

Use copies of this form to create a menu, then circulate it among team members for testing and feedback. Don't leave this to chance!

Day 1	Calories/ Serving	Servings/ Package	Calories/ Package
Breakfast			
_____	_____	_____	_____
_____	_____	_____	_____
_____	_____	_____	_____
_____	_____	Subtotal	_____
Lunch			
_____	_____	_____	_____
_____	_____	_____	_____
_____	_____	_____	_____
_____	_____	_____	_____
_____	_____	Subtotal	_____
Dinner			
_____	_____	_____	_____
_____	_____	_____	_____
_____	_____	_____	_____
_____	_____	Subtotal	_____
Drinks			
_____	_____	_____	_____
_____	_____	_____	_____
_____	_____	_____	_____
_____	_____	Subtotal	_____
		Total Calories	_____

Expedition _____   **Date** _____

	Calories/ Serving	Servings/ Package	Calories/ Package
Day 2			
Breakfast			
_____	_____	_____	_____
_____	_____	_____	_____
_____	_____	_____	_____
_____	_____		
		Subtotal	_____
Lunch			
_____	_____	_____	_____
_____	_____	_____	_____
_____	_____	_____	_____
_____	_____	_____	_____
_____	_____	_____	_____
		Subtotal	_____
Dinner			
_____	_____	_____	_____
_____	_____	_____	_____
_____	_____	_____	_____
		Subtotal	_____
Drinks			
_____	_____	_____	_____
_____	_____	_____	_____
_____	_____	_____	_____
_____	_____	_____	_____
		Subtotal	_____
		Total Calories	_____

SCRUMPTIOUS OR DIE

Palatability is super-important! It's all too common for an expedition to foist the unsavory task of menu planning upon a single member, who simply does the best that he or she can. But without active involvement from everyone during the selection and procurement stage, ruined appetites are sure to result.

Even if you think you have an iron stomach, that will change once you get to altitude and are faced with the same meals over and over. Carrying food you can't eat is a double whammy, because it also wastes energy. You may as well save the money and toss some rocks in your pack.

Though a few may disagree, the most important aspect of a menu plan is variety, variety, variety. While you personally may be able to consume macaroni and cheese every day for several weeks, the rest of the team is bound to mutiny. Even the same meal every four days gets mighty repetitious on a long expedition. More than a decade after his Ama Dablam expedition, Clyde will still not voluntarily consume a PowerBar; the expedition received several cases per climber as a donation. Another bonus of a well-stocked larder is delicacies from home give you bartering power with other expeditions.

It is well worth having a tasting party at one of the expedition meetings or pretrip excursions to try out some of the mountain foods under consideration. The more processed/engineered/marketed the food, the more likely it will taste like soggy cardboard. Test everything on the menu that is dubious. If it's only barely edible at sea level, it will be downright revolting at 23,000 feet.

Unfortunately for those who like flavorful foods, there are likely to be team members who cannot tolerate spicy meals. If that's the case, pack a freshly filled spice kit (salt, pepper, garlic, curry, cinnamon) with the stove in order to make boring dishes more appealing. Spices lose flavor with time, so don't use a kit that's several years old. If you want to warm up with capsaicin, Melinda's Habanero Dry Hot Sauce provides a lot of bang and delicious flavor (go for the XXXXtra Reserve in a bottle to really warm up). Salsa packets (Taco Bell Fire Border Sauce) and wasabi paste (in a squeeze tube) also add some kick.

FUEL PLANNING

How much fuel must be purchased and carried is a matter of cooking-system efficiency and availability of liquid water. The fuel consumption estimates provided by stove manufacturers usually do not account for the specific pots you're using, wind, and altitude. It's important to test your system in advance under conditions as realistic as possible.

As a rough estimate, if snow is the only water source, a two-person team will burn about 16 ounces (half a liter) of kerosene (paraffin) or one standard 8-ounce (225-gram) butane canister each day while melting and cooking. If a stream is nearby, or you make a solar heater to melt snow, fuel consumption can be cut in half. If the temperatures will be very cold, more fuel is required due to the dryness of the snow.

A liter of liquid fuel in an aluminum bottle weighs about 28 ounces (0.8 kg), while the equivalent amount of butane (two standard cartridges) weighs 26 ounces. This is not an inconsiderable amount if you're out for several days, so maximizing cooking efficiency is smart.

MOUNTAIN MENUS

In food, and fashion, there's no accounting for taste. However, there are meals that usually get a thumbs-up from Western climbers.

BREAKFAST
Most mornings it's a struggle to quickly eat, pack up, and get moving. Thus preparation time for breakfast should be minimal to nonexistent. The first person awake must get the stove going (or kick the tentmate awake if it's that person's turn) for hot drinks; these also help stimulate bowel movements.

Hot instant breakfasts (oatmeal, Cream of Wheat) in individual packages, in a variety of flavors, are popular and convenient. Each packet contains about 150 calories, so it takes at least two, plus milk and sugar, to start a climber's day off right.

Whole grain cereals (such as granola, muesli, Grape-Nuts) with milk don't even require hot water. While not exactly high on the nutrition scale, Pop-Tarts don't require cooking, are conveniently packaged, and provide 200 calories each. Granola bars

and other "healthy" options tend to be sickeningly sweet for many.

The dried milk usually sold in supermarkets is the nonfat variety (actually about 1 percent) that just makes a watery liquid with little flavor or energy. Powdered whole milk (26 percent fat) tastes much better and contains about a third more calories.

When weather or other factors dictate a rest day, it's nice to have a somewhat fancier breakfast, such as hash browns, scrambled eggs, or pancakes.

LUNCH
It's rare to stop for an extended lunch, so meals are designed around constant munching. If they suit your tastes and budget, energy bars offer convenience but not necessarily better performance than normal food. Beware marketing claims about superiority since test data are often limited in scope and heavily biased. Snickers candy bars, while less than nutritionally ideal because they are rather high in fat and simple sugars, get a big thumbs up for taste from many; ultimately that is more important on a long expedition.

Energy gels provide a quick pick-me-up since they are absorbed faster in the small intestine than solid fuels. Though gels shouldn't become a mainstay—slow energy is good, too—they are well suited to mountaineering (easy to consume, won't freeze). These are ideal for summit day and other times when the going is hard. However, some dentists claim they promote cavities even more than candy does so be sure to brush your teeth.

The combination of dried fruits, salted nuts, and chocolate—commonly called gorp (good old raisins and peanuts)—has probably fueled more outdoor adventures than any other snack. Also a favorite of gray jays (a.k.a. camp robbers), ravens, and chipmunks worldwide, gorp is limited in its variety and contents only by your imagination; let team members create their own blend.

Besides the trail mix, it's worth bringing an assortment of dried fruits such as apples, apricots, and bananas since they contain carbohydrates, fiber, and antioxidants. Although most fresh fruits and vegetables perish quickly, carrot sticks can be a tasty delight weeks into an expedition.

Many of the treats that you should probably limit while at home make good energy sources when climbing. Nutella is a sinfully delicious spread that contains two of the basic food groups: chocolate and nuts. A mere 2 tablespoons contains 200 calories, half from fat, the rest from sugar and protein. Marzipan is almond paste mixed with sugar that can also be used as a rich spread. Halva is a tasty snack made from sesame seeds that offers protein, calcium, and antioxidants.

Fig Newtons have long been a popular snack that travels fairly well in a pack. Certainly peanut butter, jelly, or honey are old favorites, though transport can be troublesome. An assortment of chocolate bars are standard fare on most climbs. Hard candies are just flavored sugar, but sucking on them helps combat sore throats from the dry air.

For omnivores, jerky (dried beef, turkey, or other meat) is an excellent source of protein and sodium that is fairly low in fat. Dry sausages (salami, pepperoni, landjaeger, summer sausage) tend to be higher in fat, so they pack more energy and are long lasting. Of course, many hard cheeses go well with sausage, last for about a month, and add protein and calcium to the diet. Individually wrapped string cheese sticks (mozzarella), unlike other semisoft cheeses, can survive for weeks inside a pack. Even cacklefruit (hard-boiled eggs) can be a good midday snack.

If the approach is relatively short and the temperatures mostly below freezing, bagels remain edible for a couple of weeks. But most expeditions will rely on crackers since they won't go stale, though crush-resistance can be a problem. An old standby is hardtack (also called pilot crackers), a dense, unleavened bread that strengthens jaw muscles and is good with spreads. In the western Himalaya, chapatis are popular and can be made in base camp.

DINNER

Since fuel weight is a major factor, meals that require a lot of cooking are generally not an option. Besides, climbers often don't have leftover energy at the end of the day and they want meals NOW. Therefore, boil-and-hydrate or heat-and-eat foods, plus a lot of no-cook snacks, are the mainstay of a mountain diet.

Certainly the lightest and most convenient option is freeze-dried food, since you just pour hot water in the bag, stir, and wait

10 to 15 minutes. These require no cleanup, and the new bags on better brands have resealable closures to prevent spills. Much of the freeze-dried food on the market is designer yuppie stuff that couldn't feed an anorexic fashion model, though taste has improved somewhat. At roughly $7 per bag—with a full bag having not even sufficient calories for one person—the weight savings is expensive (as is all lightweight equipment).

A somewhat heavier but far more affordable option is to use dehydrated meals purchased at the supermarket. Lipton makes a full line of rice, pasta, and noodle dinners with sauces that are quite tasty; the meals cost a couple of bucks. Each contains about 600 calories that is easily supplemented with dried milk, margarine, or a pouch (not a can) of tuna or salmon. These meals require 10 minutes of cooking and leave a dirty pot, but many climbers consider these worthwhile trade-offs.

Those with free time might consider drying their own fruits, vegetables, and meat with a food dehydrator (about $150). You can make excellent snacks, including fruit leather and jerky, that taste better than store-bought.

The development of retort packaging (an aluminum/plastic laminate) in the late 1970s for the U.S. military's MREs (Meal, Ready-to-Eat) has been a boon for expeditions. These flexible pouches are light, nearly indestructible, and don't need a can opener. They contain precooked food that is fully hydrated. Just toss the bag into boiling

The menu can make or break an expedition. Be sure what goes up will fuel the climb.

water for a few minutes, then use the hot water for drinks.

Although the standard MRE kit has too much wasted packaging to be practical for climbing, entrees are now available in many flavors. Tuna fish and salmon are available in retort pouches at many supermarkets. Long Life Food Depot (*Longlifefood.com*) offers a wide assortment of Western fare, while Tasty Bite offers some delicious Indian and Thai meals (*Tastybite.com*). These don't contain enough calories on their own (around 300) but make a great meal when mixed with instant brown rice, couscous, potatoes, or noodles.

The water content of ready-to-eat foods is both their advantage (fast) and disadvantage (heavy). The increased weight is partially offset by reduced need for fuel, but these foods are feasible only when traveling light is not essential. They can be a great way to break up the monotony of freeze-dried meals.

There are more developments in military food technology on the horizon, and these may prove beneficial to expedition climbers. Compressed Meal Entrees (CME) are partially dried, infused with a solution, then compressed into cubes for a weight reduction of three-fourths and a volume decrease of two-thirds. They are said to be easy to prepare, tasty, and much cheaper than freeze-dried. Instead of a stove, it may soon be possible to carry chemical heat sticks that work like a glow stick: break an inner vial and it generates enough heat to prepare a meal. Further out, the Transdermal Nutrient Delivery System (TDNDS) will be a skin patch that contains the nutrients needed for one to two days of optimal performance.

DRINKS

Though they do help your hydration status, drinking water or unsweetened tea is also a missed opportunity for adding calories. A great way to start the day is with hot chocolate or milk tea (black tea with milk and sugar or honey). Coffee is rather acidic so it isn't the best choice if you will be working hard, but it's a nice change on rest days. Contrary to popular belief, caffeine is not a diuretic so there is no greater risk of dehydration.

Since it requires effort to ingest adequate fluids while climbing at high altitudes, taste is of paramount importance. Some of the fancy energy drinks are okay for an occasional workout but may be tough to choke down on day 15 of constant intake. Also, they may not mix or stay dissolved well, leaving a heap of powder in the bottom of the bottle or bladder. Experiment with different brands to find flavors acceptable to everyone, but don't rule out plain old lemonade and orange drink.

Bring a *lot* of dried soups in individual packets in as many flavors as possible; these are ideal precursors to dinner. Consider ramen a soup rather than a meal, and pack a good assortment of these as well. During and after the evening meal, hot apple cider and herbal teas with honey are good choices since you don't want caffeine to disturb your sleep.

POWER SHOPPING

Most expeditions are likely to use different food types at various stages of the trip. Early on, for the approach and in base camp, bulk and canned foods are the main part of the diet. Up on the mountain, dehydrated and retort foods, along with a lot of snacks, are used in the lower camps. When the climbing gets serious, freeze-dried and energy foods become more important. At high camps on 8,000-meter peaks, only soups and drinks may appeal, though some will want something solid.

With the exception of bulk foods and some snacks that will be bought when you arrive, all of the mountain food should be purchased in advance. Though this may increase shipping costs, it assures that you will have adequate supplies. Although it is possible to arrive in Kathmandu, or even Namche, and fully outfit an expedition, this is a real gamble since you are often buying

Repackage the food into day bags before departure.

unwanted stuff. Western-style supermarkets may be surprisingly well stocked in mountain countries, but they also have a more fickle supply. It isn't wise to count on critical items unless you have a local contact who can purchase goods in advance of your arrival.

Once you have estimated the person-days and drawn up your menus, it's time to create a shopping list. Though many items will be available at your supermarket or outdoors store, others (such as whole dried milk) may be harder to track down or are far cheaper from mail order. For a large expedition, it may well be worth a trip to one of the big, bulk-discount warehouses.

PACKING THE CHOW

After all the shopping is done, a packing party should be scheduled. This is when team members get together and divide up the food into two-person-day amounts, which is all the food that a tent team of two will need for one full day. This is the easiest system for assuring that the re-quired food is in the correct place at the correct time. When you get to base camp, a tent team just needs to pack one bag, and the necessary fuel, for each day they'll be out. Using mostly dried foods, each bag will weigh approximately 4 pounds (1.8 kg).

A simple packing procedure is to use gallon-size zip-closure bags to collect breakfast items, snacks, dinner food, and drink mixes. All of the food is spread out in a large room and each member takes a bag and moves from pile to pile, gathering supplies to make up the day based upon the menu plan; be certain that the calories add up. Some expeditions will designate specific meals for certain days of the trip (best when cooking as a group), while others will just use a grab-bag system and let each tent dine on its own.

Try to eliminate as much unnecessary food packaging as possible to reduce bulk, weight, and waste. Transfer products out of cardboard boxes into resealable plastic bags. Use plastic bottles instead of glass. Resealable squeeze tubes only work for condiments like peanut butter and honey in warm climates.

CHAPTER 9

Everest (29,035 feet, 8,850 meters), Nepal/Tibet

Realizing the Dream

After months, if not years, of dreaming about an expedition, the reality can prove daunting. As the departure date draws near, the angst builds. If you have planned carefully, smooth sailing is to be expected—along with the occasional unexpected squall.

The art of expeditioning is learning to relax and enjoy the experience. Once you leave the Westernized big cities behind, you'll quickly discover that the rest of the world operates at a less frantic pace.

COUNTDOWN

The last few weeks leading up to your flight can be stressful. It's all too easy to put off seemingly minor details until you suddenly realize you have a heap of must-do's, and rapidly dwindling time.

This is also the period when your fitness training should be reaching its peak, possibly requiring 10 to 20 hours per week. It may be tempting to blow off some workouts when you're feeling the time pinch; wrong answer. Aside from helping you reach the goal while optimally fit, the workouts bring stress relief that can also improve sleep.

PACKING

For even a small expedition, you are going to be organizing a heap of gear. When deciding what goes and what stays, it's helpful to make several piles (clothes, climbing gear, accessories) that can be left on the floor; a couple of giant duffels make things tidier. As you mull over what will truly be needed, the piles will grow and shrink, so easy access is important.

Once all the group supplies are gathered, everything needs to be repackaged and divvied up. Even if everyone is on the same flight, it's wise to split up critical gear between all the members; don't put all your stoves in one basket.

Each team member must weigh his or her duffel bags as they are packing and measure the dimensions of each bag. If you will be close to the weight limit, be sure your bathroom scale is accurate. It's better to find out that you are over the baggage allowance in advance rather than at the airport while you're trying to catch a flight.

BEFORE YOU GO

Procrastination is not your friend; the more you can do two or three months in advance, the better. Immunization, passport renewal, and dental checkups are not the sorts of things you can get done overnight.

If you haven't already done so, it's wise to prepare a will. Those with significant assets should consult a lawyer to ensure this important legal document is valid. If your situation is less complicated, computer programs can help you draft a will. It may also be wise to create a living will and a power-of-attorney in case an accident renders you incapable of making decisions.

Depending on how long you'll be away, you may need to make arrangements for paying bills. Automatic payment from a bank account makes this easy. Otherwise, prewrite checks and have someone who is reliable mail them on designated dates.

Postcard writing is a popular expedition pastime, one that friends and sponsors truly appreciate. Some teams have cards made with a photo of their objective. To make the chore of addressing cards easier, print mailing labels and carry them with you.

To keep things from wandering away, mark all your personal gear with unique identifiers. Colored tape is ideal for marking climbing equipment and other hard goods;

Divvying up the group gear is a sure sign you're about to get underway.

Trango Rack Tags are very convenient. For clothing and other soft goods, use a permanent marker or a laundry pen (won't harm nylon).

For insurance purposes, take photos of your gear before you leave. Make a list of camera or computer equipment that has serial numbers. If the gear is very expensive, bring a notarized copy of the list to avoid hassles with customs agents.

On long trips, short hair is a blessing. Men may want to start a beard a few months in advance for adequate sun and cold protection; shaving can be a hassle on expeditions.

If nobody will be staying behind in your residence, you'll need to have the mail held and the newspaper stopped. It's better to have a friend take care of pets and water your plants. But if you must kennel the critters, make arrangements well in advance. Don't forget to empty the refrigerator and take out the trash before you head out the door!

TAKEOFF

Since only ticketed passengers may proceed to the gate, it's probably best to say your good-byes at home rather than at the airport. A mountain of gear invites a heap of problems, so be sure to arrive several hours prior to your flight. When checking in, do not even hint that you will be "camping." This word, or the sight of a large pack, can trigger an unpleasant search for a stove. Since rules change and airline employees are often unaware, bring a printout of the baggage regulations from their website.

Once the plane is airborne, try to rest up; you'll need energy upon arrival. Set your watch to the new time zone soon after takeoff to start adjusting your body clock. During the flight, stay hydrated, avoid alcohol, and move your legs often to reduce the risk of blood clots.

Traveling in any country where you don't speak the language can be stressful, though advance preparation can make things easier. Those who have never traveled outside North America or Europe are unlikely to be prepared for the barrage of sights, sounds, and smells in countries that are less well off. This culture shock is normal—and is probably good for you—but some people have a hard time coping and may need support from others on the team.

STAYING HEALTHY

All of that pretrip stress weakens your immune system somewhat (blood levels of stress hormones increase), and sitting on a

12-hour flight doesn't help (half the air is recirculated and you encounter many people). Some travelers take the herbal supplement echinacea for a few days prior to departure to boost immune protection.

If you are traveling east or west more than a few time zones, you will experience jet lag upon arrival (flying east is tougher). It's best to adopt the local time right away—don't take a nap—but it will take a few days for your body clock to adjust. Taking melatonin, a natural hormone that is sold over-the-counter, may reduce the effects of jet lag if the doses are taken at the proper time. Fortunately, going north or south does not cause jet lag.

During the preliminary stages of an expedition, you need to be extra vigilant about staying healthy. If you pick up a bug early on, it can be difficult to recover once the hard work starts. The best time for a run in big cities, if you feel the need, is early in the morning while the air is relatively clean. The sooner you can begin the approach, the less risk of catching traveler's diarrhea.

Though conditions have improved in areas with a lot of tourist traffic, all of the usual rules of travel in developing countries still apply. Eat at popular restaurants, not street carts, and order common dishes so the food will be fresh. Avoid any fruits or vegetables that you can't peel, even if the menu states the salads are safe. Don't trust any dairy products other than fresh yogurt; ice cream probably does the most damage.

Particularly during monsoon rains, the tap water should be considered unsafe;

Foreign cities are exotic and fun to explore but stay on guard to avoid illness and theft.

keep your mouth closed when showering. Drink bottled water, or purify your own, and use this for brushing your teeth. Do not add ice to beverages, and wipe off the tops of soda cans before sipping.

CAPITAL IDEAS

Most expeditions fly to the capital of the destination country and then take an in-country flight or other means of transportation. Since no climbing permits are required in Central and South America, there you can proceed onward with minimal delay. In the Himalayan countries, however, you will probably need a couple of days to deal with permits and to purchase supplies.

If you've hired a trekking agency in advance, someone will probably meet your team at the airport to escort everyone through the gauntlet of insistent baggage handlers looking for tips and past the throngs of shouting taxi drivers. Depending on what time you arrive and how far you've flown, the first day is often rather unproductive.

Markets the world over can fill your expedition's larder with fresh fruits and vegetables.

As soon as possible, commence with the bureaucratic process of getting the necessary permits. Though the team leader and trekking agency can do some of the paperwork, the entire team may have to make an appearance at some point, so everyone must be available at the designated time. It's important to avoid antagonizing government officials: dress neatly, be on time, accept tea if offered, act politely. If you do not appear to be respectful, your permit could be inexplicably delayed or withdrawn.

Most expeditions in the Himalaya, except to smaller trekking peaks, are required to bring a liaison officer, who is often a government official inexperienced in the mountains. Meet with him early and try to make friends, since he will be a companion for the next few weeks or months. It's important to review all the equipment and food that he intends to bring to make sure it's adequate. In fact, you will most likely be providing his gear and meals, and possibly even his boots and clothing.

It's usually cheaper to buy food, fuel, and fixed line in the capital than in gateway towns, though added transportation costs may offset this somewhat. Send a team member or two with the sirdar and cook when they shop for supplies. For transporting loads, it may also be necessary to have duffel bags sewn, to purchase padlocks, and to find plastic barrels. In some areas, porters must be given shoes, socks, and sunglasses, and possibly stoves and tarps as well, which can be bought at a market.

A visit to local bookshops may prove fruitful; they sometimes have local maps and guidebooks not available elsewhere. In cities with many foreign travelers, used bookstores can have an amazing selection of English-language paperbacks for cheap. Be sure to stock up on postcards and stamps.

Internet cafes are damn near everywhere these days, so you may want to establish a web-based email account (MSN, Yahoo) for keeping in touch with family and friends. If your trekking agency lets you use their Internet connection, keep it short, since most parts of the world still bill by the minute.

Because porters and animal drivers need to be paid in local currency, the expedition's treasurer must visit a bank to exchange money. Depending on the number of porters required, this can be a substantial wad of cash in small denominations. Be sure to bring extra funds to handle contingencies such as weather delays (porter strikes are rare now) and tips. Bridges in the Baltoro area may require a toll of 15 rupees per person that an expedition member must be ready to pay.

Whether or not you are Buddhist, expeditions in Nepal often start with a visit to Bodinath (the largest temple in Kathmandu) for a blessing by the head monk in exchange for a donation. Considering what you are about to attempt, it certainly can't hurt, and it's an interesting experience. Expeditions in the Khumbu region may also have ceremonies at Tengboche and/or Pangboche monasteries.

TRAILHEAD

Long bus or van rides are often required to reach the trailhead. Public transportation is cheap but usually very cramped, and your gear may not be safe. Your fellow passengers will often include chickens and piglets. If there are enough team members to split the cost, it's well worth hiring private vehicles. You'll arrive fresher.

Even if you plan to fly to your trailhead, some of the gear may still be trucked. Don't be surprised if weather forces a change of plans, a common occurrence with mountain airstrips.

Some people have problems with motion sickness, although this is partly mental: if you think about getting sick, you will. There are many remedies, including over-the-counter drugs (Dramamine), ginger

Receiving blessings, akata *(a prayer shawl), and* rilbu power pills.

173

Inshallah (God willing), the truck with all your gear will arrive safely.

Weigh all porter loads with a hanging scale to keep everyone happy.

root, and acupressure on the wrist.

If traveling on the ocean in boats smaller than 50 feet, there's a good chance you'll be in for a rough, yet exhilarating, ride. Those who get seasick (or aren't sure) should consider a prescription for scopolamine (Scopace, Transderm-Scop) as prevention.

Either in town or at the trailhead, everything must be repacked into porter (or animal) loads. This process is greatly facilitated by a hanging scale to weigh each load; without one, be prepared for arguments. If there is a significant disparity between personal gear that is portered, the scale can help determine how much extra a team member should pay.

Every duffel bag should be inventoried and numbered so contents can be quickly located using a master list. Numbering also allows loads to be checked in at the end of each day. Keep the trek supplies separate from base camp gear so there is less opening of bags.

Anything that can be harmed by hard impacts must be well padded (cameras, computers) or carried in plastic drums (food). The plastic jugs used for hauling kerosene (paraffin) are notorious for leaking on the hapless porter; check before leaving.

THE APPROACH TREK

At a Himalayan trailhead, if not before, the sirdar essentially takes over your expedition. Stay out of the way and let him do his job. Typically, the sirdar started out as a cook's assistant and worked his way up

Managing the porters is a crucial job of the sirdar; he makes an expedition run smoothly.

through the ranks to achieve the head guide position. Part politician, part workaholic, most likely he is remarkably talented and deserves your respect.

The sirdar will do the actual hiring of local porters, who go only as far as base camp, and ensure that the procession gets under way in a timely fashion. A four-person climbing team (with a sirdar and cook crew) spending a month in Nepal will start with approximately twenty porters. Because of remote location and the huge scale of the mountains, a ten-person expedition to a Karakoram 8,000-meter peak may head off with 200 porters and arrive at base camp with 150, having sent the others back as supplies are consumed.

Once you're on the trail, things quickly settle into a routine. A trekking day often starts early, with a pleasant fellow from the cook crew greeting you with hot tea.

After crawling out of bed, pack your gear and stumble over to be served a hot breakfast. Meanwhile, the rest of the camp is struck and the porters and pack animals start off up the trail.

As you're hiking up the trail passing heavily laden porters, the cook and his assistants will blaze on by. Not long thereafter, you will round a bend or crest a hill and find a hot meal laid out in a protected spot with a great view. The porters often catch up at lunch and proceed to cook and consume an amazing amount of chapatis or rice. The liaison officer and the sirdar never carry a heavy pack, and the LO always dines with expedition members; it's a status thing.

After a few more hours of hiking, you will arrive at the next village or camp— the end of the day's stage. This is only midafternoon, but porters straggle in for hours after the sahibs. Though your trekking crew may be more than willing to pitch your tent, if using your own, it's best to do this yourself to prevent accidents (sometimes the crews are over-enthusiastic). Once you're established, relax and look around, go take some pictures, and wait for what will likely be a huge, tasty dinner.

Prior to dinner is often the time when one or two team members will be drafted to provide medical aid for porters. Usually this just means handing out some aspirin and applying adhesive bandages to blisters. However, it also may include suturing wounds, tooth extraction, and inflating a hyperbaric chamber.

A mid-day meal with a great view is one of the pleasures of an approach.

Particularly when visiting villages, it's important to remember that you are a guest and to respect the culture. Don't be another ugly touron. Foreigners are often inundated by adorable little kids, and it's difficult to resist their pleas for pens or candy. Do not encourage this bad behavior by giving in; instead, take supplies to the local school (paper, pens, crayons, educational games) or medical clinic (toothbrushes and toothpaste, first-aid material, vitamins). Great ways to befriend local kids include games, magic tricks, or a kite.

TRAIL HEALTH

Most trekking agencies have been clued in on the need for proper hygiene. Nevertheless, keep an eye on the people you have hired to make sure water is brought to a full boil, food is thoroughly cooked, and hands are routinely washed. Though you may not be used to doing so at home, get in the habit of washing your hands before every meal. This simple precaution can prevent many intestinal problems (assuming you don't wipe your hands on a filthy rag).

If you stop at a teahouse (sometimes no more than a few bamboo walls), order stir fries, soups, or other hot dishes. Hot chai (milk tea), lemonade, or orange drink are all excellent. But hold off on the chang, the fermented rice drink, because the water hasn't been boiled.

Although the water from that trailside creek may look pristine, imbibe only after using an antiviral treatment (allow 30 minutes). Quite often a tiny village or a farmer's house is upstream, just out of sight. When using a composting toilet, do your deed but put toilet paper in the bucket that is provided for tourists, then sprinkle bark or hay over the top.

Pet lovers must remember that dogs (you'll rarely see cats) are not treated as cute, cuddly animals in many places. Consider it a given that any dog you encounter hasn't had a rabies shot and knows all about people throwing rocks at it. Although they may look gentle, yaks can be stubborn, ornery animals that have been known to gore people (sometimes fatally). When you see one lumbering up the trail, give it a wide berth. Don't stand downhill of the trail or next to a cliff; you might be bulldozed over the edge or crushed against the wall.

When the approach trek is during the dry season on heavily traveled trails, it may be wise to wear a surgical mask. All the manure from burros, yaks, or whatever gets finely pulverized and kicked up into the dust cloud that hangs in the air. There is a potential that breathing this caca can lead to illness.

Porters seldom have crampons so they must chop steps up snow slopes.

PORTERS

Be a good employer, not an exploiter. Expeditions are often required to take out insurance for porters, and it's a good idea anyway. These people are the major breadwinners in their families, and an injury can have severe consequences for many people. While the trekking agency may actually hire them, team members are responsible for seeing that porters are treated humanely.

Although high-altitude porters tend to be experienced and have good equipment, the opposite is generally true of lowland porters. These men, and sometimes women in non-Muslim regions, are often farmers from nearby villages who carry loads as a comparatively easy way to earn cash. Many are ill-equipped for working in the higher mountains. Don't assume they have the clothing for a snowstorm or know how to cross a glacier or ford a stream. Team members should assist at tricky sections and have a rope handy for rescues.

When an expedition goes above tree line or through a heavily traveled area, the wood upon which porters normally rely for cooking and warmth is not available. In these areas the expedition must issue stoves, fuel, and extra blankets to the porters. Depending on where you are traveling, it may also be necessary to issue shoes, sunglasses, warm clothing, and tarps.

177

Chapattis cooked over a fire are a mainstay of the Balti porter diet.

Distribute these only when needed, so the items won't be left behind or sold.

In areas with a lot of trekking activity, wages and the distances between camps (the stages of the approach trek) are often specified by the government. Be certain that everyone is clear on the location of the base camp you are trekking toward; ambiguously named destinations can be miles apart.

Smaller expeditions operating without a trekking agency may have to negotiate porter or animal handler wages. Try not to pay more than the local rate. Though the porters' pay may seem too little by your standards, overpaying leads to regional inflation. However, be certain that women receive equal pay.

Porters often are paid a half-day's wage when travel is not possible due to bad weather, and for their return trip home after carrying expedition supplies, but this pay should be negotiated in advance. If they have done their job well, a tip is in order and will be much appreciated; pay this separately from wages so there is no confusion.

In the past, porters have been treated little better than pack animals, though better awareness is beginning to improve their lot. The International Porter Protection Group (*www.ippg.net*) is working to build porter shelters and improve safety. Another organization, Porter's Progress (*www.portersprogress.org*), has established a lending program for clothes and stoves.

Most porters speak little or no English, but they all know how to laugh. Simple things like joining them for a game of Frisbee or horseshoes or sharing songs around a campfire can be hugely entertaining and quickly bridge cultural divides.

RIVER-CROSSING TECHNIQUE

Many climbing expeditions must cross rivers to reach the mountain, sometimes a very hazardous proposition that climbers fail to appreciate. In popular areas, sturdy cable suspension bridges have mostly replaced the rickety rope affairs. But the farther off the beaten path you travel, the greater the risk in reaching the opposite shore.

Raging rivers are relatively safe: nobody in their right mind would try to cross them. The more insidious danger lies in water that looks as if it *might* be possible to wade or hop across. Unless you have spent a significant amount of time on rivers, you likely don't comprehend the power of the water or the treacherous footing. Even if you have whitewater experience, glacial rivers are a different breed; they have flat areas a hundred meters wide braided with swift channels.

Glacial rivers are often ice cold, the rocks are rounded and polished, and visibility is nil due to glacial till. The safest time to cross is early in the morning, before the sun begins melting ice; what was a small stream can turn into a raging torrent in less than an hour.

Look for a wide spot in a straight section of river. Avoid bends, because the water will be fast and deep near the outside bank. Make sure there are no obstacles downstream of the crossing point. Fast water over your knees can easily knock a person down, but slower water can be wadeable to thigh deep or higher. If you must retreat, it's better to back up than turn around.

When fording, a pair of trekking poles (or long ice axe) are invaluable for stability and probing. Loosen your pack's shoulder straps and unfasten the hip belt so you can ditch the pack in a hurry. Wear boots, camp shoes, or sandals with wool or neoprene socks, since your feet will be numb from the cold. Don't wear anything that would be difficult to swim in (such as floppy shell gear or a down parka), just synthetic or wool underwear; no bare legs if it's overcast, since you need warmth when you emerge. Carry dry clothes for the other side in a plastic bag (seal it tight) that goes near the top of your pack.

Crossing as a group may be advisable if there are smaller or weaker people in the expedition. Linking arms and moving across with the largest members at either end of the line (strongest person on the upstream end) is effective. Stability can be enhanced by everyone linking arms and grasping a stout pole.

Unless you have been trained in the procedure, using ropes for crossing rivers can be dangerous. Trying to hold someone against swift water can force them under and result in drowning; the same can happen when using a handline. The idea is to swing them into the shore if they slip.

Wading through a wide section of river

If you get knocked over while crossing, lie on your back and get your feet pointed downstream. If you've used plastic bags to keep contents dry, your pack will remain buoyant but will ride up (your hip belt was already off); don't let go. Scull and kick with your legs to quickly reach the shore, and get into warm clothes as fast as possible.

IN BASE CAMP

On the major peaks, base camps have traditional locations—often on a rocky moraine or a flat, grassy area. This is strictly first come, first served, so late arrivals get the less desirable positions. Commercial expeditions sometimes try to push around private teams, but they have no special rights no matter how rich their clients. Send an advance team if prime location is that important.

Respect each expedition's space since base camp should be a place to unwind. Don't locate on the main trail, or other climbers will constantly wander through your camp—most annoying at 4 A.M. when you're trying to sleep in.

Expeditions to infrequently visited areas must decide on the best spot based upon many factors. It may even be worth sending a few climbers ahead to scout before the porters drop their loads. Try to keep elevation under 16,500 feet (5,000 meters) so climbers can recover better when they drop down to base camp. The spot must be free from avalanche danger. Climbing literature is full of stories of base camps flattened by avalanche wind blasts. The site should also have a good view and receive plenty of sun so that it's a cheerful place to hang out.

Ideally the real climbing should be within a three-hour hike from base, though ultralight trips can push this considerably. An advanced base camp is commonly used for greater distances so climbers are better rested for the difficulties. When climbing in the Andes, it may be wise to hire someone to guard your camp while you're up on the mountain; theft is rampant in some areas.

Among the most desirable assets of a good base camp is a stream within about 200 feet (60 meters). This can save a huge amount of fuel and hassle compared with melting snow. On Ama Dablam, Clyde's expedition placed base camp next to a pond near the Southwest Ridge. This was great for a while because it reduced the distance for carries. Eventually, however, the pond dried up and a porter had to be hired to bring water up from a stream far below.

For minimal environmental impact, it's best to camp on a moraine or on snow. If it's necessary to camp in areas with vegetation, locate the kitchen tents, sleeping tents, and gear pile in separate areas and move them occasionally. This helps prevent creation of permanent trails that scar the landscape.

CAMP CHORES

The first order of business upon reaching the site of base camp is to determine where water will come from and where the latrine will be located. The first expedition to

Base camps on glaciers have the least environmental impact.

arrive for the season makes these decisions for all others that follow. If you're not first, consult the other expeditions. Take every precaution to preserve the cleanliness of your water source, and notify everyone of the expected protocol.

The next priority is the location of the cook and mess tents (one and the same on small expeditions), since these are the largest and receive the highest traffic. Because the kitchen area is the heart of base camp, give careful consideration to this spot.

If camped on a moraine, it may take a fair amount of digging, hacking, and rock hauling to level the field. Don't tear up a nice meadow unless you want to face the wrath of the mountain gods. When you're on snow, a fully appointed kitchen can be constructed, complete with benches, shelves, under-counter cabinets for food storage, even a refrigerator to keep water from freezing at night.

Once the communal tents are up, or rock walls are built for a kitchen tarp, team members can set about making their own tent platforms. Don't get too carried away if you're on a glacier, since your platform is likely to melt out and force a move within a few weeks anyway.

Before anyone climbs, an altar is erected for the puja *ceremony to the mountain gods.*

Sherpas believe the blessings of the puja *assure safe passage for everyone.*

Ensure that the liaison officer's tent is properly pitched and that he's comfortable. This man has little to do, now that you've arrived at base camp, except hang out and compare notes with the other LOs. If he suffers for a month, you can kiss your environmental deposit good-bye.

Prior to commencement of climbing, expeditions with Sherpas will have a *puja* ceremony to pay homage to the gods and ask for their protection. This wonderful practice requires construction of a rock altar. Along with chanting of prayers, burning of juniper, and anointment of everyone with *tsampa* (barley flour), prayer flags are strung. Even in Islamic Pakistan, expeditions full of non-Buddhists often string prayer flags simply because of the good sentiment.

ENVIRONMENTAL ISSUES

If a pit toilet is to be used, this should be constructed within the first day so that stinking piles are not left all over the place. Make it big enough that it won't fill up and require building another. The latrine should be located where there is privacy, especially if there is no toilet tent. Try to find a spot that is out of the wind and that has a good view for contemplating the meaning of the universe.

Near the kitchen area, an area should be designated for collecting garbage. Divide the garbage into two piles: burnable (paper) and take-home (metal, plastic, batteries, fuel, oxygen bottles). Keep the burnable pile dry, and build a small fire about once a week to keep the pile down. Don't burn plastic or foam, since the fumes are toxic and disrespectful. The take-home pile is part of an expedition's cost of doing business; you must pay to have it hauled out for proper disposal. Leftover fuel can be sold back in town, oxygen bottles can be refilled, and empty plastic bottles can be reused by locals.

THE CLIMB

So here you are, halfway around the world, looking up at a huge monstrosity that gives normal people nightmares. Now what?

The first few days in base camp are often spent relaxing, sorting food and gear, flagging wands, doing laundry, and taking showers. Though the youngsters will be chomping at the bit, this isn't wasted time because your body needs to acclimatize. Rushing up too quickly can actually do more harm than good to summit prospects.

Some day hikes to scout the route are a good idea, but take it easy. This is also an appropriate time to conduct a crevasse rescue practice; even veterans get rusty. If team members carry avalanche beacons, do timed practice runs.

Expeditions that employ high-altitude porters on technical routes must check their skills. Although it is commonly assumed that Sherpas are great climbers, many of them have never been taught crevasse rescue technique or how to ascend and descend fixed lines on vertical rock. Everyone might find this an educational and rewarding experience.

ROUTE DECISIONS

Up until this point, all expedition styles have been essentially the same, though team size and trip duration affect the scale. Certainly the details of an expedition to Patagonia or Baffin Island differ from those to the high Andes or the Himalaya. But even extended trips to Canada's Bugaboos or Wyoming's Wind River Range share the logistical matters of getting everyone and a heap of gear to the mountain.

Members of both expedition-style and capsule-style expeditions start working on ferrying supplies up the mountain while they continue to sleep at base camp. This climb-high/sleep-low method aids acclimatization and also avoids consuming the expensive (both in cost and labor) mountain foods and fuel. After an expedition-style assault has established Camp 1, some climbers can begin pushing the line to Camp 2 while others continue to move stuff up from base camp. By definition, a capsule-style expedition must fully stock Camp 1 with everything that will be needed before it launches farther upward.

For alpine-style ascents, however, the climbers generally don't start on the route until they're ready to go to the top. Instead, the climbers make forays onto nearby peaks for altitude conditioning and to get a better view of the intended route. If the summit is under about 22,000 feet (6,700 meters), it may take only a week or so of these excursions to acclimatize. Taller peaks will necessitate spending a few nights at around 6,000 meters—possibly higher if you're really going big—to give

Without high-altitude porters, moving supplies up the mountain is a laborious chore.

your body a fighting chance.

Big-wall climbs often adopt an alpine or capsule style, but because the pace is so slow, sometimes only three pitches per day, there is little danger of going too high, too fast. Just getting all the gear to the base of the wall frequently offers plenty of opportunity to acclimatize.

Many expeditions are likely to utilize a combination of styles. When you read the climbing accounts closely, even some of the extreme alpine ascents employ less-than-pure tactics. While the armchair ethicists may debate, use whatever makes sense at the time: just be honest about it afterward.

The best-laid plans don't mean squat until you reach the mountain and *feel* the current conditions. Perhaps a heavy snow year has turned the slopes into avalanche death traps. Or there is so much snowmelt

that your proposed route is now a waterfall. On the other hand, it may have been a very dry winter and sections that usually are relatively safe are raked by rockfall. Sometimes the limited photos available don't show the hideous icefall down below.

For any of these reasons and more, it may be necessary to switch to Plan B, then Plan C, then Plan D. . . . Clyde recalls reaching Plan W on a Canadian ski mountaineering expedition that started out as a traverse from Jasper to Banff but kept evolving due to severe weather and horrendous depth hoar. Even dreams must be flexible.

GLACIER PRIMER

Here are some basic considerations for climbing on glaciers. Read *Glacier Travel & Crevasse Rescue,* by Andy Selters (The Mountaineers Books, 1999), for details. As with all lifesaving skills, it's important to practice crevasse rescue technique.

By midday on a glacier at mid-latitudes, even at 19,000 feet (5,800 meters), the sun can be baking hot, and firm snow turns to postholing mush. Thus days start and end early, with climbers heading out at first light wearing a lot of insulation and finishing by noon stripped down to underwear.

When hiking as a rope team, it's the responsibility of the person on the sharp end to find the route and stay out of holes. Whoever is behind the leader has the primary jobs of keeping slack out of the rope and anticipating the direction of a fall. With a good belay, any fall should be easily caught by the belayer just leaning backward, and the leader should rarely pop in over his or her head. But it still can be unnerving for the person in front.

Two-person teams are especially vulnerable on glaciers with hidden crevasses and must be fully prepared. Each should tie in about 25 feet (8 meters) from the center of a 60-meter rope and coil the long tail so it's available for rescue. Everything needed to perform the rescue must be easily accessible.

Try to find a path that avoids crossing beneath seracs. All too often you'll return later and see sections of trail that have been wiped out by one of these towers of ice that has fallen. It's best to stay strung out when taking short rest breaks and to regroup only for meetings in a safe spot that has been probed (the last person is belayed in and the leader is belayed out).

Place wands no more than a rope length apart and at any possible trail junction. Pack down soft snow and make a deep hole with an ice ax or ski pole without a basket; a wand is useless if it melts out and falls over.

Skiing downhill on a glacier while roped and carrying a heavy pack relies greatly upon bombproof snowplow technique. On steep slopes where the consequences of a fall are grim, leave the skins on your skis to slow the descent. If the situation looks particularly dire, strap the skis to your pack and don the crampons.

When crossing glaciers while pulling sleds, the lead and middle climbers should attach a prusik sling from the tail of their respective sleds to the climbing rope so their sled won't land on top of them in a crevasse fall (potentially fatal). The last person on a rope should either travel

Massive snow dumps can bury tents and change plans.

without a sled or stay behind the sled at snow bridges so it can be pulled across the bridge by others.

Descending with a sled can be an exciting time since the beast has a mind of its own. This is where the commercial models with rigid traces and fins prove their worth, as they allow you much more control. No matter the sled, it may need to be lowered on steep drops, and two people must control it on sidehills. Riding the sled down is ill-advised when you're a long way from the hospital.

FIXED ROPES

Though it may be tempting, never trust your life with an old fixed line from previous expeditions. Often just a few strands remain, or they are only frozen in place and cannot hold the weight of a climber. Even ropes that were recently placed can be damaged by rockfall, and old anchors may weaken.

When fixing lines, the team generally climbs on a dynamic rope and carries a spool of static rope to a solid anchor at the top of the difficulties. Then on the descent,

Old fixed lines cannot be trusted and are difficult to remove once frozen in place.

Anchors for fixed ropes should be located at a secure stance.

the static line is tied off to intermediate anchors so it becomes a series of short, independent sections that can take one climber (only!) at a time. A common method for tie-offs is to make a figure-8 knot in the rope and then pass webbing through the loop and tie the webbing directly to the anchor, eliminating the need for a carabiner. Leave a couple feet of slack at anchor points as kink traps (fixed lines often twist up horribly).

The anchors should be located where there is a good stance so a climber carrying a heavy pack can safely make the knot pass: clip the daisy from the harness to the rope above, unclip the ascender, then reclip it above the knot. Pitons or chocks pounded in rock are always the preferred anchor points since they are the most secure. Keep an eye out for sharp edges or abrasion points; redirection of the rope may be necessary to prevent disaster. If using snow pickets or ice screws as anchor points, try to locate them in the shade and bury them with snow to minimize melting out—and recheck them frequently.

Some mountain routes, such as Gasherbrum I and II from Pakistan as well as the south side of Everest, have major icefalls that must be overcome before the real climbing begins. This can take considerable effort, several spools of fixed rope, dozens of ice pickets, and a lot of wands to establish safe passage. Likewise, the Trango Towers and other high-altitude big walls often require many pitches of fixing just to reach the start of the climb.

These days, Everest's Khumbu Icefall is fixed and maintained by a team of Sherpas and every climber pays $300 to use the ropes—a fair deal. Above the icefall, however, and on most other mountains, the first expedition to arrive gets stuck with the task and the bill. It costs roughly $20,000 to fix ropes to the top of the world (3,000 meters of rope, 500 ice pickets, 200 ice screws, and Sherpa salaries). In theory, other expeditions would chip in to share the costs, but this rarely happens.

It may be possible to obtain a list of expeditions with permits for your route from the Ministry of Tourism. If it looks like you'll be the first to arrive, contact the other expedition leaders far in advance to negotiate a deal. They may be more amenable to paying if they know about the expense in advance and don't have to bring their own ropes.

An equal problem is that few expeditions bother to help maintain the fixed lines in an icefall. The anchors melt out in the sun, but people mindlessly clip in and never inspect them. Granted, many of these "climbers" don't have the gumption to look at a snow picket that's halfway out of the snow and realize that it wouldn't hold a fall. So the team that put in the ropes often has to maintain them for a hundred other people who never even say "thanks."

LOCATION, LOCATION

Among the most important decisions that your expedition will make is where precisely to place the high camps and bivy sites. Looking at maps and photos is great, but you'll also have to use gut instinct when you're there.

187

Narrow ridges call for narrow tents; big domes may not fit.

Finding a spot suitable for a tent isn't always easy, so compromises are often made. Because snow sluffs off and doesn't accumulate, the snow in the middle of a steep slope may not be thick enough for hacking out an adequate-size ledge. The base of a vertical cliff often has a good pile of snow, but beware of falling projectiles (a snow cave may be a better option here). A site beneath a rock overhang is ideal. The convergence of two ridges sometimes offers a big enough, albeit very exposed, location. Just below a ridge on the lee side can provide a good spot if it isn't snow-loaded and ready to avalanche.

If you'll be camping on a glacier, start with a thorough probing of the area for possible crevasses, using a ski pole without its basket (an ice ax is too short). Then mark the perimeter of the safe area with wands, to prevent falls into a hidden crevasse. Also decide where the latrine will be located (well away from any campsites) and probe the entire path leading there.

High Camps

For camps up on the mountain, stomp or excavate a firm tent platform and erect the tent with the door on the lee side of the prevailing winds. In exposed locations, it may be necessary to build a snow wall around the entire tent; the ends of a straight wall can erode away in the wind until it falls over.

During heavy snowfall, you may have to dig the tent out every few hours. If the tent is right next to a cliff, spindrift can build up and start pushing it and its occupants into the void. Bring a shovel inside, and sleep with your head at the door, ready to escape. In 1996 two climbers died of suffocation on Annapurna IV when their tent was buried by 10 feet of snow in a two-day storm. The tent had one door, and their heads were at the opposite end.

Even as one person is finishing campsite chores, the other tent mate should get the stove roaring and start melting snow. Begin rehydrating with soups and hot drinks as soon as possible. Once the first round of drinks is done, move right on to making dinner, more drinks, and enough water to fill bottles before bed.

For extended stays at a campsite, it's worth comfortizing with a nice kitchen and a snow pit at the tent door (making it easier to get in and out). To escape midday heat, secure your sleeping bags over the tent for insulation from the sun. If you have a Grand Shelters IceBox tool (fast, easy way) or a snow saw (slow, hard way), you can build an igloo. Expeditions on the Nepal side of Everest often hire, or share, a cook who stays at Camp 2 to prepare meals.

Condensation inside a tent is inevitable when it's well below freezing, but using vents will reduce the problem. Much of the moisture comes from exhaling. It's important to not breathe into your sleeping bag since that pumps water right into the insulation. In the morning, as soon as you leave the bag, roll or stuff it twice to force warm, moist air out before it freezes; doing this can prolong the loft.

After moving up to a higher elevation, each climber should subtly monitor the health of the other person sharing a tent. Altitude illness can creep up on someone without their knowing it, so stay alert for the signs. Slurred speech, confusion, or balance difficulty can be early indications of high-altitude cerebral edema (HACE), while trouble with breathing, excessive tiredness, or coughing up blood are harbingers of high-altitude pulmonary edema (HAPE).

A real danger when cooking inside a tent is carbon monoxide poisoning. This odorless, tasteless by-product of combustion has killed many climbers. When the stove is running, always keep vents open or the snow-cave entrance unblocked, no matter how nasty it may be outside.

When climbing an 8,000-meter peak, it's a wise policy to never get separated from your sleeping bag, even if you hire porters. Without it, surviving a night in the open unscathed is questionable.

Summit day often begins at 1 or 2 A.M., possibly earlier, so try to have everything ready to go with minimum hassle. Make yourself as comfortable as possible the night before, and try to get at least a couple hours of sleep. Place your alarm where you can hear it—not on your wrist, deep inside the sleeping bag!

Be aware that on Everest and elsewhere, a disturbing number of climbers have discovered that it's easier and cheaper to freeload off of others. Not only do they use fixed lines without paying a share of the cost, but some have also borrowed other people's tents and sleeping bags and stolen food, fuel, and oxygen from high camps.

High Bivouacs

An unplanned bivy is simply a night of making do and hoping for the best. But a planned bivy is a matter of trying to reduce the suffering, while using as little gear as possible. According to veteran climber Jack Tackle, "We'd read in Yvon Chouinard's book *Climbing Ice* that 'if you bring bivouac gear, you will bivouac.' Turns out, if you don't bring bivouac gear, you will bivy too."

Ledges sometimes aren't big enough for even one small tent. If it's likely that ledges

With a huge void below the bivy, it's wise to stay tied in at night.

will have to be chopped into an ice slope, cutting a long, skinny ledge for bivy sacks can be faster than making a short, wide one for a tent. String an anchor rope across the ledge so that packs and critical items can be secured; dropping a boot would be ugly.

Narrow ridges tend to have few sheltered spots. As the winds picked up on Ama Dablam, Clyde and his three teammates bivied in a cul-de-sac at the base of the Mushroom Ridge at 21,000 feet (6,400

meters). It had room for a Bibler I-Tent (a snug two-man tent) into which three people crammed, while Clyde huddled outside in a bivy sack. While chopping out a ledge, he punched a hole through to the other side of the ridge, and the wind rushed wildly through. It was a long night.

A snow cave can be a wonderful retreat from the fury of a storm, though it takes a lot of work to build—roughly three hours of digging for two people, leaving the workers soaked. If you're lucky, you can avoid the work and get the same benefits by escaping into a crevasse. It's warmer (just below freezing) and quieter in a snow cave than in any tent or open bivy. If you're relying on snow caves, bring a larger shovel, wear synthetic insulation, and use lighter synthetic-filled sleeping bags; a saw for cutting snow blocks may also be helpful.

While the excavation is under way, even in nasty weather, one person should stay outside the cave to move snow out of the way; if the cave collapses during the dig, they can effect a rescue. The only real design requirements for the cave are a vent in the ceiling and an entrance trench that is lower than the sleeping area, for cold air to collect. When burning candles (a nice touch for ambiance, and also an air quality indicator) and stoves, be certain of good ventilation.

Caches

It's sometimes convenient to stash supplies for retrieval on the descent or during a traverse. Place the cache where it can be easily spotted when you're coming from the opposite direction. Use extra-long wands that won't bend to mark the cache. On Denali write your name and expected return date on duct tape. If there is a good view of the horizon for accurate positioning, a GPS receiver can be a useful tool.

The nemesis of climbers throughout the alpine world, ravens are remarkably smart birds with large, nasty beaks. These black beasts mock from a distance with their *caw-caw*, then assault your food when your back is turned. Neither plastic nor nylon will stop their attacks. Pile rocks on top of your cache or bury it at least a foot below the snow surface without leaving a mound, and place the wands five paces away in a specified direction.

If you must leave tents unattended for more than a day, it's best to collapse them by unhooking the poles, which can then be used as wands to mark the spot. Otherwise the tents risk being irreparably flattened by heavy snow or strong winds. Leave the fly in place and the doors zipped up so meltwater won't get inside.

THE DESCENT

So you tagged the top—good job! Now start thinking about how to get down. Only after you have a plan of action for descent can you allow a moment for congratulations and enjoying the view.

Getting down is the most important skill that any climber can possess. During the past fifty years in North America, a third of all climbing accidents occurred on the descent. Since you are mentally and physically drained after reaching the summit, it's all too easy to let your guard down. Wait until base camp to relax.

RAPPELS

Arguably the most dangerous of all climbing activities, rappelling should never be treated lightly. Be afraid. In addition to the lethal risk, a stuck rope is one of those nightmares that climbers seek to avoid.

Use an overhand ring bend (a.k.a. the Euro Death Knot) to connect two rappel ropes, even of dissimilar diameter, because it is much less likely to get stuck and is easily untied. It is critical to always leave long tails (at least 12 inches; 30 cm) and snug the knot very tight before trusting your weight to it; do not use a figure-8 knot since it can unroll.

When the two connected rappel ropes are a single climbing rope (10 to 10.5 mm dynamic) and a haul line (8 mm static is best), the thin rope goes through the anchor, and you will pull down on the fat rope for retrieval. This way, if a rope does get stuck, you have more of the good rope in hand to deal with the issue. Using skinnier static line is not recommended because the wind will play havoc with it.

If descending long snow climbs, you can do a single-rope rappel on your 120-meter half rope. The rope is run through the anchor webbing and a loop is tied in the end; clip a carabiner to the loop and around the rope. After the rappel, retrieve by pulling the carabiner down with a 3-millimeter cord brought for the purpose. This method works only on snow slopes, not rock, because you can't pull hard enough on the 3-mil if there is a lot of friction. In high winds, stick with shorter rappels.

An anchor failure can ruin your day, so do everything possible to make each secure. Oftentimes in the alpine realm, it's necessary to rap off a single piece of protection; otherwise there won't be enough gear to make it down. The standard procedure is to make the anchor solid, install a backup piece, send the heaviest person down first, then have the lightest person retrieve the backup and descend last—gently.

If you know you will be rapping, bring plenty of sling material (at least 6 mm rope or $^{11}/_{16}$-inch nylon webbing) and a sharp knife so that anchor material can be trimmed to fit. When possible, use natural anchors such as rock horns or chockstones and sacrifice a sling for easier rope retrieval.

If there is solid ice and you brought a hook tool (bent coat hanger or similar), a V-thread hole (made by intersecting two ice-screw holes) can provide a secure rappel anchor. These are typically faster and more secure than chopping a bollard out of ice. In snow, it's best to use pickets or deadmen (a buried shovel, snow-filled stuff sack, or helmet) for rappel anchors. If nothing is available, try chopping a large bollard that is 3 to 10 feet (1 to 3 meters) in diameter, depending on firmness of the snow.

When rappelling into unknown territory or through loose rock, it's wise to employ a backup system. Extend the rappel device to about face level with a daisy chain on your harness. Attach a prusik loop to one leg loop with a girth hitch, then make an autoblock knot by taking about three upward wraps around both ropes and clipping the sling ends together with a carabiner. With your brake hand over the knot, the rope slides easily, but if you lose control, the knot grabs. Once the harness is rigged, it takes only a few seconds extra to add this backup knot. When descending past an overhang, be sure the rap device makes it past the lip or you could become trapped.

Knotting the ends of the rappel rope is a pseudo-safety procedure, but the knots like to jam in cracks and it's possible for them to pull right through the rappel device. This last point is obvious with a figure-8, due to its size, but even a tube-type device (ATC, Jaws) might not stop a fall on skinny half ropes. Do not tie the ends of the ropes together or you will end up with a tangled mess at the bottom.

When tossing a rope, hang on to the ends and toss the middle down first to reduce tangles. In very windy conditions, it's sometimes best to tie the ends of the ropes to your harness and descend with the stack in your lap.

If three climbing ropes are available, a team of four can make a rapid descent with a system that keeps everybody in motion and minimizes hassles with wind. The first climber is lowered a full rope-length and establishes the next anchor. The second climber is lowered on another rope while carrying the third rope in a coil. This leaves two strands in place for the third and fourth climbers to simulrap (both rappel at the same time on a single strand and counter-balance each other) and retrieve the ropes. Meanwhile, the first and second climbers are already starting the next lower, and so on. Needless to say, everybody must have their act together.

EMERGENCIES

Hey, bad things happen. We're all gamblers, and sometimes the dice—and stones and ice chunks—don't land the way we would wish. Unfortunately, the consequences of even a minor accident can quickly snowball into a major epic.

Although many expeditions bring extensive medical kits to base camp, little of this makes it up onto the mountain where injury is more likely to occur. In short, climbers need to be able to deal with most situations on their own—hence all that first-aid and rescue training that you've accumulated over the years (right?!).

Before you start the climb, have a discussion with those who stay behind about how long they should wait for your return. There have been quite a few cases in which climbers or explorers survived an extended struggle, only to find that others on their expedition had given up hope and removed camp, leaving them stranded. If you are ever in the position of having to retreat and leave missing teammates behind, always make a food cache—and a prominent note on where they can find it!

During the climb, team members need to keep the communication channels between each other open. It's all too easy for climbers to secretly harbor fears and doubts, afraid to speak up because the others might think less of them. Instead of keeping mum, respect your inner voice and make your concerns known. Have a discussion about the worsening weather, the avalanche potential, or personal health problems. Talk these things through, and you may find that the sixth sense of others is also setting off alarm bells.

RESCUE PROCEDURES

Should a situation suddenly deteriorate into an emergency, pause for a moment and take a couple of deep breaths. Resist the urge to panic. As quickly as possible, gather the pertinent facts, weigh the possibilities, consider any and all solutions, and make a plan of action. Depending on the circumstances, all of this could take place in a matter of seconds or a couple of hours.

Under most circumstances, self-evacuation is the best procedure. Delaying for help to arrive wastes precious time. Even with badly mangled legs, it's possible for climbers to escape their predicament; recall Doug Scott on the Ogre (*The Everest Years*, by Chris Bonington) and Joe Simpson on Siula Grande (*Touching the Void*).

If there are disaster survivors in critical condition on the mountain, outside help needs to be called in. Think hard about the necessity of a helicopter before calling for one, because this triggers a cascade of events over which you'll have little control. And unless the victim is covered by rescue insurance, the bill can be enormous.

Improved communication to the outside world allows inexperienced climbers to call for help for relatively minor injuries. In places like Denali, where there is cell phone coverage from much of the mountain, calling in the troops is easier than ever. In the spring of 2002, there were nineteen chopper evacuations from Everest Base Camp in Nepal, which makes one wonder whether people are getting careless with their health and safety (or if rich people are taking a fast ride home).

Elsewhere you may have to send out a runner to notify authorities of an emergency. Since you were a good scout and did the research in advance, you know the necessary contacts and procedures for getting help. Your trekking agency and your embassy can assist.

Helicopters

Small helicopters routinely fly loads to the Conway Saddle, at 19,000 feet (5,974 meters) in Pakistan, so rescue is theoretically possible while quite high up. At these altitudes, however, the air is too thin to support vertical takeoff and landing. Hovering and one-skid touchdowns work only under ideal conditions, which are rare in the mountains. Cable rescues are even tougher because the choppers lose ground effect (a lifting air cushion from the rotor wash).

In general, choppers at high altitude need a landing zone about the size of a football field—100 feet (30 meters) wide by 300 feet (90 meters) long—that is oriented into the wind. Because the rotor wash is in excess of 100 miles per hour (160 kph), the site must be clear of anything that can fly up into the rotors, such as jackets or foam pads. If a snowfield is used, heavy objects must be laid down to provide the pilot with depth perception.

Ideally the pilot wants a steady, gentle breeze (about 12 mph; 20 kph), because still air has less lift. A landing may not be possible if the wind speed is over 50 miles an hour (80 kph), or if the gust-spread exceeds about 20 miles an hour (32 kph)—with the wind dropping, for example, to 10 miles per hour and then peaking at 35.

Hand signals can lead to confusion unless you know the procedures. Waving your arms to get a pilot's attention is actually a signal, called a wave-off, that indicates a dangerous landing; he may abort the mission. It's better to crouch well out of the way and shield your eyes from flying dust and pebbles.

With most helicopters, always approach from the front, where the pilot can see you. When the rotors are moving, under no circumstances ever go past the rear of the skids; go around the front to reach the other side. The exceptions to these rules are Chinook helicopters and other giants with two rotors on top and the door at the rear (the front rotor dips, so you never stand in front of these machines). Crouching is usually a good idea to avoid decapitation, but always keep your eyes on the pilot. Be ready to jump clear, because a pilot may have to suddenly take off.

ALTITUDE PROBLEMS

The strategy for dealing with altitude problems can be summed up in three words: *get down fast.* Once the onset of

HACE or HAPE has become noticeable, things can deteriorate quickly if the affected climber does not get down to a lower elevation. It's much better to take preventive action by descending early than risking death.

Even if your expedition brought along an air-pressure chamber, like a Gamow Bag, it's unlikely to be in the right place when it's needed. More practical when climbing to extreme altitude is to carry a small kit with dexamethasone (both pills and injectible) for HACE and nifedipine pills for HAPE. Neither medication is a cure, but they can buy some valuable time if you must wait out a storm or if avalanche danger makes the route too dangerous to descend.

THE GRIM REAPER

Death is a distinct possibility in the high mountains. When someone dies, it is usually not in itself an emergency: once they are gone, there is little more you can do. If the death occurred during a difficult situation (a storm; an avalanche) that still endangers others, the first priority is safety of the survivors. The time for mourning will come later, but in the critical moments of crisis, action takes precedence.

In many cases of death at high altitude, body disposal won't be an issue because it either is not retrievable or would involve too much danger to the people trying to reach the body. If the body is accessible but cannot be brought down, it should be moved well off the route and buried under rocks or dropped into a crevasse.

If the victim was lower on the mountain, expedition members should try to respect

The Gilkey Memorial to those who have died on K2.

the wishes of the climber, if they are known. (See the Expedition Medical Questionnaire in Appendix A.) Burial at base camp is perhaps the best solution for everyone. Having the body flown back to the home country can cost well over $10,000 and may not be covered by insurance, increasing the stress on survivors. Cremation is another option, though this can cost several thousand dollars as well.

AFTER THE CLIMB

Once the decision is made to go home, whether you reached the summit or not, it's time to start cleaning up the mountain. It typically takes several days for this task, so don't count on getting out of there overnight. Unless someone's life is in peril, high camps must be removed. Wands should be collected and burned in base camp.

Fixed ropes should be taken down by the expedition that installed them, unless another expedition agrees to handle the job. Ropes that are left will not be trustworthy the next season, so they just become litter. Some routes have a dozen old ropes crisscrossing crux sections, not one of which is usable.

As base camp is deconstructed, each

Abandoned tents litter many high camps on the world's great mountains.

member should take the time to wander the area with a trash bag and pick up litter. Stone walls can be left in place if others will use the site, but collapse the walls of a pit toilet. If you sorted your garbage all along, there won't be much left to burn. But you may still be looking at several porter loads of trash that need to be hauled out.

To head off further regulations, you should discreetly police other expeditions. Climbers from other cultures may not understand the need for protecting the environment. Without being confrontational, some gentle encouragement, and leading by example, can do wonders.

Before everyone goes their separate ways, the team should dispense tips to the support staff. While money is always appreciated, they might prefer fleece or down jackets, boots (if they fit), packs, good sunglasses, plastic tarps, or other useful items. If your sirdar, cook, and high-altitude porters have done a good job, write letters of recommendation for them.

On the approach and during the climb, you may not have seen much of the country; everyone tends to stay focused on the goal. If there is time at the end and you aren't burned out, it's well worth taking the time to look around. Perhaps visit your sirdar's home and enjoy a party with a lot of chang and a Sherpa line dance. In the Karakoram, try to go out over the Gondogoro La (instead of back down the Baltoro) for spectacular new views accented with wildflowers. Go visit Machu Picchu in Peru or the Taj Mahal in India. Years later, you'll be glad you did.

The safe conclusion of an expedition is reason enough for a party.

Back in the capital, the expedition leader may have to meet with officials for a debriefing. Group supplies (tents, stoves, rope, food, fuel, pickets, drums, etc.) can be sold off in a gateway town or the capital. This is also the time for souvenir shopping.

AFTER THE EXPEDITION

It ain't over when it's over! After the expedition, the spirit that motivated everyone begins to evaporate as each person reenters the real world. Suddenly those pre-expedition commitments seem trivial: they get put on the back burner, then forgotten.

This scenario is so common that sponsors have become reluctant to support newcomers, no matter how sincere they appear. When you don't follow through on obligations, you screw up future trips for yourselves and many other people.

Generally within a month of your return, sponsors who provided gear expect a detailed report on the conditions you encountered and the performance of their products. They also want photos of the equipment in action, as well as shots of the banners that you carried. Be sure to send them a thank-you letter signed by the whole team.

The expedition leader should make a report on the trip to the national alpine club of his or her home country (even if those on the expedition are not club members) so that historians can keep track of climbs. Whether or not the trip was eventful or historically significant, this information can still be useful. Expeditions that received grants are also expected to turn in a report.

After all the travails of your expedition, it would be a tragedy to lose all your film in a lab accident. Find yourself a pro photo lab, but entrust them with the fruits of your labor in batches. If you have a good story to tell, contact the editors of magazines with a brief query letter. Try to figure out what makes your story unique from all the other submissions. Give them the gist of your proposed article—sell it in the first paragraph—and enclose photo samples. Do not send original slides or anything else that you want returned, until the publication requests them.

SLIDE SHOWS

Expedition members often receive requests for slide shows from community organizations, local stores, and clubs. It's a lot of work to sort slides and assemble them into a sequence that tells the story.

No matter how long your expedition, the entire show should fit into a single 120-slide carousel (or two trays of 80 if you use cardboard slide mounts or are doing dissolves). This means you must edit ruthlessly! Leave them wanting more rather than falling asleep.

Avoid the excessive use of music (no more than 5 minutes at the beginning and end); it can turn off more people than you realize. If you are doing the show for profit, you legally cannot use copyrighted music (all your favorite tunes) without paying a royalty. There's no real need for whiz-bang effects since these tend to distract from the actual content.

Use a bright laser pointer (with fresh batteries) to show the route and other important details. For audiences larger than 100, depending on acoustics and your voice, it's generally best to use a microphone. Bring a spare bulb for the projector. Don't rely entirely on wireless remotes; pack a hard-wire backup.

Unless you are an exceptionally riveting speaker—a rare individual—the show should seldom last more than one hour and never longer than 90 minutes. Resist the temptation to tell your life story or every detail of the approach (hint: nearly all expedition treks sound the same). Whether or not they are climbers, people want to hear about the country, the personalities, and the major obstacles more than anything else. Minutiae about crux moves on each pitch will bore even your most ardent admirers.

Even if the expedition ended in tragedy, try to end on an upbeat note. Provide a strong message about your environmental commitment and social awareness. Slide shows are both educational and inspirational, and a great show will be remembered for years.

HEALTH

Be sure to continue any courses of medications, particularly antibiotics and antimalarial drugs. If you forget, you could be setting yourself up for a mysterious illness several weeks after your return.

Odds are you lost weight and are very fit. Keep the momentum going. It isn't uncommon to lose 20 pounds or more on an expedition, though some of this is from chronic dehydration. Still, expeditions are an effective way to lose fat that you'll probably want to keep off. Unfortunately, some of the weight loss may also have come from muscle mass, particularly in the upper body. Resistance training (weight lifting) is the fastest way to regain strength.

After going through a starvation episode, your body has a tendency to prepare against another by adding fat stores. What's more, you are still used to eating huge quantities of food, even though your energy output has dropped dramatically. If at all possible, try to maintain your aerobic conditioning with such activities as running, cycling, skiing, and snowshoeing.

Even during an expedition, you can't help dreaming about the next.

FUTURE DREAMS

Of all the things you do in your life, few will be more life-altering than going on an expedition. Whether large or small, long or short, mountaineering or otherwise, an expedition offers adventure and camaraderie that has a long-lasting effect on everyone, hopefully for the better.

After your return, normal life takes over, for a while. But eventually the wanderlust deep inside begins to nag, like an unquenchable thirst. Resistance is futile. It's all but certain that you will join another expedition—or create your own—so start saving and planning.

Appendix A: Questionnaires

Make copies of the following forms (Expedition Application, Medical and Diet Questionnaire) and have each prospective team member fill them out. Some of the questions are intended to provoke conversation that might head off future problems. They could be uncomfortable to answer now but may be even more so halfway through the trip.

EXPEDITION APPLICATION   Date_____

Name _____

Home address _____

City _____ State _____ Zip _____

Occupation _____

Work address _____

City _____ State _____ Zip _____

Day phone _____ Evening phone _____ Fax _____

Email _____ Website _____

Age _____ Date of birth _____

For International Travel

Name as it appears on passport _____

Passport number _____

Place of issue _____

Date of issue _____ Expiration date _____

Citizenship _____

Qualifications

What rating can you comfortably lead?

Traditional rock _____   Sport rock _____   Ice _____   Mixed _____

List previous expedition and alpine climbing experience.

What is the highest altitude you have reached on a climb, and where?

Rate your physical conditioning (1=couch potato, 5=animal)
Aerobic _____   Strength _____   Carry heavy pack uphill for hours _____

Rate your ability (0=no experience, 1=minimal, 5=expert)
Avalanche safety _____   Crevasse rescue _____   Emergency medical care _____
Escaping a belay _____   Swimming _____

Teamwork
Will you make air and hotel reservations with the group or on your own?

Will your husband/wife/boyfriend/girlfriend join the expedition as a member or trekker?
If so, are you certain you have a strong relationship?

What is the longest you've been cooped up in a tent or snow cave? How was the experience?

Do you snore? _____ If yes, rate the volume (1=minor snorts, 5=rattle the walls) _____
Do you smoke tobacco? _____   marijuana? _____   drink alcohol? _____

Have you ever received psychological counseling or medication for depression or other
psychological challenges?

What languages do you speak?

What unique qualifications would you bring to the expedition?

Motivation and Commitment

Why do you want to join this expedition?

Has anyone encouraged you to go?

Has anyone discouraged you from going? Is this a problem?

What are your current interests and pursuits?

What is your greatest joy in life?

What three words best describe your personality?

How important is returning to your job on a specific date? Is there any flexibility?

Can you make a deposit on expenses now?

Will you be able to meet the timeline for payments?

How much time each week can you offer for preparation?

EXPEDITION MEDICAL QUESTIONNAIRE

Name _____

Medical Biography

Date of birth _____ Height _____ Weight _____

Blood type _____ Tetanus shot (date) _____ Polio _____

Describe major sicknesses or injuries in the last twelve months.

Have you been hospitalized in the past two years? If yes, please explain.

List medications taken regularly or intermittently and reason.

Have you ever had frostbite? If yes, please describe.

Have you ever experienced a major altitude illness? If so, please describe the circumstances.

Do you wear eyeglasses or contacts?

Have you had eye surgery (LASIK, LASEK, PRK, RK) within the past year?

Have you ever experienced vision problems at altitude?

Please check all that apply:

- ❏ Ankle problems
- ❏ Arm or shoulder problems
- ❏ Asthma
- ❏ Back/neck problems
- ❏ Bleeding disorder
- ❏ Blood disease
- ❏ Cancer
- ❏ Colitis, ulcers, or stomach problems

- ❏ Chronic infections
- ❏ Hernia
- ❏ Diabetes
- ❏ Epilepsy/seizure disorder
- ❏ Head injury
- ❏ Hearing impairment
- ❏ Heart condition
- ❏ High or low blood pressure

- ❏ Kidney problems
- ❏ Knee problems
- ❏ Respiratory problems
- ❏ Intolerance to heat or cold

If you marked any of the above, please explain (include date, length, severity, current symptoms, and limitations).

Do you have any life-threatening allergies? If yes, please list them and any medications that you carry.

Describe any other health-related facts your teammates should be aware of.

EMERGENCY CONTACTS

Name _____

Relationship _____

Day phone _____ Evening phone _____ Fax _____

Email _____

Name _____

Relationship _____

Day phone _____ Evening phone _____ Fax _____

Email _____

Name of physician _____

Address _____

Day phone _____ Fax _____

Email _____

BODY DISPOSAL

If I die, I prefer:

_____ Burial on mountain   _____ Cremation   _____ Funeral at home

If I elect cremation or home funeral, the following insurance policy will pay for the substantial costs incurred:

Insurer _____

Policy # _____

DIET QUESTIONNAIRE

Name _____

Height _____   Weight _____

Estimated calorie intake on a normal day _____

Estimated calorie intake on a day with a hard workout _____

Do you have any food allergies? If yes, please list them.

Please check the item that applies to you:

❑ Omnivore (it's all good)

❑ Semi-vegetarian (dairy, eggs, some seafood and poultry but no red meat)

❑ Lacto-ovo vegetarian (dairy and eggs okay, but no meat or seafood)

❑ Vegan (no animal products)

If vegetarian, will you eat meat while on the expedition? If yes, please list acceptable meats.

List any foods you absolutely cannot eat.

List any foods you prefer not to eat.

List any foods you absolutely cannot live without.

Do you like spicy foods?

What are your favorite energy bars/gels/drinks?

What are some favorite treats?

Rate your cooking skills (1=burn water, 5=gourmet) _____

Appendix B: Resources

TRAVEL WEBSITES

Centers for Disease Control Travelers' Health *(www.cdc.gov/travel)*. Here is up-to-date information on all the nasty bugs around the globe and how to avoid them.

CIA World Factbook *(www.cia.gov/cia/publications/factbook)*. This free resource is an amazing collection of recent information (within a couple of years) for every country on the planet.

Embassyworld.com. A great resource that contains links to every consulate and embassy for any country. It also has visa requirements and an international phone directory.

Fodors.com. This guidebook publisher has good online travel tips for many destinations around the world. Useful even if you're just passing through Cuzco or Kathmandu.

Lonelyplanet.com. The famous guidebook publisher for off-the-beaten-path destinations also operates a great website chockful of up-to-date info.

MDTravelhealth.com. This site is more user friendly than the CDC's and has good information for doctors and patients.

Medical Advisory Services for Travelers Abroad *(www.masta.org)*. A good U.K.-based website providing useful information for anyone heading overseas.

U.S. Embassies *(www.usembassy.state.gov)*. Direct links to all U.S. embassies and consulates around the globe.

CLIMBING WEBSITES

High Mountain Info *(www.planetfear.com/climbing/highmountainmag/mountaininfo)*. This takes over where *Mountain* magazine left off after its demise. It's an excellent compendium of expedition activity in the greater ranges since 1995.

Himalayan Index *(www.himalaya.alpine-club.org.uk)*. Here is a tremendous resource for any climber thinking of heading to that part of the world. It contains abstracts of nearly 5,000 articles in the *Alpine Journal, American Alpine Journal,* and *Himalayan Journal* covering 2,600 peaks above 6,000 meters.

Peakware.com. The best part of this website is the online summit registry for more than 1,700 major peaks around the world. You might be able to contact someone who was just there to get tips.

UIAA *(www.uiaa.ch). The Union Internationale des Associations d'Alpinisme,* the International Mountaineering and Climbing Federation, is the world body for our sports. Their website contains the latest information on permits for the Himalaya (look in Commissions) as well as a lot of other good info.

BOOKS

Baume, Louis. *Sivalaya*. Seattle: The Mountaineers Books, 1979. Although dated, this book chronicles the history of the 8,000-meter peaks. The bibliography contains nearly 400 books on the early years of the great peaks.

Bonington, Chris. *Everest the Hard Way*. New York: Random House, 1976. A classic account of a successful climb of the Southwest Face using siege tactics. The 100 pages of appendix material provide detailed information on how to organize a behemoth expedition. Many of the participants became advocates of small, lightweight expeditions.

Graham, John. *Outdoor Leadership*. Seattle: The Mountaineers Books, 1997. Superb information on what it takes to lead groups.

Mason, Kenneth. *Abode of Snow.* London: Rupert Hart-Davis, 1955. The definitive history of climbing in the Himalaya.

Neate, Jill. *Mountaineering and Its Literature.* Seattle: The Mountaineers Books, 1986. Helpful for finding climbing books that are long out of print.

Sale, Richard, and John Cleare. *Climbing the World's 14 Highest Mountains.* Seattle: The Mountaineers Books, 2000. Both a history and a climbing guide for the big ones. It's a must-read if you are considering any of them.

Salkeld, Audrey, ed. *World Mountaineering.* New York: Bulfinch Press, 1998. Useful information on fifty-two major peaks around the globe—an alpinist's dream book.

Selters, Andy. *Glacier Travel & Crevasse Rescue.* Seattle: The Mountaineers Books, 1999. Walk not on glacial ice without reading this manual.

Soles, Clyde. *Climbing: Training for Peak Performance.* Seattle: The Mountaineers Books, 2002. If you are serious about climbing, get serious about fitness.

Soles, Clyde. *Rock & Ice Gear.* Seattle: The Mountaineers Books, 2000. Detailed information on selecting the right equipment for all types of climbing.

Twight, Mark. *Extreme Alpinism.* Seattle: The Mountaineers Books, 1999. An excellent instructional book for aspiring alpinists. Though it may be too hard-core for your tastes, there is still plenty of good info.

Wilkerson, James, ed. *Medicine for Mountaineering.* Seattle: The Mountaineers Books, 2001. A great text for anyone going into remote regions.

MAPS

The following websites are good sources for maps: *Adventuroustraveler.com; Chesslerbooks.com; Geokatalog.de; Maplink.com; Stanfords.co.uk.*

Nakanishiya Shuppan Company
2 Nihonmatsu-cho, Yoshida, Sakyo-ku
Kyoto 606-8316, Japan
075-751-1211
Fax: 075-751-2665
iihon-ippai@nakanishiya.co.jp
Recent mountaineering maps of the Karakoram (9) and Hindu Kush (4) in 1:150,000 scale with 170 photos.

National Geophysical Data Center (*www.ngdc.noaa.gov/cgi-bin/seg/gmag/fldnsth1.pl*). Use this website to find the current magnetic declination for old maps.

Space Imaging
12076 Grant Street
Thornton, CO 80241
303-254-2000
Spaceimaging.com
Satellite images and maps for almost anywhere.

LIBRARIES

Alpine Club Library
55 Charlotte Road
London EC2A 3QT, England
0171 613 0755

American Alpine Club
710 Tenth Street, Suite 100
Golden, CO 80401
303-384-0110

Map Library
The British Library
Great Russell Street
London WC1B 3DG, England
0171 636 1544

GRANT SOURCES

Alpinist B-Team Climbing Grant
alpinist magazine
www.alpinist.com

American Alpine Club
710 Tenth Street, Suite 100
Golden, CO 80401
303-384-0110
www.americanalpineclub.org
For information on the following:
  Mountaineering Fellowship Fund
  Scott Fischer Environmental Expedition
    Fund
  Research Grants
  Helly Hansen Adventure Grant
  Lyman Spitzer Climbing Grant

CMC Grant
Banff Centre for Mountain Culture
Box 1020, Station 38
107 Tunnel Mountain Drive
Banff, Alberta TIL 1H5 Canada
www.banffcentre.ab.ca

Everest Environmental Project Grant
3730 Wind Dance Lane
Colorado Springs, CO 80906
719-277-7133

John Lauchlan Award
Canadian Himalayan Foundation
P.O. Box 61063
Kensington Postal Outlet
Calgary, Alberta T2N 456 Canada

Mount Everest Foundation
Gowrie, Cardwell Close, Warton,
Preston, PR4 1SH, England
01772 635 346

Mugs Stump Award
Patagonia
259 West Santa Clara Street
Ventura, CA 93002
805-643-8616
www.patagonia.com

National Geographic Society
Expeditions Council
1145 17th Street N.W.
Washington, DC 20036-4688
202-862-5200
Fax: 202-862-5270
www.nationalgeographic.com/council

Nick Estcourt Award
24 Grange Road, Bowden,
Cheshire WA14 3EE, England

Polartec Challenge
P.O. Box 582
Jackson, NH 03846
603-383-0945
www.polartec.com

Shipton/Tilman Grant
W. L. Gore & Assoc.
105 Vieves Way
Elkton, MD 21921
www.gore-tex.com

MEDICAL SUPPLIES

CERTEC
69210 Sourcieux-les-Mines, France
33 4 74 70 39 82
www.certec.fr
Mam'out hyperbaric chamber.

Chinook Medical Gear
3455 Main Avenue
Durango, CO 81301
800-766-1365
www.chinookmed.com
Gamow Bag and other backcountry emergency
  medical gear.

Life-Assist
11277 Sunrise Park Drive
Rancho Cordova, CA 95742
800-824-6016
www.life-assist.com
Offers a wide range of emergency medical
  equipment.

Treksafe
P.O. Box 53 Repton
NSW 2452 Australia
+61 2 6653 4241
Fax: +61 2 6655 4130
www.treksafe.com.au
Portable Altitude Chamber (PAC).

HIMALAYAN PERMITS

Indian Mountaineering Federation
Benito Juarez Road, Anand Niketan
New Delhi 11002 India
Fax: +91-11-688 3412
indmount@del2.vsnl.net.in

Mountaineering Association of China
9 Tiyughan Road
Beijing, China
Fax: +86-10-67111629
cmaying@263.net

Mountaineering Association of Tibet
No. 8 East Linkhor Road
Lhasa, Tibet, China
+86-891 6333687/6333720
Fax: +86-891 6336 366
ctma@public.ls.xz.cn

Mountaineering Association of Xinjiang
312 Guizhou Road, Urumqi
Xinjiang, China 83011
+86-991 3812422
kongtrvl@mail.w.xj.cxn
climbing@xj.cninfo.net

Nepalese Ministry of Tourism
Mountaineering Division
Kalamati, Kathmandu, Nepal
Fax: +977-1-227758
Information on mountaineering peaks.

Nepalese Mountaineering Association
Sports Council Building
P.O. Box 1435
Kathmandu, Nepal
Fax: +977-1-434578
peaks@nma.wlink.com.np
Information on trekking peaks.

Tourism Division
Government of Pakistan
Islamabad, Pakistan
+92-51-9212760
+92-51-9202766
Fax: +92-51-9204027
tourism@isb.comsats.pk
tourism.gov.pk

Appendix C: Gear Checklist

The following list can be copied double-sided onto legal-size paper. Remember—the fewer things you check, the simpler life will be. Just don't leave out items critical to success (or escape). Every expedition has its unique demands, so adjust the list accordingly.

TRAVEL GEAR

Packed / Planned

- ❑ ❑ Address book or PDA
- ❑ ❑ Airline tickets and itinerary
- ❑ ❑ Cable lock
- ❑ ❑ Credit cards
- ❑ ❑ Day pack or fanny pack
- ❑ ❑ Diarrhea medicine (motion sickness remedy)
- ❑ ❑ Dressier clothes for meeting officials
- ❑ ❑ Exchange-rate calculator or PDA
- ❑ ❑ Extra passport photos (4 to 6)
- ❑ ❑ Film X-ray shield
- ❑ ❑ Gifts for exchanging
- ❑ ❑ Guidebooks and maps
- ❑ ❑ Hotel reservation
- ❑ ❑ Immunization documentation
- ❑ ❑ Inflatable pillow
- ❑ ❑ Language dictionaries
- ❑ ❑ Luggage locks and zip-ties
- ❑ ❑ Notarized list of camera and computer equipment serial numbers
- ❑ ❑ Passport
- ❑ ❑ Passport/money carrier
- ❑ ❑ Photos of family, friends, and home
- ❑ ❑ Serial numbers
- ❑ ❑ Toiletries (comb, shampoo, shaving supplies, nail clippers, etc.)
- ❑ ❑ Travel alarm or PDA
- ❑ ❑ Travel duffels (2)
- ❑ ❑ Traveler's checks and computer serial numbers
- ❑ ❑ Visa
- ❑ ❑ Voltage converter/adapters
- ❑ ❑ _____
- ❑ ❑ _____
- ❑ ❑ _____

TREKKING GEAR

Packed / Planned

- ❑ ❑ Extra boot treatment
- ❑ ❑ Folding chair
- ❑ ❑ Hat with full brim
- ❑ ❑ Insect repellent
- ❑ ❑ Lightweight boots
- ❑ ❑ Long-sleeved shirt
- ❑ ❑ Loose-fitting pants
- ❑ ❑ Medium-weight socks (2 pair)
- ❑ ❑ Mosquito net hat
- ❑ ❑ Neoprene socks
- ❑ ❑ Rain cover for pack
- ❑ ❑ Rock shoes and chalk bag
- ❑ ❑ Sandals
- ❑ ❑ Shorts
- ❑ ❑ Sunglasses
- ❑ ❑ T-shirt (2)
- ❑ ❑ Trekking poles
- ❑ ❑ Umbrella
- ❑ ❑ _____
- ❑ ❑ _____
- ❑ ❑ _____
- ❑ ❑ _____

PERSONAL GEAR

Packed / Planned

CLOTHING
Inner Layer

- ❑ ❑ Glacier glasses
- ❑ ❑ Heavyweight wool socks (3 pair)
- ❑ ❑ Liner gloves
- ❑ ❑ Midweight long underwear bottoms (2)
- ❑ ❑ Midweight long underwear top (2)
- ❑ ❑ Sport bra (3)
- ❑ ❑ Synthetic liner socks (3 pair)

Packed
Planned

- ❑ ❑ Underwear (3)
- ❑ ❑ _____
- ❑ ❑ _____
- ❑ ❑ _____

Mid Layer

- ❑ ❑ Belt or suspenders
- ❑ ❑ Down or fleece vest
- ❑ ❑ Fleece or Primaloft jacket
- ❑ ❑ Hat or balaclava
- ❑ ❑ Long pants
- ❑ ❑ Long-sleeved wind shirt
- ❑ ❑ Midweight gloves
- ❑ ❑ Neck gaiter
- ❑ ❑ _____
- ❑ ❑ _____
- ❑ ❑ _____

Outer Layer

- ❑ ❑ Down pants
- ❑ ❑ Down parka
- ❑ ❑ Face mask
- ❑ ❑ Gaiters
- ❑ ❑ Heavyweight gloves
- ❑ ❑ Insulated booties
- ❑ ❑ Insulated mittens
- ❑ ❑ Mountain boots
- ❑ ❑ Overboots or supergaiters
- ❑ ❑ Waterproof/breathable jacket
- ❑ ❑ Waterproof/breathable pants or bibs
- ❑ ❑ Windshell
- ❑ ❑ _____
- ❑ ❑ _____
- ❑ ❑ _____

CAMPING GEAR

- ❑ ❑ Bivouac sack
- ❑ ❑ Bowl

Packed
Planned

- ❑ ❑ Fork
- ❑ ❑ Hydration bladder
- ❑ ❑ Insulated cup
- ❑ ❑ Internal frame pack
- ❑ ❑ Pee bottle
- ❑ ❑ Sleeping bag(s) with stuff sack
- ❑ ❑ Sleeping pads (2)
- ❑ ❑ Solar shower
- ❑ ❑ Spoon
- ❑ ❑ Stuff sacks for organizing gear (6 to 8)
- ❑ ❑ Thermos bottle
- ❑ ❑ Water bottle and insulated case
- ❑ ❑ _____
- ❑ ❑ _____
- ❑ ❑ _____

CLIMBING GEAR

- ❑ ❑ Ascenders
- ❑ ❑ Belay/rappel device
- ❑ ❑ Climbing shoes
- ❑ ❑ Crampons with anti-balling plates
- ❑ ❑ Daisy chain
- ❑ ❑ Dynamic ropes
- ❑ ❑ Helmet
- ❑ ❑ Ice ax
- ❑ ❑ Ice protection
- ❑ ❑ Ice tools (2)
- ❑ ❑ Locking carabiners (3 to 5)
- ❑ ❑ Portable 2-way radios
- ❑ ❑ Prusik slings (2)
- ❑ ❑ Ratcheting micro pulley (2)
- ❑ ❑ Rock protection
- ❑ ❑ Roller gauze, 2-inch
- ❑ ❑ Snow protection
- ❑ ❑ Static ropes
- ❑ ❑ Sit harness
- ❑ ❑ _____

Packed
Planned

Packed	Planned	
❏	❏	_____
❏	❏	_____
❏	❏	_____
❏	❏	_____
❏	❏	_____
❏	❏	_____
❏	❏	_____
❏	❏	_____
❏	❏	_____

SNOW GEAR

- ❏ ❏ Avalanche transceiver and probe
- ❏ ❏ Climbing skins, waterproofing spray, and extra adhesive
- ❏ ❏ Glacier glasses
- ❏ ❏ Goggles
- ❏ ❏ Poles
- ❏ ❏ Skis
- ❏ ❏ Sled
- ❏ ❏ Snowshoes
- ❏ ❏ Snow shovel
- ❏ ❏ Wax kit (waxes, cork, scraper)
- ❏ ❏ _____
- ❏ ❏ _____
- ❏ ❏ _____

ADDITIONAL GEAR

- ❏ ❏ Altimeter
- ❏ ❏ Batteries
- ❏ ❏ Binoculars
- ❏ ❏ Birth control
- ❏ ❏ Books
- ❏ ❏ Camera equipment and film
- ❏ ❏ Camp towel
- ❏ ❏ Candle
- ❏ ❏ Compass
- ❏ ❏ Contact lens supplies

Packed
Planned

- ❏ ❏ Earplugs
- ❏ ❏ GPS receiver
- ❏ ❏ Headlamp (with extra bulbs)
- ❏ ❏ Journal and pen
- ❏ ❏ Lighters (4)
- ❏ ❏ Lip balm
- ❏ ❏ Personal medications
- ❏ ❏ Sleep mask
- ❏ ❏ Solar charger
- ❏ ❏ Spare glasses or contact lenses
- ❏ ❏ Sunscreen
- ❏ ❏ Swiss Army knife
- ❏ ❏ Tampons
- ❏ ❏ Thermometer
- ❏ ❏ Toilet paper
- ❏ ❏ Toothbrush and paste
- ❏ ❏ Trowel
- ❏ ❏ Watch with alarm
- ❏ ❏ Whistle
- ❏ ❏ _____
- ❏ ❏ _____
- ❏ ❏ _____
- ❏ ❏ _____
- ❏ ❏ _____
- ❏ ❏ _____

PERSONAL FIRST-AID KIT

- ❏ ❏ Ace bandage, 4-inch
- ❏ ❏ Adhesive bandages (Band-Aids, 8)
- ❏ ❏ Adhesive tape, 1-inch
- ❏ ❏ Blister kit (Second Skin, foam, etc.)
- ❏ ❏ Collapsible scissors
- ❏ ❏ Gauze pads, 4-inch by 4-inch (3)
- ❏ ❏ Pain reliever (aspirin, ibuprofen)
- ❏ ❏ Povidine iodine packets (5)
- ❏ ❏ Roller gauze, 2-inch
- ❏ ❏ Safety pins (4)

Packed
Planned

- ❑ ❑ Throat lozenges
- ❑ ❑ Tweezers
- ❑ ❑ _____
- ❑ ❑ _____

Packed
Planned

GROUP EQUIPMENT

SHELTER

- ❑ ❑ Snow stakes
- ❑ ❑ Sponge or brush
- ❑ ❑ Tents (with rain fly, poles, and stakes)
- ❑ ❑ _____
- ❑ ❑ _____
- ❑ ❑ _____
- ❑ ❑ _____

KITCHEN GEAR

- ❑ ❑ Biodegradable soap
- ❑ ❑ Fuel
- ❑ ❑ Fuel funnel with filter pot
- ❑ ❑ Lighters (2)
- ❑ ❑ Plastic trash bag
- ❑ ❑ Pot grips
- ❑ ❑ Pot scrubber
- ❑ ❑ Pot set
- ❑ ❑ Resealable plastic freezer bags
- ❑ ❑ Spice kit
- ❑ ❑ Stove (and spare parts)
- ❑ ❑ Stove pad (for non-hanging stoves)
- ❑ ❑ Water filter or purifier
- ❑ ❑ Water sack
- ❑ ❑ Windscreen
- ❑ ❑ _____
- ❑ ❑ _____
- ❑ ❑ _____

Packed
Planned

BASE CAMP GEAR

- ❑ ❑ Clothesline and pins
- ❑ ❑ Cutting board and knives
- ❑ ❑ Games (cards, backgammon, Frisbee)
- ❑ ❑ Guidebooks and field guides
- ❑ ❑ Lantern(s)
- ❑ ❑ Large thermos
- ❑ ❑ Paper towels
- ❑ ❑ Parachute cord
- ❑ ❑ Portable shower
- ❑ ❑ Radio and antennae
- ❑ ❑ Solar panels
- ❑ ❑ Spotting scope
- ❑ ❑ _____
- ❑ ❑ _____
- ❑ ❑ _____
- ❑ ❑ _____
- ❑ ❑ _____
- ❑ ❑ _____

REPAIR KIT

- ❑ ❑ Baling wire
- ❑ ❑ Crampon and ski binding screws
- ❑ ❑ Duct tape
- ❑ ❑ Epoxy and steel wool
- ❑ ❑ Pole patch kit
- ❑ ❑ Seam grip
- ❑ ❑ Sewing kit
- ❑ ❑ Spare binding parts
- ❑ ❑ Spare pole basket
- ❑ ❑ Tools (pliers, vice grip, multitool)
- ❑ ❑ _____
- ❑ ❑ _____
- ❑ ❑ _____
- ❑ ❑ _____
- ❑ ❑ _____
- ❑ ❑ _____

Appendix D: Medical Supplies

MINOR MEDICAL KIT

The following are all available without a prescription. As with gear lists, the medical kit carried in the field must be tailored to the trip. As the expedition gets longer or more remote in location, greater quantities will be required and major medical items are recommended.

Ace bandages or vet wrap (Coban) for compression.

Adhesive bandages (Band-Aids). Bring a lot for porters and team members who run out.

1-inch adhesive tape. Has a lot of uses; be sure it's easy to tear.

Antacid tablets. For acid reflux, which is common at high altitude.

Aquaphor or Blistex for chapped lips and fever blisters.

Betadine or Hibiclens for cleaning wounds.

Bismuth subsalicylate (Pepto-Bismol) tablets to soothe the digestive system.

Compeed (aka Blister Block) or Cushlin for preventing and treating blisters.

Digital fever thermometer.

EMT shears. To cut clothing.

Gauze pads and rolls.

Hydrocortisone acetate (Anusol HC) and witch hazel pads (Tucks). To treat hemorrhoids, which are common on expeditions.

Hypothermia thermometer. Reads to 86° F.

Labiosan or other complete sunblock for nose and lips.

Latex or nitrile gloves.

Loperamide (Imodium). Invaluable for stopping active bowels on long bus or jeep rides.

Loratadine (Claritin). Nonsedating antihistamine for allergies.

Medicine for Mountaineering or other good manual.

Miconazole nitrate (Monistat) suppositories. Using antibiotics can make women more suseptible to yeast infections.

Moleskin. A cheaper alternative for preventing and treating blisters.

Nonin Pulse Oximeter. To check oxygen saturation of blood.

NSAIDs (nonsteroidal anti-inflammatory drugs): ibuprofen (Advil) or naprosyn (Aleve). Bring a lot for porters and team members.

Oral rehydration solution packets (Jeevan Jal, Infalyte). An improvised solution can be made with half a teaspoon of salt, 8 teaspoons of sugar, and 1 liter of water. Helpful for those stricken by dysentery.

Oxymetazoline hydrochloride (Afrin) or similar nasal decongestant.

Paper and pencil.

Pseudoephredine (Sudafed) or other oral decongestant.

Psyleium (Metamucil) laxative to aid bowel movements.

Safety pins in assorted sizes.

SAM splints, both full-length and finger sizes.

Snakebite kit (Sawyer Extractor).

Sterile applicators.

Steri-Strips (multiple sizes) for sealing wounds.

Stethoscope. Double tube to help in noisy environments.

Superglue for closing skin fissures.

Tegaderm or OpSite. Good for protecting abrasions.

Throat lozenges. Bring a lot.

Tongue depressors.

Uncle Bill's Tweezers. Great for splinters.

Dental Kit

Benzocaine (Orabase-B). Topical anesthetic, anti-inflammatory.

Cavit or Super-Dent, for temporary fillings.

Dental probe.

Elevator.

Eugenol. Topical analgesic for teeth, derived from clove oil.

Filling instrument.

Floss.

IRM (intermediate restorative material) powder for recementing crowns.

Mouth mirror and explorer.

Universal extractor.

MAJOR MEDICAL KIT

Most of the following items require a prescription and medical training; consult your doctor and *Drugs.com* for details. While not needed by all expeditions, these are likely to be taken for major journeys far from professional medical services.

Abdominal and Genitourinary
Ducosate (Colace). To soften stools.

Fluconazole (Diflucan). Yeast infections.

Foley catheter (16 French with 30 cc balloon). Can be used as a urinary catheter, improvised chest tube, posterior nasal pack, or tourniquet.

K-Y Jelly for rectal or vaginal exams.

Prochloroperazine (Compazine) suppositories and tablets to control nausea (added benefit of respiratory stimulant at altitude).

Urine pregnancy test. To rule out ectopic pregnancy in a woman with pelvic pain or vaginal bleeding.

Urine test strips (ChemStrip, DiaScreen). The 10SGs offer ten tests at once.

Airway Management
Endotracheal tubes (7.5, 8.0) for nasal intubations without a scope. Be sure the bottles and regulator are compatible.

Laerdal Pocket Mask for CPR.

Laerdal V-Vac. Lightweight suction device.

Laryngoscope with disposable blades.

Medical oxygen tanks with regulators, nasal cannulas, and 100% non-rebreathing mask with reservoir. Be sure the bottles and regulator are compatible.

Oral airways, at least medium and large.

Altitude Illness
Acetazolamide (Diamox). For prevention of AMS.

Dexamethasone (Decadron). For treatment of cerebral edema.

EPAP (Expiratory Positive Airway Pressure) mask and PEEP (Positive End Expiration Pressure) valve. Compact system for temporarily treating HAPE.

Furosemide (Lasix). For treatment of peripheral edema.

Analgesics
Botorphanol tartrate (Stadol NS). Powerful pain relief delivered nasally.

Hydrocodeine (Vicodin). Pain relief, cough suppressant.

Hydroxyzine (Atarax). Potentiates pain relief; sleep aid.

Antibiotics
Azithromycin (Zithromax). Upper and lower respiratory infections.

Cephalexin (Keflex) or cefadroxil (Duricef). Skin and soft-tissue infections.

Ciprofloxacin (Cipro). Bacterial diarrheas.

Mebendazole (Vermox). Hookworm, roundworm, and tapeworm.

Mefloquine (Lariam), doxycycline (Vibramycin), or atovaquone/proguanil hydrochloride (Malarone). Malaria prevention.

Tetracycline or doxycycline. Tropical fevers, tick fevers.

Tinidazole (Fasigyn) or metronidazole (Flagyl). Giardia.

Central Nervous System
Diazepam (Valium). Tranquilizer to aid sleep (not recommended at high altitude) that is also useful for low back pain.

Haloperidol (Haldol). Antipsychotic, in case somebody goes off the deep end.

Modafinil (Provigil). For combating sleep.

Scopolamine patches (Transderm-Scop). For motion sickness.

Eyes, Ears, Nose, Throat, and Dental
Benzocaine (Orabase-B). Topical anesthetic for teeth, anti-inflammatory.

Corticosporin solution. For swimmer's ear on river trips.

Cyclopentolate HCI (Cyclogyl). Dilates the pupil to eliminate spasms from photokeratitis.

Dental syringe with bupivacaine (Marcaine) ampoules.

ENT scope kit for seeing what's in there.

Eye patches for corneal abrasions and photokeratitis.

Fluorescein strips. For detecting corneal abrasion.

Nasal tampons (Rhinorocket). Lightweight, simple method for treating nosebleeds.

Tetracaine ophthalmic solution. Pain relief for snow blindness (photokeratitis).

Tobramycin (Tobrex) or other antibiotic drops.

Injectable Medications

Ceftriaxone (Rocephin) or imipenem/cilastatin (Primaxin). For controlling life-threatening infections.

Diazepam (Valium). For sedation.

Diphenhydramine (Benadryl). An antihistamine; also helpful for sleep.

Epinephrine (EpiPen). Vital for allergic reactions.

Lidocaine 1-2% (Xylocaine). To numb an area before working on it.

Methylprednisolone (Depo-Medrol). Trigger-point injection for severe tendinitis.

Morphine for severe pain relief and naloxone (Narcan) to prevent complications from morphine.

Prochlorperazine (Compazine). For severe nausea and vomiting, plus sedation.

Promethazine (Phenergan). An alternative antiemetic and sedative.

IV Kit

Anticoagulated blood collection bags if group transfusion is considered.

Bacteriostatic normal saline or heparin flushes.

Blood solution administration sets.

Heparin locks.

Intraosseous needle, for when an IV isn't possible.

IV fluids. Normal saline or lactated Ringers for volume restoration; D5W for administration of medications.

Microdrip administration sets.

Multiple sizes of angiocaths (16, 18, 20 G).

Respiratory/Cardiovascular

Albuterol inhaler (Ventolin, Proventil). For relieving cold-induced or exercise-induced asthma and helping treat lower respiratory tract infections.

Nifedipine (Procardia). For HAPE, angina, hypertension; also Raynaud's Syndrome.

Nitroglycerin (Nitrostat/Transderm Nitro). For chest pain or myocardial infarction.

Propranalol (Inderal). For chest pain or myocardial infarction.

Surgery/Trauma

1 cc TB syringes for administration of lidocaine.

14 G angiocath and a condom for pneumothorax (collapsed lung).

20 ml syringe with 18 G catheter tip for high-pressure irrigation.

No. 11 scalpels for incision and drainage.

Air or gel casts for sprained ankles; lightweight splints that can be worn inside a boot.

Bandage scissors, tissue scissors, needle drivers, and forceps.

Blood pressure cuff.

Disposable shavers to remove hair prior to cutting.

Disposable skin stapler and removal tool. Better than sutures for the untrained.

Fiberglass splints (3M One Step). For broken bones.

Kendrick Traction Device. Lightweight system for a broken femur.

Paper drapes for a clean theater.

Sutures in multiple sizes, both nylon and absorbable.

Topical Medications

Corticosteroid cream (Aristocort, Kenalog). Itching.

Ketoconazole cream (Nizoral). Athlete's foot and other fungi.

Murpirocin cream (Bactroban) or Polysporin ointment (nonprescription). Topical antibiotic.

Silver sulfadiazine cream (Silvadene). To prevent infection of burns.

Index

About the Authors

Clyde Soles

Clyde Soles is a freelance writer, photographer, and consultant with a passion for adventure.

For seven years, he was an editor at *Rock & Ice* magazine, during which time he wrote most of the gear reviews and several feature articles. He is also the founder of *Trail Runner* magazine and has contributed many articles to that publication.

After three decades of climbing, Soles enjoys all aspects of the sport—from bouldering to Himalayan summits. He is equally devoted to trail running, road biking, mountain biking, telemark skiing, track skiing, and scuba diving.

Soles has a B.A. in nature photojournalism from the University of Colorado in Boulder and attended graduate school (ABD) at the Brooks Institute of Photography in Santa Barbara, California.

Phil Powers

Phil Powers owns and operates Jackson Hole Mountain Guides in Jackson, Wyoming. During his career as an outdoor educator, he has served as course leader and chief mountaineering instructor for the National Outdoor Leadership School (NOLS) and as President of the American Mountain Guides Association (AMGA). He is a certified AMGA guide.

Since 1979 Phil has led more than thirty expeditions to the mountains of Alaska, South America, and the Karakoram Range. He made the first ascents of Lukpilla Brakk's Western Edge (Pakistan) and Denali's Washburn Face (Alaska). In 1992 he and his partners made the first winter traverse of the Cathedral Group in the Grand Tetons, and in 1993 Phil became one of a handful of Americans to summit K2.

THE MOUNTAINEERS, founded in 1906, is a nonprofit outdoor activity and conservation club whose mission is "to explore, study, preserve, and enjoy the natural beauty of the outdoors. . . . " Based in Seattle, Washington, the club is now the third-largest such organization in the United States, with 15,000 members and five branches throughout Washington State.

The Mountaineers sponsors both classes and year-round outdoor activities in the Pacific Northwest, which include hiking, mountain climbing, ski-touring, snowshoeing, bicycling, camping, kayaking and canoeing, nature study, sailing, and adventure travel. The club's conservation division supports environmental causes through educational activities, sponsoring legislation, and presenting informational programs. All club activities are led by skilled, experienced volunteers who are dedicated to promoting safe and responsible enjoyment and preservation of the outdoors.

If you would like to participate in these organized outdoor activities or the club's programs, consider a membership in The Mountaineers. For information and an application, write or call The Mountaineers, Club Headquarters, 300 Third Avenue West, Seattle, WA 98119; 206-284-6310.

The Mountaineers Books, an active, nonprofit publishing program of the club, produces guidebooks, instructional texts, historical works, natural history guides, and works on environmental conservation. All books produced by The Mountaineers Books fulfill the club's mission.

Send or call for our catalog of more than 500 outdoor titles:

The Mountaineers Books
1001 SW Klickitat Way, Suite 201
Seattle, WA 98134
800-553-4453
mbooks@mountaineersbooks.org
www.mountaineersbooks.org

The Mountaineers Books is proud to be a corporate sponsor of Leave No Trace, whose mission is to promote and inspire responsible outdoor recreation through education, research, and partnerships. The Leave No Trace program is focused specifically on human-powered (nonmotorized) recreation.

Leave No Trace strives to educate visitors about the nature of their recreational impacts, as well as offer techniques to prevent and minimize such impacts. Leave No Trace is best understood as an educational and ethical program, not as a set of rules and regulations.

For more information, visit *www.LNT.org,* or call 800-332-4100.

Other titles you might enjoy from The Mountaineers Books

Available at fine bookstores and outdoor stores, by phone at 800-553-4453, or on the Web at *www.mountaineersbooks.org*

Mountaineering: The Freedom of the Hills, 6th Edition, edited by Don Graydon and Kurt Hanson. $35.00 hardbound, 0-89886-426-7. $24.95 paperbound, 0-89886-427-5.

Extreme Alpinism: Climbing Light, High, and Fast by Mark Twight and James Martin. $27.95 paperbound. 0-89886-654-5.

Rock & Ice Gear: Equipment for the Vertical World by Clyde Soles. $24.95 paperbound. 0-89886-695-2.

Climbing: Training for Peak Performance by Clyde Soles. $18.95 paperbound. 0-89886-682-0.

Medicine for Mountaineering: & Other Wilderness Activities, 5th Edition edited by James A. Wilkerson, M.D. $19.95 paperbound. 0-89886-799-1.

Fifty Favorite Climbs: The Ultimate North American Tick List by Mark Kroese. $32.95 paperbound. 0-89886-728-2.

Staying Alive in Avalanche Terrain by Bruce Tremper. $17.95 paperbound. 0-89886-834-3.

Glacier Travel & Crevasse Rescue, 2nd Edition by Andy Selters. $18.95 paperbound. 0-89886-658-8.

Aconcagua: A Climbing Guide, 2nd Edition by R. J. Secor. $16.95 paperbound. 0-89886-669-3.

Bolivia: A Climbing Guide by Yossi Brain. $16.95 paperbound. 0-89886-495-X.

Ecuador: A Climbing Guide by Yossi Brain. $16.95 paperbound. 0-89886-729-0.

Mexico's Volcanoes: A Climbing Guide, 3rd Edition by R. J. Secor. $16.95 paperbound. 0-89886-798-3.